Imagery and Symbolism in Counselling

companion volume

Dictionary of Images and Symbols in Counselling
ISBN 1 85302 351 5

of related interest

Inner Journeying Through Art-Journaling
Learning to See and Record your Life as a Work of Art
Marianne Hieb
ISBN 1 84310 794 5

Using Interactive Imagework with Children
Walking on the Magic Mountain
Deborah Plummer
ISBN 1 85302 671 9

Narrative Approaches to Working with Adult Male Survivors
of Childhood Sexual Abuse
The Clients', The Counsellors' and the Researcher's Story
Kim Etherington
ISBN 1 85302 818 5

Counselling and Psychotherapy with Refugees
Dick Blackwell
ISBN 1 84310 316 8

Little Windows into Art Therapy
Small Openings for Beginning Therapists
Deborah Schroder
ISBN 1 84310 778 3

Imagery and Symbolism in Counselling

William Stewart

Jessica Kingsley Publishers
London and Philadelphia

First published in 2005
by Jessica Kingsley Publishers
116 Pentonville Road
London N1 9JB, UK
and
400 Market Street, Suite 400
Philadelphia, PA 19106, USA

www.jkp.com

Printed digitally since 2005

Library of Congress Cataloging in Publication Data
A CIP catalog record for this book is available from the Library of Congress

British Library Cataloguing in Publication Data
Stewart, William
Imagery and Symbolism in Counselling
I. Title
361.323

ISBN-13: 978 1 85302 350 7
ISBN-10: 1 85302 350 7

Contents

Preface   vii

Preface

This book explores the fascinating world of imagination and its use in counselling. For me, it has been a personal journey that has added depth to my work but, more than that, it has been a liberation. Prior to 'discovering' imagery, my work as a counsellor had relied very much on feeling and thinking, and my intuition had not been allowed to develop fully. When I started using imagery, I was aware of entering a whole new world, full of exciting and totally unpredictable possibilities and truths.

My 'baptism', as it were, came through two channels: transpersonal psychology training and a dream analysis by a Jungian counsellor. I date my 'conversion' to the meeting of those two channels, about fifteen years ago. As I say, the experience was personally liberating, but it also revolutionised the way I worked with clients. I like to think that I was fairly empathic before that, but what the conscious use of my intuition did was to enable me to 'think' in terms of images to represent the client's feelings and to present these images as a possibility. It would be arrogant of me to suggest that I was always right – far from it – but not being always right doesn't matter; it is not always possible to say the right thing. What this method does is to let the client see that we are *trying* to get somewhere near.

One of the very first incidents which is etched on my memory was of Jane,[1] a lady who had come to see me because of tensions between herself and Barry over Jane's inability to have children. This was the focal point; underlying was the fact that Jane was a very tense person, always working and living under great pressure. I taught both Jane and Barry the technique of deep relaxation, which helped ease the general tension. When Jane had mastered the relaxation, and she and I were together, I introduced her to imagery, and found that she was adept at using her imagination. In one scene, she found herself on a path that led into a wood, and then into a clearing. She was visibly distressed as she looked around the clearing, particularly as she looked at one large tree.

A Freudian counsellor may have said to himself, 'Aha, a phallic symbol', and it may well have been, but I rarely interpret symbols, either to myself or to the client. Instead, I asked her to view this tree from all angles, and to describe how she felt. Jane had her eyes closed, concentrating on her inner pictures; had they been open, my guess is that she would have looked terrified, and certainly her face was flushed. I encouraged Jane to get as close as she felt comfortable. 'Can you put your arms round it?' Jane shook her head. 'It'll hurt me,' she said. 'Can you just reach out towards it?' As she reached out towards it, although not yet touching it, she started to cry and shake. I am not sure why I asked her, 'How old are you?', but I did. She

---

1   Names have been changed throughout

replied that she was two years of age, standing in a cot in a hospital, crying for her mummy, who had left her. By now she was really sobbing, as she relived that memory of nearly thirty years before, a memory of which she had never consciously thought until that moment. She had gone in to hospital to have her tonsils out.

I would like to say that this solved all Jane's and Barry's difficulties, but counselling is seldom like that. So far as I am aware, they never did have children, but through that one incident, both Jane and I had been taken into the realms of possibility, and both of us were aware that deep within there is tremendous potential for growth. From then until now, I have gone on to develop this wonderful power, a power that is within all of us, the power of the imagination. Some people are certainly more adept at using it than others, and I hope that throughout this book you and I will share some of the journeys I have been privileged to accompany people on in their quest for wholeness.

I hope that you will decide to travel with me in your imagination, and I sincerely trust that this journey will be as liberating for you as it is for me. I hope that the introductory chapters, that deal with theory, will not be desert-dry, or as laborious as climbing a mountain, or as depressing as going down into the deepest cave, but if it is like this, please try to use your imagination to understand what is happening, and seek for ways to change the image into a feeling that is more acceptable to you and more enlightening.

This book is written as Journeys, rather than chapters, for the word seemed in keeping with the basic idea of journeying towards greater understanding. Certainly for myself, the writing of this book has proved to be a fascinating journey, and I hope that you, too, will experience something of the thrill as we travel together.

Many of the concepts, ideas and themes in this book are universal, and have been worked by other people. What I have done is to show how I use them, even though this may not coincide with the work of other counsellors or therapists. A concluding point is that in the References I have quoted only those authors whose work I have consulted, rather than to provide a comprehensive bibliography or to show how other counsellors use imagery.

PART ONE

Twelve Journeys Through Imagery

Setting Out

This book is in two parts: Part One introduces the reader to the principles and practice of imagery, drawing on personal case studies to illustrate the principles; Part Two consists of illustrative case studies.

Much of imagery is tied up with myth, and in order to understand myth, one has to make use of imagination. Indeed, in order to use imagery, one has to be able to suspend that most vital of functions, 'thinking' and its close cousin, 'logic'; there is nothing 'logical' in imagination! This particular mode of working may present difficulties to some people, who must always look for explanation, who always see things in black or white terms.

This goes for clients as well as for counsellors. Some clients are so caught up in the material, thinking, and the logical, that for them to be asked, 'What does that look like to you?', or 'Imagine yourself on top of a mountain, what can you see?', produces a blank stare or obvious signs of discomfort. Such clients will then have to be worked with *at the level at which they feel comfortable*. In my early enthusiasm at my own new-found liberation, I imagined that every client would be able to work in this way, but that is not so, any more than to say that all counsellors can.

What imagery does is to cut through the control of the mind, which so often blocks tapping into the feelings. This does *not* mean that the client is *out of control*; that would be too frightening to contemplate, and would certainly not be therapeutic. At all times clients are totally aware of what is happening and of where their imagination is taking them, although the *why* and the *outcome* is obscured.

The psyche is in control of the operation, and the more I work with imagery, the more convinced I am of the principle that the psyche, if trusted, will work towards wholeness and integration. This means trusting the client, and that something within the client works towards the client's best interest. It means something else: a partnership between the psyche of the client and the psyche of the counsellor.

Before travelling further, there are three concepts that must be considered: conscious, unconscious, and collective unconscious.

Conscious

The conscious of one of Freud's regions of the mind which, with the preconscious and the unconscious, make up the psyche. Freud described the conscious as the sense

3

organ of the ego. The conscious is open to immediate awareness, unlike the preconscious and the unconscious which are not. The functions of the ego – reality testing, perception, observation and evaluation – are all at a conscious level. Some of the superego functions – criticism and conscience – are also mainly conscious. The defence mechanisms and censorship are not within the conscious. Behavioural, humanistic and cognitive therapies all emphasise working directly with the conscious in the belief that only what is observable can be accurately interpreted.

The preconscious is the area of the mind between the conscious and the unconscious – the 'ante-chamber' to consciousness. It is also referred to as the descriptive unconscious or the fore-conscious. The contents of the preconscious, knowledge, emotions, images, although not immediately in the conscious, are accessible to it because the censorship is absent. Material can be described as temporarily forgotten; suppressed, and not repressed. The preconscious is important in the process of working through, a process necessary to consolidate the insight gained through interpretation.

Unconscious

This refers to mental processes of which the subject is unaware. In psychoanalysis it is a division of the psyche and the storehouse of repressed material of which the individual is not consciously aware. The discovery of the clinical importance of the unconscious became the cornerstone of psychoanalysis.

In *analytic (Jungian) psychology*, the unconscious is represented by:

1. The personal unconscious: the surface layer of the unconscious. It is everything that the person acquires throughout life; everything forgotten, repressed, subliminally perceived, thought and felt, as well as complexes.

2. The Collective Unconscious: those aspects of the psyche that are common to humankind as a whole. It is part of everyone's unconscious and is distinct from the personal unconscious, which arises from the experience of the individual. The Collective Unconscious contains *Archetypes*, which express themselves as universal primitive images, accumulated down the ages and across cultures. The *Archetype* is to the Collective Unconscious what the complex is to the personal unconscious. Because the material in the Collective Unconscious has never existed in the conscious, it has not been repressed. Jung's evidence of the Collective Unconscious is found in myths, legends, folk tales, fairy tales and dreams. During sleep, the material in the Collective Unconscious is not under the control of the conscious mind, and material from it pops through in the form of dreams or visions.

Conscious versus unconscious

The differences between the conscious and the unconscious could be thought of as contrasts between rational and irrational behaviour, or between voluntary and involuntary action. It can also be where we decide to focus conscious attention, contrasting with what we dismiss or fail to notice.

Symbolic language, whether in myth or fairy story, through allegory or metaphor, often calls attention to the unconscious content of the psyche. We may have our attention drawn to the dark and destructive potential of the unconscious, or as an incentive to discover the treasures that lie buried, to enrich our conscious life.

There is no clear boundary between the conscious and the unconscious. It is not like the Berlin Wall, that was, or the barbed-wire fence of a prison, rather more like an imaginary line. Most physical functions fall within the sphere of the unconscious. An illustration of this is the 'autonomic nervous system' of the body which controls all the vital functions and operates without our conscious control. At the same time, however, its effective functioning is strongly influenced by our behaviour.

An example of this would be: Joe *thinks* he has cancer, and this pushes up his anxiety level. This in turn works on the gastric secreting part of the autonomic nervous system, so increasing the supply of gastric juices to the digestive tract. Too much acid, for example, may cause heartburn, and worse, ulcers. The pain from the ulcers, plus the heartburn, confirm to Joe, even more, that he has cancer. Various tests reveal the true cause, but Joe's anxiety level is so high that he *thinks* the doctors have misdiagnosed his case, and the condition becomes chronic.

This is presenting a fairly simple, but common enough, illustration of the interplay between the conscious and the unconscious. The *thinking* is in the conscious realm, but the influence extends into the unconscious processes of the body.

Another important facet of the unconscious is what we inherit, and this is where we start tapping into Jung's Collective Unconscious, and, indeed, where the boundary between the personal unconscious and the Collective Unconscious is decidedly fuzzy. Something of which I am not personally proud, but which certainly exists in my personal Collective Unconscious, is the fact that some of my forebears were involved in the slave trade between the West Indies and Britain. This fact was not known to me until I was well into middle age, yet from an early age I had been troubled by the plight of the underdog, and got very hot under the collar whenever slavery, in whatever form, was mentioned. I now believe that I was tapping into the Collective Unconscious.

Evoking one's ancestors is one way of gaining access to the conflicts of one's own inner world. The blood of my ancestors runs in my veins, the blood of the brilliant and courageous ones, as well as the black sheep and the criminals. We must be prepared to come to terms with the shadow side of our ancestors as well as the bits we like.

The real difference between the conscious and the unconscious lies in the difference between the rational and irrational. Symbolism seeks to bring what is irrational and involuntary into the light so that it can be transformed into an appropriate relationship with the rational side. All the while elements remain in the unconscious, they will act like fifth-columnists, who pretend to be loyal, but are ever waiting to betray.

Symbolism is not an aim in itself; it is a tool for us to work with to extend the boundaries and to broaden the sphere of consciousness. Far better to go out to meet the potentially hostile forces of the unconscious, armed with all the weapons there are, than to try to fight a rear guard action with inadequate weapons.

It is now time to introduce two more terms: *psyche* and *Archetypes*.

Psyche

The oldest and most general meaning of 'psyche' comes from the early Greeks, who regarded it as the 'soul', or the very essence of life; in classical mythology, it is the eponymous heroine in the story of Cupid and Psyche. A certain Greek king had three daughters, of whom Psyche, the youngest, was so beautiful that people worshipped her and neglected Venus. Venus (Aphrodite) was so jealous that she sent her son Cupid (Eros) with instructions to make Psyche fall in love with some ugly, old man. Cupid, instead, fell in love with Psyche himself. He told her that she must never see him, but one night, while she was looking at him by the light of a lamp, a drop of oil fell on him, and he awoke and fled. Psyche was desolate and searched far and wide for him. She finally submitted herself to Venus who set her four impossible tasks: to sort a huge pile of different seeds into their respective piles; to acquire some golden fleece from the terrible rams of the sun; to fill a crystal container from an inaccessible stream; to descend into the underworld and fill a small box with beauty ointment. This last task was made all the more difficult because Psyche would have to harden her heart to compassion. Psyche completed all her tasks, the first three with assistance from ants, a green reed and an eagle. The final task she accomplished by saying 'No' three times to people's pleas. Cupid persuaded Zeus, the Father of the Gods, to let him marry Psyche; Zeus agreed and Psyche was made immortal. The Greek word for soul is psyche and in Greek folklore the psyche or soul (or spirit) is depicted as a butterfly: the soul or spirit, distinguished from the body; the mind functioning as the centre of thought, feeling and behaviour, and consciously or unconsciously adjusting and relating the body to its social and physical environment.

In analytical psychology the psyche is the sum total of all the conscious and unconscious psychic processes. The soul is regarded as the sum total of personality, comprising the persona – the outward face or attitude, the mask – the Anima (in men) and the Animus (in women) – the inward attitude or face.

The mythical romance of the maiden Psyche and Cupid is really an allegory of the union of soul and body and their subsequent separation.

Archetypes

An Archetype is a primeval image, character or pattern that recurs in literature and in thought consistently enough to be considered a universal concept. An Archetype is an inherited disposition to perceive and experience typical or nearly universal situations or patterns of behaviour. Archetypes are the basis for Jung's Collective Unconscious. They correspond to such experiences as confronting death or choosing a mate and manifest themselves symbolically in religions, myths, fairy tales, dreams, and fantasies.

Archetypes tend to cluster around the basic and universal experiences of life, such as birth, marriage, motherhood, death and separation. Archetypes remain hidden until recognised and acknowledged, and carry a strong charge of energy which the person finds difficult to resist. Archetypes arouse feelings, blind one to realities and take possession of the will.

All psychic imagery taps into the archetypal to some degree, which is why dreams have a strong spiritual content. At times of crisis, when the Ego is most vulnerable, when the normal mechanisms of control are not in operation, Archetypes are able to appear and may take over. Archetypes are not static nor fixed; each new generation adds to the reservoir of Archetypes in the Collective Unconscious. (The Appendix lists some examples of Archetypes.)

Working with imagery releases the client's energy, because much of the material is attached to Archetypes and the Collective Unconscious. Added to this, the imagination works with symbols, and symbols, like dreams, reflect the state of the unconscious. Like any faculty, the imagination can be used wisely or misused; for positive or negative. Faulty use of the imagination can lead us into feeling negative about ourselves. What the therapeutic use of imagination does is to clothe feelings with images, which then makes it possible to work with them.

The four main functions of the psyche are intuition, sensing, thinking and feeling. Each approaches reality from a different point of view and with a different question. Each grasps a different part of reality. In order to move on to study creativity and its relevance to imagery, these four functions are now dealt with in some depth, and the final stretch of this first journey is to explore what Jung says about personality.

Jung's Personality of Type Theory

Carl Gustav Jung (1875–1961), the Swiss psychiatrist, developed his theory of psychological types to help people recognise and understand basic personality differences.

Jung's three dimensions were:

1. Extraversion/introversion

2. Sensing/intuition

3. Thinking/feeling

This book will consider only the four functions of sensing, intuition, thinking, feeling.

By becoming aware of these basic differences, we can better understand our own and others' motivations and behaviours and can expand tolerance and respect for those whose styles are different. Jung recognised that people make clear choices from infancy onward as to how they use their minds. Although each person has some of each kind of orientation, he or she generally favours one type over the other. Types seem to be distributed randomly without regard to sex, class, level of education, and so on.

Summary of Jung's four basic preferences

Sensing perceives through the five senses, works with facts, and tells us a thing *is*. It gives the immediate reality – the *now*. It informs us of the existence of the object which impinges upon the senses at the present moment. We are aware that something is here in our immediate environment.

People who are more sensing than intuitive prefer the concrete, real, factual structured, tangible here-and-now. They become impatient with theory and the abstract, mistrusting intuition. Sensing people think in careful, detail-by-detail accuracy, remembering real facts, making few factual errors, but possibly missing an understanding of the overall picture.

Intuition perceives through hunches, works with possibilities, deals with the potential, the thing which will develop. It is the function which has to do with the element of *time and space*. It is not concerned with what *is*, but with what is *going to be*, or *has been*. It is the 'hunch' by which we estimate the possibilities of a given situation.

People who are more intuitive than sensing prefer possibilities, theories, patterns, the overall, inventions, and the new. Intuitive people tend not to relate to fixed concepts. Intuitive people think and discuss in spontaneous leaps of intuition that may leave out or neglect details. Problem-solving comes easily for this type of individual, although there may be a tendency to make errors of fact.

Thinking makes head judgments and gives something a name, a concept. It tells us *what* a thing is. It is a process of understanding by which we become aware of the nature of the thing with which we are dealing. People who are more thinking than feeling make judgments about life, people, occurrences, and things based on logic, analysis and evidence. They consider it irrational to make decisions based on feelings and values. As a result, thinking people are more interested in logic, analysis and verifiable conclusions than in empathy, values, and personal warmth. Thinking people may step on others' feelings and needs without realising it, neglecting to take into consideration the values of others.

Feeling makes heart judgments, and gives us a sense of values. It tells us whether a thing is agreeable or disagreeable. Feeling helps us decide to accept or reject something by determining its value to us. People who are more feeling than thinking make judgments about life, people, occurrences, and things based on empathy, warmth and personal values. As a consequence, feeling people are more interested in people and feelings than in impersonal logic, analysis, and things, and in conciliation and harmony more than in being on top or achieving impersonal goals. Feeling people get along with people in general. Of course, none of these types should be regarded as superior to any of the others; they are just different.

Summary

In this first journey we have looked ahead at the structure of the book, and touched on how imagery may be used to benefit both counsellor and client. We have seen how imagery is more linked to myth than to reason and logic; and how the lack of structure may prove a stumbling block to some people who have difficulty moving in fields without clearly defined boundaries.

Some important concepts have been introduced: conscious, unconscious, and collective unconscious. Counselling, although it deals in the main with the conscious mind, cannot ignore what lies beneath, in the unconscious. In imagery, one moves in and out of the Collective Unconscious as images raised from the Collective Unconscious are brought to the surface, images that are charged with powerful feelings.

Along the first journey we met the psyche and Archetypes, two important concepts in counselling, and crucial when working with imagery. The idea of psyche being a butterfly illustrates how delicate it is to handle, so easily damaged. The Archetypes are so closely associated with the Collective Unconscious that to consider one is to think of the other. A study of Archetypes would provide work for many years to come.

We saw that imagination and imagery may not come easily to some people, so some time was spent exploring Jung's four functions: sensing, intuition, thinking, and feeling. Generalisations are notoriously flawed, and when considering the use of imagery, there are many other factors, such as experience, which may compensate for, or limit the use of, the functions that favour imagery, such as intuition and feeling. Yet, the other two functions, sensing and thinking, are just as essential, for they provide different inputs. Just as we ignore the non-dominant hand at our peril, so we must not ignore the functions with which we feel less comfortable.

In the next journey we shall explore the principles of imagery as something which can be used at any time during counselling, often triggered off by words that create pictures.

Exploring the Principles of Imagery

Imagery can be used at any time in the counselling session. However, its effectiveness is dependent upon the psychological awareness of the counsellor. This awareness is the product of personal therapy, training and experience. I hope that this book will add to both your personal development and your experience. If you wish to develop your imagery skills, I would strongly recommend that you undertake either a course of personal therapy with a counsellor who focuses on imagery or that you find a group that is working along these lines.

Certain words evoke images. It is useful, therefore, to pay attention to the words the client uses to express feelings and to say something like 'Could you use your imagination to put that word into a picture to describe how you feel?'

One person might say of the word 'trapped': 'Oh, I imagine myself in a swamp'. Someone else might say: 'I see myself in a dark, underground dungeon'. Each of these answers gives both counsellor and client a little more understanding. Some words are powerfully evocative.

A Case Study – Anna

During a workshop demonstration of counselling, Anna, the client, said, 'I feel very insecure at present'. When she was asked to put this into an image, she imagined herself faced with five closed doors, uncertain as to what lay behind any of them.

When she was asked, 'So you are in a room with these doors all round you ?', she realised that the doors were in the open and arranged in a half-circle. Using the principle of *extension* (Task four – see The Eighth Journey, Exploring Twelve Herculean tasks), I asked her to turn and face away from the doors. This instruction was based on the principle that if the doors represented the future, then turning around she would be facing the past. As she did so, her face lit up in total surprise and delight, as she exclaimed, 'The landscape is all beautiful and light and green. What lovely country!'

When she had admired the scenery, and still in her imagination, she was encouraged to identify the doors, which she did. One of the doors she wanted to open, just a little way, but didn't want to go beyond the threshold at that time. She then decided to close the session.

During discussion with the group, Anna commented on the revelation of turning round and looking at her past. She had thought of her past as being dark, difficult and traumatic. Looking at it at the crossroads of her life, she realised for the first time that although there were scars on the countryside, the overall feelings were good and comfortable and the scars had healed. She felt, having realised this, that she had greater freedom to start exploring what lay behind the doors of the future.

Some people seem to have a natural gift for creating inner images. If you are one of these, using imagery is likely to prove very rewarding for you and your clients. For many of us, the imagination we were born with has been overlaid with left-brain activities. Careful nurturing and use will help it to resurface.

Therapeutic imagery has several names – guided imagery, symboldrama, active imagination, visualisation – but whatever its name, it means working with images, where imagination is facilitated by the therapist, who prompts, encourages, develops and brings the fantasy experience to a close. The material may then be analysed in terms of its meaning and symbolism – as in dream analysis. A word of caution must be introduced here: interpretations of symbols must always be tentative, and not delivered from a purely theoretical standpoint. While it is true that certain symbols mean certain things – red usually means danger, for instance – circumstances alter the meaning. To a red colour-blind person, red means nothing, so taking this as an analogy; interpretations should be 'What do you think of this meaning?' or 'The books offer this as an interpretation, what do you think?' or 'What does that image (symbol) mean to you?' It is arrogant to assume all knowledge, and by so doing, to ignore the insights of the client.

Symbols, which may conceal or reveal, always derive from Archetypes. The fundamental truth of therapeutic imagery is that the psyche will always strive to represent itself in fantasy using images. Imagery takes us into the realms of such richness, in which the psyche is given freedom to explore, unhampered by the conscious mind, whose language is reason and logic.

I rarely set out to work with imagery, for this would mean that the client would have to fit in with my preconceived ideas. Rather, as I indicated earlier, I will introduce the idea of imagery when the client gives some indication that she/he is already working in terms of pictures.

Glen was a surveyor who had been referred to me because of panic attacks that were interfering with his work and his daily living. At one stage he said, 'When I think what I was like…' This indicated to me that he was looking at something in his mind's eye, so I said, 'If you were an artist, and you were painting a 'before' and 'now', what would you paint?' 'That's strange', he said, 'I do like painting, and often take myself off down the river.' He then went on to talk about two pictures, one of himself as a happy-go-lucky chap, with bright colours on the canvas; the second picture was him all screwed up, looking haggard, and the scene was cloudy and overcast. Towards the end of six months of counselling, he looked again at the paintings; the second had changed, bright colours had replaced the dull colours, and he was standing with his hand to his eyes, looking into the future. The image he had created clearly depicted the dramatic change in his outlook and in his feelings.

One of the fascinating characteristics of the imagery journey is that the client is all the characters in the inner theatre – the script writer, producer, director, and players. What is often surprising is that clients produce complicated images they have no knowledge of ever having seen, and these are in full, glorious Technicolour and delicate hues. Sometimes the scene is taken from actual memory, and that, too, is perfectly acceptable; if that is what the client wants, then that's where the client needs to be at that particular moment. Others create scenes that could very well fit some particular science-fiction movie. What is important to remember is that what the client produces from the imagination is what is significant to the client, in some way.

Categories of Symbols

As imagery works with symbols, now is an appropriate time to introduce some structure into how we can look at symbols. There are many groupings, but I have decided on eight.[1]

1. Nature

2. Animal

3. Human

4. Man-made

5. Religious

6. Mythological (The Gods and Goddesses are given their Greek names, please turn to Deities to find their equivalent Roman names.

7. Abstract

8. Individual/spontaneous.

It is not necessary to categorise a particular symbol produced by a client's imagination; at the same time, it is useful at some stage to be able to slot them into a category. This might apply, for example, where a client has produced a certain image, then feels stuck in exploring it further. Here the counsellor may suggest a linking symbol. For example, a client who produces an image of a prehistoric altar-stone, and is unable to take it further, may be prompted, 'That sounds as if it has something to do with sacrifice.'

Familiarity with the eight categories is also a way for you, yourself, to work on certain groups of symbols. This 'homework' is crucial in the development of a repertoire of explored symbols which you can feel confident in working with. In any form of counselling, self-knowledge, and psychological awareness are essential. We must never rest on what we have accomplished, there is always more to enlarge our field of awareness. I believe that it is, therefore, in our own interests to enlarge our working base with symbols, for as we engage each new symbol, and expand

---

1   For a more detailed exploration, see *A Dictionary of Images and Symbols in Counselling* (Stewart 1996)

our awareness of it, as we saw in the previous journey related to liberation, our intuition will be deepened and we shall become more sensitive and alert to symbolic words that the client is using.

This self-training, or self-exploration, may take us into unexpected and previously unexplored areas of our inner world. We may need to confront the devil within us, and, as did Dante, go through hell, before we can reach a degree of wholeness, if not Paradise. Unless we can travel these roads, we will fail our clients when we try to travel with them on their journeys.

Six Guiding Principles of Imagery

1. The principle of confrontation

The client is encouraged to be courageous and to confront images that cause anxiety. Successful confronting causes transformation and removal of anxiety. The feared symbolic figure is generally a part of the self and confrontation takes courage (Jane, referred to in the Preface, had to draw on her courage to be able to confront the tree). Very often confrontation occurs with frightening creatures – the dragon that emerges from the cave, the swamp or the sea; or with the snarling animal that dashes out from the forest. All of these – swamp, marsh, sea, and forest – may be said to represent the unconscious.

The natural instinct when startled is to freeze or turn and run. One of the curious aspects of imagery is that although the client knows it is imagination, the reactions are still *very* real. I have seen clients blanch with fear, tremble, flush with anger, shrink back into the chair, and present all the indications of panic. Although I have never taken the pulse or blood pressure, I am quite sure that there would be physiological indications of what they were experiencing. I have seen clients at the end of a session dripping with sweat; I have seen them cry and rock in their chair, as a child would when distressed. Imagery is certainly never a soft option!

How should the counsellor continue, when the client is confronted by something terrifying? First, it is vitally important to remember that, *at the moment*, what the client is imagining is as real as the chair in which she or he is sitting; in exactly the same way as when we are dreaming, the edge of the precipice on which we are teetering is real, as is the one hundred-foot drop. Should we advise the client to run, fight, kill the creature by putting a sword in her hand? Confrontation is not attack, it is standing one's ground, determined to be in control, and this may require a lot of encouragement from the counsellor. However, it is not a simple thing like saying, 'Stand your ground; look at it; be in control'. What the client is imagining represents some aspect of the unconscious, something that holds some power over him or her. It presents in this fearsome form to exert the maximum effect.

Sometimes it is necessary for the counsellor to take control, but rarely have I had to do this, and would only do so if there were indications that the client had become too terrified to do anything. Normally I would say something like, 'What do you want to do?' This leaves the client firmly in control, and I think this is essential. If the client says, 'I want to run away,' my next response might be, 'Where do you want to run to?' Again this leaves the client in control. I would probably follow it up with, 'What would happen if you didn't run away?' If the client says something like, 'I want to kill it,' I would advise against this by responding with, 'What would happen if you did kill it?' This type of probing response encourages the client to explore the symbol further, and not accept it at face value.

From my knowledge of symbolism, and of some of the workings of the unconscious, I know that fighting the creature and killing it are not the answer; for that would only be destroying a vital part of the client's self. I would probably say, 'What name would you give this creature?' Naming something often removes much of the fear attached to it.

Before engaging in imagery which is potentially dangerous (although danger can appear from the most unexpected quarters), I would suggest that the client look around for some sort of talisman to offer protection. Again, the choice of talisman is interesting and revealing. So, when the client needs to confront, I would draw attention to the talisman, but also ask, 'Is there anyone you would like to be with you just now as you confront [using the name given to it by the client]?' As with the talisman, who the person brings into the scene is interesting. Sometimes I will suggest that there is a wise person approaching, someone who will be there just for them. I will then suggest that the client enter into a dialogue with the wise person about what to do.

If there is no such wise person, and if the client wishes to confront, rather than flee, I would then suggest that the client studies the creature closely, in great detail. This often leads to a change in the client's feelings, as critical analysis is used to bring the creature into some sort of reality. What often happens is that the creature diminishes in size and fearsomeness, or it may spontaneously be transformed into something more acceptable and less frightening.

2. The principle of transformation

While transformation may take place in confrontation, as we shall see with Margaret and the dragon, sometimes the transformation has to be more clearly directed. Changing the feared object into something more acceptable is not just a way of coping; the new object often reveals significant psychological growth.

Margaret was confronting a dragon in a clearing in the forest. She was presenting every indication of terror. 'Do you want me to do anything?' I asked, not wishing to intrude on the scene. 'Hold my hand, please.' Holding hands is not necessarily age-related, but often such a request indicates an age-regression. As Margaret stood her ground, fingering a cross around her neck, the dragon changed spontaneously into an eagle, which was still frightening to her, then into a black cat. As she reached out to stroke the cat, it was transformed into her step-mother holding a switch with which she used to beat Margaret. For years Margaret had been troubled by nightmares of a dragon, pursuing her out of a dark wood. Confronting the dragon in this way revealed to her how her unconscious had held control over her in the same way as her step-mother had. Now that the dragon had been unmasked, the fear went; it served no useful purpose.

3. The principle of feeding

Where confrontation is inappropriate, or unacceptable – the challenge may be too great – the counsellor may suggest that the client feeds the frightening figure to make it lazy and sleepy. Feeding is often a more gentle way for the client to deal with the dangerous creature and it is also easier for the counsellor. At the same time, it does mean that the client has to take control, and to take risks. Feeding is often an appropriate action to take. A ferocious animal suddenly coming out of a cave, with every intention of devouring the client needs to be fed.

A general principle can be identified here. Where the creature seems all bluster, breathing out fire, like the dragon, confrontation may be more appropriate than feeding, even though the fear it inspires is just as real. Where the creature comes from reality, like a lion or a grizzly bear, and it looks hungry, I would suggest that feeding is the more appropriate action to take. Feeding the grizzly on its favourite food – honey – would be a good start. Bears also like fish, big fish such as salmon. In such a scene I would suggest, 'Just to your right hand is a gigantic jar of honey; throw it at the feet of the bear, and while he's eating it, go and catch some salmon in that river. You will find a fishing rod on the bank. Come back with your catch and give it to the bear. When the bear is eating it will become less angry, and when he has been overfed, he will lie down and sleep'.

4. The principle of reconciliation

This is where the client makes friends with a hostile symbolic figure, by addressing it, touching it, making friends with it. This is what Jane (in the Preface) was prepared to do. Making friends with this symbolic figure means assimilating the part which has been rejected and split off, so that it no longer represents a negative force in the client's psyche.

Jim had been coming to me for personal growth work for well over two years, and during that time he had worked with many different themes and images. One theme that kept recurring was how he thought other people perceived him. He was a tall, pleasant-looking man in his mid-twenties, extremely good-natured, a graduate of mathematics who had changed direction and had come into nursing. His self-image and self-esteem were poor, and this was an area he often concentrated on.

In one session, towards the end of our relationship, he said, 'I feel apprehensive, as if I've come to a crunch point, and I know it's something to do with integration'. He was a man who read a great deal, and spoke of psychological ideas with great accuracy and insight. Over many months we had looked at the possibility of some part of himself he wasn't really in touch with, and instinctively I felt that we were about to confront this, whatever it was. If a client feels not fully in touch, then the image of a mirror is useful to present to them, and this is what I did with Jim. 'Imagine you are walking through a big store, and you suddenly come face to face with yourself in a full-length mirror. What do you see?' His face slowly crumpled and he began to sob. Through his tears he said, 'I see this horrid person, all covered in suppurating sores, like leprosy, or boils, ugly, ravaged with disease and neglect, and with such an evil expression, of hate and loathing. That can't be me, can it?'

Even now, as I write this, some two years afterwards, I am once again caught up in Jim's distress. I have witnessed clients weep, and have cried with them; I have seen them angry, terrified and broken, but I have never seen one so blasted as Jim was, as he confronted the despised part of himself. Reality does not enter into it; and how useless it would have been for me to have said something like, 'But that's not really how you are.' That is how he felt he was. I said, 'Can you integrate this other Jim?' 'I'll try,' he said.

Normally I say, 'Keep me in touch with what's happening', but in this instance it was a long time before Jim spoke, but he didn't need to, for his face and his general body language told be what was happening, as he began to relax. This is what he eventually said. 'There was this other Jim, who walked out of the mirror, and that was really scary, and he stood at about arm's length from me. I wasn't sure if he wanted to be integrated, but I knew it had to be done. I had a conversation with him, and discovered that although we spoke the same language, he was coarse, and swore a lot. I knew he was my shadow, and I also knew that I'd been blaming him for lots of the bad things I felt, so I told him. 'That's all right, you weren't to know, but what are you going to do about it? You can't ignore me now.'

'I moved closer to him, and reached out to touch him, and that took a lot of courage, for I felt he would contaminate me. So I managed to touch a bit of his arm that wasn't so bad, and when I did, it was if he'd been touched by a miracle, and the skin on his arm began to heal. I moved closer to him, and put my arms around him, not knowing what to expect, and it certainly wasn't what happened. It feels really strange talking about it, as if I was watching it happening, but it was really happening to me. You know how it is when two images are brought together to make one, well it was like that. We moved closer together, and then we weren't two any more. We had integrated.'

I make no apologies for quoting this account in detail, for it is one of the clearest accounts of reconciliation I have experienced. I know that for Jim this was a turning point in his experience, as he came to accept this other part of himself. All the time the other Jim was split off, Jim could not feel whole. He may not have liked what confronted him in the mirror, but if was to make progress, he would have to accept what he did not like, and he could only do this as and when he was ready to be reconciled.

5. The principle of the magic fluid

We shall be dealing with the stream later, but for now, the brook or stream represent the flow of psychic energy and the potential for emotional development. Bathing in the stream or drinking from it often proves therapeutic. Bathing in the stream can be very revealing, from what is felt and from what one discovers in the depths.

It is worth pointing out here that some clients cannot trace the stream to the ocean, and this signifies a significant blockage which needs to be worked on. In the natural world, a stream may get lost underground to reappear later, so it is important to trace the route. Another variation of blockage is where the stream peters out, symbolic of a severe lack of psychic energy, or of staying power; this might be an appropriate point from which to trace the stream to its origin, back to the source of psychic energy.

6. The principle of exhausting and killing

This should only be used by an experienced counsellor, because it is very often an attack against the client's self. Although it has been included for completeness, it is not something in which I have ever actively engaged. It is quite a different matter when death of the symbol occurs spontaneously. If, for example, the creature becomes so exhausted in the chase that it dies, and this happens without any suggestion from the counsellor, then it would seem that this is the psyche's way of completion of the image.

Guidance and Direction

From my experience the counsellor is there as a guide, not in any sense as a controller; suggestions should be made tentatively and should not intrude. To be the unobtrusive guide means entering the client's imagery. This is always problematic, for two people looking out of the same window see things slightly differently. This being so, what I produce in my imagination, based on the feedback the client gives, gets me somewhere near what the client is imagining, and my perception can always be tested out. When the client says, 'I can see a mountain', I might say, 'Where exactly? To your right? Left? In front? Behind? How far in the distance?' For this helps me to 'ground' the image I have. It also helps me to be able to relate this to the concept of direction – north, south, east or west – all of which have psychological significance.

Thus a general principle emerges; the less the counsellor gives explicit guidance, the more the client's psyche is in control, and can plot its own course. The six principles, explored above, are used only when the situation demands it. There are no hard and fast rules; experience and intuition should be the guidelines. As introduced above, the wise person may act as the guide. The wise person may be in the form of a magic horse, or other animal. When the woman client chooses a male guide it can be a representation of her Animus; and when a man chooses a female guide it can represent his Anima. This choice may or may not be important to talk through after the imagery session. What is significant is that the woman is prepared to trust the male part of herself, and the man to trust the female part of himself; each can gain strength from the representation of the opposite gender.

The next Journey will take us into an exploration of some of the standard themes used in imagery. What has been described so far could be called 'free imagery'; what is dealt with in the next Journey are themes that can be used to start the client off, or to work with them as they appear spontaneously during the client's journey.

Summary

Imagery is not an easy option; it demands a high degree of skill, experience, sensitivity, and a well-developed intuition. It would be arrogant and insensitive to suggest that other counselling approaches do not require these, they do – however, it is also fair to say that every approach requires different qualities and skills. Possibly the one major difference is the use of symbols, many of them abstract or deriving from mythology.

What therapeutic imagery has in common with most other forms of counselling is that interpretation of symbols, when offered, must be tentative. There is the literal interpretation which is obvious – a key opens a door. For the counsellor, the key may be a sexual symbol; for the client, it may represent freedom, coming of age, leaving emotional adolescence behind and moving into emotional adulthood. So, it is not a matter of the counsellor telling the client from an authoritative stance, but rather asking 'What do we think this symbol means *to you*?'

Summary of the six guiding principles:

1. The principle of confrontation: the client is encouraged to be courageous and to confront images that cause anxiety. Successful confronting causes transformation and removal of anxiety. The feared symbolic figure is generally a part of self.

2. The principle of transformation: changing the feared object into something more acceptable is not just a way of coping: the new object often reveals significant psychological growth.

3. The principle of feeding: where confrontation is inappropriate, or unacceptable the therapist may suggest that the client feeds the frightening figure, to make it lazy, and sleepy.

4. The principle of reconciliation: this is where the client makes friends with a hostile symbolic figure, by addressing it and touching it.

5. The principle of the magic fluid: the brook or stream represents the flow of psychic energy and the potential for emotional development. Bathing in the stream or drinking from it often proves therapeutic. Bathing in the sea can be very revealing.

6. The principle of exhausting and killing: this should only be used by an experienced therapist, because it is very often an attack against the client's self.

Therapeutic imagery is possibly one of the least directive of all therapies yet it taps into, and uses, the insights from many other approaches. It is possibly the approach where the counsellor is most closely involved in the client's inner world. For this reason, those who use it may have to do a great deal of work on their own inner world.

This particular Journey prepares the way for the next Journey, and a more detailed look at the main themes or motifs in imagery.

Exploring First-Level Themes

The previous two journeys have talked in general terms about imagery and symbols; the Third, Fourth and Fifth Journeys present a structure to the eighteen themes, illustrated by case studies.

My reason for talking about three levels of theme is that some of the themes, such as the cave, or the woods, or Sleeping Beauty, deal with the deeper regions of the unconscious, and to explore these symbols requires insight and experience on the part of the client, when the client has explored many of the elements in the other two levels. However, this is a general statement, and not a unqualified rule which is never to be broken. The experience and insights of the counsellor are taken for granted. I would like to stress that these themes are not original; they are used by many other authors. How I use them may be different.

Eighteen Principal Themes in Guided Imagery

Book	Cave	Container
House	Dragon	Lion
Meadow	Mountain	Rosebush
Sub-personalities	Sleeping Beauty	Stream
Wilderness	Sword	Volcano
Witch/wizard	Mentor	Woods

Themes can be used in two ways: they may be allowed to arise spontaneously, or the therapist may direct the client to work with them. Both methods are appropriate and every one of the motifs works with something different.

The 18 themes are divided into the three levels as follows:

Level One	Level Two	Level Three
Meadow	Book	Lion
Stream	Cave	Sub-personalities
Mountain	Container	Sleeping Beauty
House	Sword	Volcano
Woods	Dragon	Wilderness
Rosebush	Mentor	Witch/wizard

If the stated intention is to concentrate on imagery, and if the client has never worked in this way before, this is how I would continue, although every one must work out his or her own way of working.

The Process

As I indicated earlier, it is not always necessary to devote the entire session to imagery; it is often more effective to move between imagery and dialogue. With a new client I will wait until an 'image word' is used, as was the case with Anna, at the start of the previous Journey, and her use of the word 'insecure'. I would then take the client through a quick relaxation session; head resting back in the chair, legs arms and hands resting comfortably.

Some therapists believe that during imagery, the client's eyes should be closed and should remain closed until the imagery is over, and if the eyes are opened, the client should be told to close them. This is in the belief that outside stimuli will interfere with the process. This may be true; however, it is important to remember that we are all different and that some people feel very threatened closing their eyes in the presence of someone else. Janet was such a client. When I suggested she closed her eyes to relax, I sensed a tension, then added, 'But only if you want to.' This 'permission' allowed her a choice. I noticed that as the relaxation exercise went on, her eyes gradually closed. When the imagery session was over, she said, 'Thank you, I did feel afraid, now I feel really comfortable with you'. Janet was a victim of sexual abuse by her father. For her, closing her eyes in the company of comparative stranger felt too threatening.

The belief about outside stimuli interfering with inner visualisation may be justified. Someone who is very extraverted, who relates to the external world, may have difficulty with imagery if the eyes are kept open. Likewise an introverted person may have difficulties of a different kind; such a person may get so carried away with the inner pictures that the counsellor is left far behind. So, as with most activities, I would point this out to the client, and let the client decide.

Jim, also mentioned in the previous Journey, was quite introverted, and the first time we engaged in imagery, he kept his eyes open and worked very well with what he could obviously imagine happening somewhere within him. This was characteristic of Jim, though there were many times when he did close his eyes, and these were generally related to painful images. Generally I have found that the more extraverted a person, the more he or she will need to close the eyes; and the more introverted the person, the more he or she will need to keep the eyes open.

As I have said, there are no hard and fast rules, and often I'm asked, 'What about silences, how do you deal with them?' They are no more easy to deal with than silences in any counselling. However, it is important to remember that the client is processing information coming through as images and symbols. At the same time the client is struggling to make sense of what often seems nonsense, and may also be struggling with some deep emotion, or with some disturbing memory, triggered off by an image that seems to come from nowhere. A minute's silence seems a long time; two minutes' silence seems an age; longer silences can seem like eternity.

Knowing when to say something comes from a mixture of experience and intuition; even then what we say may be an intrusion at a particularly sensitive stage. Although I say, 'Keep me in touch with what's happening, please', my guess is that the client often forgets I'm there, and that presents its own difficulties. What does the counsellor do, think, feel while the client is lost in his or her own world? The client is never totally passive; there are changes in facial expressions, head movement, shifts in the chair, hand and leg movements, all indicators of something happening. But what? To make the link, I will say softly (for if the client really is lost in the image, my speaking could be an unwarranted intrusion) something like, 'Just now your right hand made a fist, I wonder what was happening'. Or, 'Your face flushed as if you were angry'. Often this, or 'I wonder what's happening right now' is enough to 'bring the client back'.

Imagery can be a deeply emotional experience for the client, and as there is close similarity between working with imagery and deep relaxation, plenty of time should be given for the client to readjust to 'reality'. I would normally allow fifteen minutes for this readjustment, during which time the client and I would discuss what was taking place during the imagery, though this would not necessarily mean interpreting the images or symbols. It is also important to make links between the present and preceding sessions. 'Last week you imagined you were walking through a desert, this week you'd left the desert behind and were confronted by a massive rock. What do you think that means?' Counselling, in whatever format, is a partnership, and an imagery session should be no different.

Theme One – The Meadow

Starting a session

'Now that you are relaxed I want you to imagine you are in a beautiful meadow somewhere; it can be somewhere you know, or you can create it out of your imagination. It is a warm, sunny afternoon, past midday, there is a slight breeze blowing and you feel at peace and comfortable. You look around, and somewhere you hear a stream, the water is tinkling on the stones as it makes its way through the meadow. As you look around you see a wood, a mountain, and a house. You like this place, you feel happy, and you decide to lie down on the grass. You look up at the blue sky, and watch the fluffy white clouds drifting slowly across the sky. You listen to the humming of the insects and the song of the birds, you hear the rustle of the grass shaken by the breeze. You feel drowsy and you begin to day-dream; what is going through your mind?'

This open-ended question helps to put the client in a relaxed frame of mind, and enhances the feeling of being in control. The images the client discloses will influence the way the session goes. I might say something like, 'Imagine a time in your life when you did something similar to this. Can you describe it to me – the place, the occasion, the people? This may evoke either pleasant or unpleasant memories. For one client it evoked the time she was lost, and the terror she felt as she wandered around the beach looking for her parents, a memory she hadn't consciously thought of for years.

When a few minutes have passed, and when there are no further memories evoked, I will say something like, 'Time is getting along now, and before you leave the meadow, take a look around it and describe what you see'. I will recreate part of the first session with Jim, whom we met earlier. When he did this introductory exercise, he wandered round the edge of the meadow, and described in great detail the hedges, the fences and the various trees in it. Some boundaries were broken, allowing animals to stray in and out; some were bounded entirely by fierce-looking barbed wire, or chain link. Jim's boundary was made of a well-kept hedge, and this was characteristic of Jim, who was a precise and well-ordered man.

WILLIAM:　　Are there any animals or people in the meadow?

JIM:　　　　No animals, but I can see two figures over there.

　　　　　　He walked over to them and a sad look came over his face.

　　　　　　It's my parents, but they're not real, they're statues.

WILLIAM:　　And how do you feel looking at them? You look quite sad.

JIM:　　　　I am, I don't understand this at all. If they were dead I could understand it, but they're not. They're cold stone.

WILLIAM:　　Perhaps they seem dead to you?

JIM:　　　　That's very true. I don't like it here. May we move on, please?

Discussion of Jim

It is not always appropriate to explore there and then what the client discloses, and the deeper the psychological issue, the less it is appropriate to explore it. My feeling is that it takes time for the image to work within the client's psyche. Time, as we know it, is not something the psyche understands; the psyche does not have a clock that measures time in twenty-four hour segments. I believe that the psyche is like eternity, where time has *no* meaning. When something is ready to happen, it will.

For example, when Jim lay down in the grass, he imagined it so tall that he was completely hidden. It would have been inappropriate for me at that stage to make suggestions as to the possible meanings of that. Some months later, however, when we were discussing symbols in general, Jim said, 'That long grass, it had to be tall, for I didn't want to be seen by *them*, although I didn't know they were there.'

This illustrates the idea in the above paragraph. Some part of Jim, probably his inner child, wanted to keep his presence secret from his parents, although there was no reason for him so to do. Then when he 'found' his parents, they were lifeless and cold. We spent many sessions talking through his relationship with his parents, and how distant he felt from them. So, in the first session, we see the seeds being sown of what was to come.

Sometimes the client may imagine the meadow exactly as it was in the previous session, in every detail; other clients introduce changes – clouds, rain, animals, people. Every change indicates something happening in the emotions. A cloud passing over the sun, throwing shadows on the landscape, is a frequent image which indicates difficulties. Where the original image was a sunny afternoon, the subsequent image may be of another season, much less inviting, or a snow scene with all the surrounding images. The weather is a reliable indicator of mood.

In the early stages I 'set the scene' by describing the weather, but that is about all. Occasionally the client will say something like, 'I can't get a picture of a meadow', in which case I will respond, 'That's fine, what do you imagine?' Some imagine the seashore, with long stretches of sand, washed by the sea; others a desert island, barren and dry. Each of these 'pictures' shows part of the inner world of the client. The latter picture might be interpreted as depicting emotional dryness.

The word 'meadow', to most people, conjures up images of childhood, a return to nature, of simple beauty. For some it has suggestions of Paradise; a home base. It is for this reason that most people who work with images choose to start the journey of inner exploration with the meadow. I repeat, not all counselling starts in this way; more often it starts by latching on to an image word or a feeling that evokes an image in me. Then I find it a good time to ask, 'If you were an artist, or just using your imagination, what picture would you paint to describe that feeling?' This gives a useful clue as to how the client might use imagery.

The idea of the 'home base' is quite an important one, for when we are engaged in definite imagery journeys, rather than what could be called 'spot imaging', we will always start with the meadow scene. This return to familiar ground is important, to give a sense of security. There is another reason for the home base. As we reach the end of the meadow scene, I will say something like, 'Just before you leave the meadow, take a good look round, familiarise yourself with it; hear the sounds, smell the warm earth, the flowers; listen to the birds. Look again at the stream, the mountain, the wood and the house, for you will be returning here, probably many times. There is something else, this is your secret place, nobody can violate it, no one can come uninvited, you have invited me, and I thank you. In times of stress or difficulty, you can be here in an instant, and here you can feel safe. Now, in your own time, when you are ready, return to this room on (say) Tuesday the (say) seventh of May 1996 at (say) three o'clock.' This last part should not be neglected, for it is important that the client is 'grounded' in the present. The client may have been a million miles away, in a totally different time scale, and to be brought 'back to earth' suddenly could be very disorientating.

An anecdote will suffice to draw this theme to a close. My client, Mark, had been in imagery for well over half an hour, and was deeply engrossed in navigating a way through a marsh, when suddenly his bleeper went off, startling us both. Normally he left the machine at reception, but had forgotten to do so. The reaction of us both was like suddenly being wakened in the middle of a dream. I trust that this story will alert you to the dangers of modern technology.

A final point about the meadow. I have found that people who cannot work with the meadow image have difficulty with imagery in general, so for them, this may not be an appropriate way of working. This does not mean that they may not be able to do 'spot imagery', but their strengths probably lie in other areas.

Theme Two – The Stream

Either in the first session, if there is time, or in the second, I will say, 'Of the other images, the stream, mountain, house or wood, which would you like to explore first?' This leaves the psyche in control. For the purpose of this book, however, I will keep to the plan.

It is useful, fairly early on, to get the client to make a sketch of the meadow, with the other symbols; this helps to 'fix' it in the mind. For instance, a stream starts from somewhere and goes somewhere; that is an obvious statement but it needs to be explored. Symbolically the stream has a beginning and an end, beyond where the client is, and a middle, where the client is now. A stream that flows from the client's left to right is moving from the feminine to the masculine, from the creative to the thinking side of the brain, from the Yin towards the Yang. Why is this important? It suggests that if the client wishes to explore the origin of the stream, the journey will take her or him into the intuitive part. If the client wishes to explore to the right, towards the sea, it will explore the logical part. On the other hand, if the stream flows from right to left, it is flowing from the masculine towards the feminine, from the thinking, logical part towards the intuitive part, from the Yang towards the Yin. The direction of the flow is a possible indication of where the psyche is directing the exploration.

The next question would be, 'If you were to explore this stream, which way would you go?' Upstream is often regarded as the easier option, and equates to ascent; downstream equates to the descent, into the unconscious.

When Rhona was asked this she replied, 'I don't want to explore it; I just want to paddle in it and enjoy myself'. As she paddled she began to talk about two abortions she'd been through and the pain and shame of them. There was something about her play in the water that reminded me of baptism, and the fact that her two 'children' were not baptised. 'It sounds as if maybe you want to raise some sort of memorial to your two children, and maybe baptise them,' I suggested. 'Could I? Wouldn't it be sinful?' she asked. It would have been easy to offer reassurances that it would be 'all right', yet Rhona was hesitant. 'Who's telling you it's sinful?' I asked. She was silent for quite some time, then said, 'I am, nobody else. So I'll do it'. Rhona chose two stones, from the streambed, picked them up and then held them under the water. 'What do you want to do with them now?' I asked. 'I'll take them with me.'

Until that time, Rhona had denied any pain attached to the abortions. The scene by the stream allowed her pain to wash over her in symbolic cleansing. There were many times afterwards that Rhona needed to return to the stream scene. Seldom is such healing accomplished in one session.

Rhona didn't wish to explore the flow of the stream, but Carole did. There was no hesitancy when I asked the question. For her the origin called, and that was to her left. To explore the origin has a certain regressive quality about it, going back to the source, which has overtones of the mother–child relationship and a return to the womb.

For Carole the return to the origin happened in a strange way, and highlights another psychic trick. In all imagery there is the possibility that the client makes the particular journey an idyllic one, where all is bright and cheerful, although I have rarely encountered this. More often it is the opposite, where, in the case of the stream theme, there are gigantic rocks, waterfalls or even rapids to overcome.

For Carole, it was a hill that got in the way, and the stream disappeared into a steep cliff, and if she were to continue, she would have to part company with the stream for a while. While she toiled up the hill, through woods, I said, 'It sounds like really hard work.' 'Ah, that's me, William. I always make hard work out of things. I wonder why?' This led to a fruitful discussion about the difficulties she had experienced when her parents divorced and she went to live with her autocratic grandmother whose strictness and insistence on discipline left little space for Carole to develop the more intuitive side of her personality, which is possibly why she chose to journey towards the origin.

One of the exciting features about imagery is that nothing is predictable. The stream is included in the primary level themes because it is reckoned to be 'safe'. We have already seen with Rhona how it can tap into very deep feelings, and so it was with Carole. As her guide she took a cocker spaniel who led her to the top of the hill where she 'discovered' a clearing with a large tree and a seat, with a name carved on it which she was not able to decipher. This suggested that either it was from the past and it didn't matter, or that it wasn't yet ready to be deciphered.

At the base of the tree Carole found a door which led into a tunnel. There was every indication at this stage that this would lead underground, and my hunch was that it was a passage to a cave. This was not how 'directed imagery' therapists would have it, at least not in the client's fifth session. This was a second level image, but it would have been highly inappropriate to have stopped the process, so I went with it. The tunnel was dark, so Carole found a lantern on a shelf, which lighted the many steps that led her down, through a door and into a huge cavern. In the middle was a large pool, the source of the stream. The water was grey and uninviting, but warm to the touch. Another door beckoned her, which led her outside onto the hill again.

I asked if she wanted to do anything about the lack of colour in the cave. She broke a hole in the rock, thus allowing a shaft of light to shine directly on the source, which now looked blue. 'How would you interpret that?' I asked. 'The cave is my emotional life, colourless and vast, but I've opened it up to allow some light in.'

Discussion of Carole

This was only Carole's fifth session, and she was demonstrating very accurate insight in interpreting what was happening. Her comment about her 'emotional life' was a recurring theme; she felt an overwhelming need to be in control, and never to cry. She felt, as a result of her upbringing, that her emotional life was very underdeveloped; she had a good brain and prided herself on that, but desperately wanted to be able to express how she felt.

It is interesting that although this was only the fifth session, and we had done very little imagery work, her psyche decided she was capable of handling the journey to the cave to find the origin. At the same time, it was obvious that having discovered the source, Carole didn't want to stay to explore the cave, and that was fine. She achieved the breakthrough she needed *at that time*. Carole stayed in counselling for around eighteen months.

To return to the stream image: it may be a trickle over rocks and pebbles, shallow and clear, deep and rapid, brown with peat; it may have fish in it. All these spontaneous images have their meanings, and while it may not be appropriate to explore every one, they should be noted. The question 'Are any of these things important to you?' may trigger off a memory.

Hamish originated in the Western Isles, and his stream issued from the hills high above his native croft, and the water was a dark brown that frothed with peat deposits as it bubbled down the steep hill into a waterfall. I was prompted to ask, 'What does the water taste like?' His face screwed up in disgust, but that question triggered off a memory of when he nearly drowned in the waterfall. So for Hamish the stream, almost entering into the sea, meant that he had some unfinished business to deal with related to that incident.

Some clients want to take off their clothes and swim. This suggests the throwing off of restraints. In imagery, anything goes; for in imagery they may do what in the real world they would not dare to do. Crossing the stream, in itself, suggests adventure. Following the stream towards the sea may seem a long way, and sometimes it is, but it need not be. If the aim is the sea, it is the journey that is important; the road travelled, the people met on the way, the events, the objects, the trees and plants. For example, what is it like on the opposite bank? Does the path suddenly end? Where does it continue? Are there any bridges? What does the client see in the water as it flows under the bridge? Standing in the middle of the bridge, what lies behind, what lies ahead?

Sometimes the stream becomes dammed up and then it is important to explore the cause and the purpose. In the natural world, streams and rivers are dammed up and form lakes or reservoirs, in order to supply water elsewhere. On the other hand, if the client cannot discover the outlet, then the whole region around the dammed up part should be examined, until the outlet is re-established.

Most often the stream in imagination follows the same sort of course as it would in the natural world, even though it may have to overcome obstacles. Sometimes it does strange things, such as going uphill or going round in circles, so that the client keeps returning to the same spot. This suggests that there is unfinished business to attend to before it is possible to continue.

What happens when the stream joins with another stream? How does the client feel? This is symbolic of losing one's identity in the vaster identity of the universe, the great unconscious. This can be scary, but the idea can be built in that even if there is only one drop left, that drop represents part of the original, so although it may be changed, it is never lost, never destroyed.

The sea is a natural extension of the stream or river, but on a much wider, deeper scale. The sea is an endless reservoir of water with unfathomable depths, symbolising the unconscious. Although the boundaries of the sea are not so rigidly defined as those of the lake, river or stream, the sea does have its bounds. Heavy downpours often cause streams and rivers to break their boundaries and flood the surrounding land. Seas often break over their boundaries when the waters are whipped up by fierce winds or by high tides. The sea can be a friendly place, thronged with people, bathing and relaxing; or it can be a place of danger, where bathing would be foolhardy.

When the client reaches the sea, I would say something like, 'What do you want to do now you are here?' There is no guarantee that if in the real world the client is a non-swimmer that she or he will be afraid of the water, or vice versa. For the psyche recognises that the sea is the unconscious. Some clients, even though they are still early on in the imagery process, have enough psychological awareness to be able to cope with what may lie in the waters of the sea.

I would certainly recommend getting in gradually, not diving, unless the client is well-versed in the psychology of the unconscious. Diving into water is symbolic of penetration, probing, or invasion of another element, and the diver may be confronted with terrifying images and symbols that represent monstrous, archaic figures from either the personal unconscious, or from the Collective Unconscious. However, it can be fruitful.

Phil *was* well-versed in the work of the unconscious, and came with the explicit aim of learning to work with imagery. I introduced the sea theme, and there was no fear of diving in. Down in the depths he found a cave. The bottom of the cave was silted over with sand, and sticking out was the foot of a skeleton. Scraping away the sand he found a complete skeleton. When I asked him what it represented to him he immediately linked it to a broken relationship many years before in Australia. He had tried to bury the pain of that, but now he was having to confront it.

Theme Three – Mountain

Although the principal theme is the mountain, I want to extend this to include landscape in general. A mountain does not stand in isolation, it is part of a landscape, and all that the client imagines gives clues to the emotional state or mood.

Landscape

Landscapes are invariably connected with journeys, and the significance of the various features of the landscape are linked to their emotional content. Various landscapes, such as gardens, fountains, lakes, rivers, hills and rocks, are the haunts of people who love nature. Just as in life, we 'discover' a site, rather than 'choose' it, so in imagery; we do not deliberately set out to create a particular landscape, it simply happens.

The landscape may be verdant, green and fruitful; it may be dry and parched like the desert; it may be rocky, with only sparse growth; it may be bounded by rivers, or the sea, or mountains. It may be some frozen waste, or an island sweltering under the tropical sun. The sky may be brilliant, dark with clouds, or lit only by the moon, or no light at all. It may be a park in the middle of a city, surrounded by skyscrapers, fences and traffic. The landscape may be colourless or full of natural or exaggerated colours. It may be deluged by rain or snow. All of these have their own meanings, and normally give a clue to the client's mood or view of life now or for the future. Only the context in which the symbol is placed can help determine its possible meaning.

Valleys are important symbols of the landscape. A valley is a low area more or less enclosed by hills and usually with a stream flowing through it. The valley is a fertile place, as distinct from the surrounding hills, and is in direct contrast to the nature of the desert. Thus, the valley symbolises life and fruitfulness. The valley is associated with death: 'Yea, though I walk through the valley of the shadow of death, I will fear no evil: for thou art with me; thy rod and thy staff comfort me' (Psalm 23:4).

The valley of death is used to symbolise the slaughter in *The Charge of the Light Brigade* by Tennyson; in *Pilgrim's Progress* John Bunyan says, 'It is an hard matter for a man to go down into the valley of Humiliation, and to catch no slip by the way'.

Without the surrounding hills and mountains there would be no valley, so mountains and valleys are linked images. It is from the hills that the water drains down into the valley. While there is growth on the mountain, it is generally a stark place, a place of effort and hardship. Yet it is also a place of victory, aspiration and thrill, where we can see views hidden from us when we are in the valley. Yet it is down in the valley where the work has to be done. This does not imply that in the personal quest that the work in the valley is any less or more important than the work on the mountain. What it does mean is that the valley should not be ignored. This ascent and descent in imagery are important related symbols which will be discussed in the Eighth Journey (Exploring the Heights and the Depths).

We sometimes refer to a 'valley experience', the mundane, the everyday, when the routine things of life press down on us, when we long for the mountain-top experience. From time to time we need to climb the mountain again, and take a look at what lies below and beyond; but in order to reach there we have to descend. Martin Luther King (1929–68) said, 'I just want to do God's will. And he's allowed me to go up to the mountain. And I've looked over, and I've seen the promised land. So I'm happy tonight. I'm not worried about anything. I'm not fearing any man'.[1] Was King's psyche speaking on that occasion?

Generally, when the client first encounters the meadow scene, the mountain is at a distance, thus implying that there is a journey before the mountain is reached. At this early stage it is helpful to ask the client to describe the mountain from that distance, for each of the associated symbols has a bearing on the potential journey. The mountain can be bare, or forested; grassy, or of sheer rock; clad in snow or bathed in sunshine. These are not mere picturesque images, but they don't need much interpretation, particularly when they are related to the future.

---

1   Speech in Memphis, 3 April 1968 (the day before his assassination), quoted in the *New York Times* 4 April 1968, page 24.

A related exercise is to ask the client to imagine what the scene would be like from half-way up, then again from the top of the mountain. Very often the two panoramas are quite different, when the client is actually climbing the mountain, and much will depend on the amount of inner work done between the two. Very often, when viewed from a distance, the top seems a long way off, and no path is visible.

When asked to do this, the client may imagine the sort of atmosphere or 'feel' given out by the mountain; approachable, jagged, aloof, and so on. These descriptions are what we often apply to people (or people apply to us). An interesting point is to ask the client who he or she would associate with this mountain. Often the term 'man-mountain' is given, and then linked with some hero, or heroine, although more often the association is with male figures. A related question would be, 'What sort of animals or birds live there?' The answer is an indication of the nature of the creatures. Are they friendly or not? Would they act as companions or as enemies?

When Jim looked at the mountain he felt fear rise within him; it looked forbidding, and strange. He described as, 'All angular and sharp, and it keeps shifting. Nothing stable about it'. I did not interpret it, neither did he, and it was not until many sessions later that he ventured towards the mountain.

Thinking about it now, it would seem that while some people would talk about their foundations shaking, Jim was actually experiencing that sort of feeling. He set great store by his brilliant brain, not that he was conceited or vain; he just accepted it as fact. So in a sense, coming into counselling, and electing to work for most of the time with imagery, intuitively he felt that his strong point – his mountain – was not going to see him through this experience without being subjected to much shaking. The mountain image is more masculine than feminine, more thinking than intuitive, and Jim was having to re-evaluate these other parts of himself. So the mountain that was once firm and secure was now being shaken as if in an earthquake.

Mountain climbing is symbolic of the exploration and conquest of the aspirations. The Indians believed the peaks of the Himalayas to be the home of the gods, in the same way as the Greeks regarded Mount Olympus as the place where their deities resided. For the Japanese, Mount Fujiama is invested with sacred meaning. And of course there is the significance of Moses receiving the Ten Commandments on Mount Sinai. So it is no coincidence that in imagery, climbing the mountain represents the striving for higher or spiritual values.

Sometimes the top of the mountain is hidden by clouds; this symbolises mystery, there is more to be revealed. When Glenn climbed his mountain it was not an easy climb, for in life he didn't like heights. His psyche made it so difficult for him, and put him at one stage on a precipice, from where he had to be rescued by someone throwing him down a rope and pulling him up. He reached a plateau, not uncommon in this theme, from where he looked back along the path he had laboriously climbed and at the several obstacles to get where he was.

A plateau is a place to rest, to gather strength. It is not the top; it is a place to take stock. As Glenn looked up at the mountain top, it became shrouded in mist. 'Oh, no! Not something else to deal with. Why can't things be straightforward,' he groaned, literally. The summit of Glenn's mountain was reached only after another difficult climb, but as he climbed, the mist cleared, and by the time he reached the top, it had disappeared totally. 'What do I do now, William?' I suggested he look for a cave. My hunch was that he needed a reward for the difficult climb, and where better to look than in a cave. What he found was a 'visitor's book' to sign. His was the first name, and he proudly wrote, 'I made it!' 'What would you like to take away with you?' I asked. 'I'll take this illuminated scroll with me, testifying that I have been awarded this because I made the difficult climb.'

Discussion

The difficult ascent reflected Glenn's studies, which had not been easy, and had been made more difficult by the attitude of his parents who did not approve of his choice, compounded by his having to retake part of his degree. I would have been surprised if the ascent had been easy; too easy a journey, or one accomplished too quickly is an indication of the client's unwillingness to confront the inner world. In reality, climbing a mountain takes time and effort, and so in imagery. If there were no effort, no struggle, I might wonder why the client was seeking counselling.

There is the possibility, in such a case, that climbing the mountain is mistimed, that there needs to be an exploration of the stream, or possibly to go back to a previous journey. It is also interesting that the more difficult the climb to the summit, the more likelihood that the person is driven by a demanding and exacting personality. This was certainly so in Glenn's case, driven as he was by parents who set impossible standards.

Sometimes the client can become lost on the mountain; the path disappears, or is blocked by a wall of rock. In this instance the counsellor may need to step in with assistance, although not immediately. 'If you look around you will see something that will take you out of this predicament', is often enough for the climber to discover a rope, a ladder, or something else to help them 'escape'. Even an animal may be used as part of the escape. Sometimes the journey has to be terminated there and then. 'Perhaps you've had enough for today?' gives the client the option not to feel under pressure, and this is important. Glenn was lifted off the mountain top by a helicopter and transported to his favourite beach. Whatever happens, whatever form the climb takes, it is essential that the client returns to his or her chosen place as a transition back into the outside world.

Theme Four – The House

The house, a chest, a walled garden are all accepted symbols of the feminine principle. The house is credited with being the storehouse of all wisdom. The house represents different layers of the psyche. The outside signifies the outward appearance; our personality, the façade we put up, the mask we wear. The roof and upper floor represent the head and the mind, as well as the conscious will and the mind. The cellar corresponds to the unconscious and the instincts. The kitchen is a place of work, the place where substances are transformed. Stairs are the links between various levels, and are particularly significant whether they ascend or descend.

The principal symbolism of the window is separating inside from outside. In this respect it is similar to a door or a wall, but the main difference is that it is transparent, so its purpose is to let light in. If the house is taken as representing the person, then the window represents the eye, and the eye is said to represent the person's soul. The Virgin Mary is alluded to as the 'window of heaven' (Walker 1985). When one is outside looking through a window, this is symbolic of a desire to see into the unconscious, the unknown; looking out is symbolic of moving into the conscious and the known. An open window symbolises invitation, a closed window symbolises privacy. A broken window suggests violence; if broken from the outside it represents intrusion; if broken from the inside, it suggests escape. A window dressed with light net is symbolic of a degree of openness; when dressed with heavy net, it suggests exclusion. A lighted window is symbolic of hope; a darkened window suggests death. A light shining of a window is symbolic of a beacon, or a homing device.

The house theme is generally accepted to represent the person, and for this reason, if the six themes in the first level were taken in order of complexity, they would be in the order presented here. However, as I have said several times, the psyche doesn't always subscribe to our order of things. So when in the meadow, although not generally in the first imagery session, I ask the client, 'Which of these would you like to explore first?' I have to be prepared for the psyche to choose; sometimes that choice is the house.

If the house is regarded as the self, then it is also symbolic of the feminine part of us, or at least more feminine than masculine. Very often it is a 'remembered' house, at first, but after a time, the psyche seems to take over and takes the client into parts that did not exist in the original house. One of the fundamental principles of working with the psyche is that one has to be prepared to go where the psyche leads, work with what the psyche reveals. For the counsellor this can be scary, for one cannot plan. If *you* don't feel comfortable with 'free-floating imagery', that which is unplanned, then try working with guided imagery, where you direct the client to look at specific symbols or parts of the scene.

It would be considered unwise for the client to enter the house suddenly, in much the same way as diving into the sea suddenly is unadvisable. Now follows what would be a typical scenario, working from the meadow. I would say something like, 'We've explored the meadow, stream, and mountain, we still have the house and the woods; which of these two would you now like to explore? (Although the rosebush is included in the first level, this is a theme I would introduce as a linking with the next level). I shall assume the client has elected to explore the house. 'From where you are, how would you describe the house? How far is it from you? What is the feeling you get as you look at it?' (These questions are similar to the questions asked about the mountain). I would listen carefully to the replies, but rarely interpret, or ask for an interpretation, at this stage. Interpretation calls on a certain amount of 'thinking' and analysis, and too much could interrupt the flow of the imagination and intuition. I would then say something like, 'Now walk towards it and tell me if anything changes.'

Beverley was doing this exercise and imagined a big brick-built house, with a fairly high wall around it, and a gravel path leading up to a white-painted gate in an archway in the middle of the wall. This was a house she had seen in Ireland, but had never been in. She had looked at it through the gate, but that is all. A gate or a door is often the first hurdle or barrier to overcome, particularly if it is shut, as this one was. It is at a time like this that we must be patient, and not hurry the client.

The client may decide to explore the garden first, and that is acceptable, for the garden can reveal a great deal about the client's inner world. Gardens may be formal, with neat, well-kept beds and immaculate lawns, with carefully trimmed edges; or they can be overcrowded and fussy; or they can be wild, where nature has taken over. There may be orchards, and the trees and bushes may be in blossom, heralding fruitfulness, or already bearing fruit. It may be winter and the trees are stripped of leaves. It is not unusual for the client to imagine a fountain, or a pond or lake. If it is a lake, the absence of wild life maybe an indication of the barrenness of the client's inner world. As the house and garden are inseparable, a thorough exploration of the garden and its surroundings is useful; however, an overlong exploration *before* exploring the house could be a means of putting off this part of the exercise. In which case, a remark such as, 'We have lots to discuss about the garden, and you can always come back to it; how do you feel about exploring the house now?' keeps things moving forward.

Beverley was a mature woman, yet she had been transported back to her childhood, and was now about eight, she said, looking wistfully through the gate, not daring even to press the bell. This is characteristic of imagery, and one has to tread carefully, remembering constantly to check out exactly where the client is, and what age. An adult would ring the bell, or walk through and knock on the door.

I said, 'What does this child want to do?' To which she replied, 'I want to go in, but mother might be cross with me'. In discussion later, it emerged that her mother was the one who did the disciplining in the family, and was held in great awe by her children. 'So you need permission even to ring the bell, is that it?' She struggled with that question before she said, 'No, I don't!', with a defiant lift of her chin. There was no reply, so she opened the gate and as she walked up the long drive, she described the garden which was pleasantly unkempt.

It is always advisable to be courteous when dealing with the psyche, so I advised Beverley to knock; she did, but no one came. 'Try the handle', I advised. She did, and the door opened into a darkened hall. 'It's spooky', Beverley said as she looked around. I suggested she pause for a moment, while she thought which part of the house she would like to look at first.

Some counsellors might direct the client to specific levels. This is based on the theory that the cellar relates more to the unconscious and feelings; the ground floor to the conscious, or Ego, and the attic to the superego or conscience, and to the intellect and thinking. Every room has its own symbolism, as one would expect: the living room symbolises comfort and leisure; the bedroom symbolises intimacy and rest; the kitchen symbolises transformation of raw ingredients, and work; the study symbolises intellectual work and recreation; the dining room symbolises meeting the physical needs; the cellar represents the foundations of personality; the attic represents knowledge stored away. Treasure can be discovered anywhere, but often in both cellar and attic.

To my question, 'Where would you like to start to explore?' Beverley replied, 'Am I allowed to? It's not my house'. I replied, 'If the owner had given you permission, where would you like to start?' This suggests that the owner has given permission, although it is not stated. Personally, I find this tentative approach works really well. If Beverley had said, 'I still need permission', I might have suggested that somewhere in the house or outside, she would find the person she could ask permission from. Not until the house had been explored for the first time would I speak about it representing the client and even then it would normally take the form of, 'Having spent some time in the house, have you any ideas what it represents?' Then it would be, 'How would you feel if I said it represented you?' As much as possible it is better for the client to discover what's what, rather than to be told.

Beverley had her first real clue as to the identity of the house when she visited the 'library', and found a diary, entitled, 'The private diary of Beverley –.' As she 'read' some of the pages, she started to cry over long-forgotten memories, of thoughts recorded twenty years before. Whether these were actual memories is unimportant; what is important is that they released a great deal of emotion about her childhood.

When Phil explored his house, the front and the back presented two different appearances. The front was well-kept, rather traditional, and pleased Phil. When I invited him to 'look round the back', he was so taken aback at its ramshackle appearance that he started to cry. His 'front', as a doctor, was conformist, and he recognised that there was a shadow side, kept well out of sight.

When he explored the house, he stopped at a door, tried the handle and found the door to be locked. The 'locked door theme' is often introduced later in counselling, if it does not occur spontaneously, as it did with Phil. A room where the door is closed is a symbol of privacy, of private thoughts. A locked room symbolises secrecy; dark secrets, skeletons. A room with windows allows light in and permits the person to see out. Windows not clean enough to see through speak of disuse.

'What do you want to do with that door? I asked Phil. 'Part of me wants to break it down, but that wouldn't be right, I know that, so I must find the key.' This expression, 'find the key' can refer to an actual key or a symbolic key, such as 'Open sesame', or some other magical key. But here there was a lock, so it could be assumed that Phil needed to find the key. I said, 'What do you think could be in that room? Or who?' He had no idea, although some clients do have an inkling.

It could be postulated that the locked room has a sexual symbolism, particularly as the lock is the female to the male key. Was Phil to discover something about his sexuality? Where was the key? The feeling that it was something to do with sexuality was strengthened when he found the key in a large china urn, standing in the hall. In symbolism, containers are generally regarded as representing the feminine.

Phil said, 'I'm holding this "golden" key and admiring the intricate pattern on the handle; this is no ordinary key and no ordinary door. I feel a bit scared at what I might find. Here goes!' The room was curtained and only dimly lit, and 'it smells really musty. It hasn't been opened for a long, long time.' 'What can you see in it?' I asked. He drew the curtains, and opened the window, then said, 'A chest, with "Phil" written in large letters. Gosh that's weird. Does it mean that's me, or does it belong to me?' 'Perhaps it means both?' I suggested. 'If that trunk is me, then I'm opening me up to see what's inside. But that's exactly what I am doing.'

He opened the trunk and found only one item, a hand mirror, but no ordinary mirror; this one, like the key to the door, was golden, beautiful and obviously precious. Who can resist looking in a mirror? Not Phil. He picked it up, but what he saw reflected was not his own face but the face of himself as a woman. Was the psyche playing a trick on him? He sat on a chair, still looking in the mirror and said, 'Is this telling me I'm gay?' This certainly could be one interpretation, but experience has taught me not to go for the first interpretation. 'It could, but what else could it mean?' I asked, aware that Phil was looking quite shocked, having his sexuality confronted in this way. 'I don't know, William. I'm stuck.' Answers rarely come neatly packaged, ready for pulling off the shelf to be handed out to the next customer; rather the answer develops; although writing about it now, it loses some of the mystery, the thrill of mutual discovery.

'Is the mirror reflecting you, Phil, the man?' I asked. 'No, it's reflecting someone very like me, who could be my twin, but it's female.' 'So, male and female. What does that suggest to you?' 'Two, partners, Adam and Eve, opposites.' When he said the last word, we both knew that was the answer. When such an answer comes, one wonders why it often takes so long for the truth to dawn! 'My female part, the feminine?' Phil asked. 'I've hidden my feminine part away, locked her in a room, for all these years, yet she comes to me in a gold key and a gold mirror. Wow!'

This was not the end of Phil's journey in the integration of his feminine principle, however; his work as a doctor was greatly enhanced as he learned to make use of the what he had hidden away for so many years.

Sometimes the client will meet people in the house, and this would not be surprising. I shall be dealing in more detail with significant people in Theme Fourteen. Significant people tend to occupy specific rooms in a house, and often represent Archetypes, rather than actual people, although real people often do appear. When they do, it is likely that they represent something in the client's immediate life, whereas archetypal figures represent something much deeper.

When Jenny knocked at the door of her house, it was opened by a witch. This took both Jenny and me totally by surprise. When the witch screeched at Jenny, 'Go away you horrid child' (reminiscent of a fairy tale), I encouraged Jenny to stand her ground, to speak politely and firmly, and tell her she had every right to come in. Though it took a lot of courage, Jenny did it, and the witch was transformed into a mouse that scuttled away out of sight.

Other archetypal figures are Mother and Father, and grandparents, step-parents, particularly the step-mother, giants, religious figures, the Devil; the list could go on. A browse through the *Dictionary of Images and Symbols in Counselling* (Stewart 1996) might prove a fruitful study, for many of the items there are supplemented with possible psychological interpretations. Before we leave the house theme, there is one final observation to be made. If the house is revisited, and often this is helpful, particularly when there has been significant personal development, it may have changed considerably since the first visit.

Beverley had been in counselling for many months and towards the end she went back to the house. On her first visit she encountered the witch; on this visit, as she approached the house, she said, 'There's smoke coming out of the chimney and the gate is open.' her knock was answered by a kindly old lady, who welcomed her with a smile and called her by name. Although Beverley didn't recognise the old lady, they had a good rapport, and Beverley was invited to 'afternoon tea'. As Beverley left, the old lady handed her a red leather book, which Beverley recognised as her old diary. The old lady thumbed through the pages, then took out a pen and wrote on one blank page, 'The past is finished' and on the facing page wrote, 'The future is starting'. I don't think further comment is needed.

Theme Five – The Woods

The Oxford English Dictionary defines a wood as 'A collection of trees growing more or less thickly together (especially naturally, as distinguished from a plantation), of considerable extent, usually larger than a grove or copse (but including these), and smaller than a forest; a piece of ground covered with trees, with or without undergrowth'. A forest is defined as 'An extensive tract of land covered with trees and undergrowth, sometimes intermingled with pasture' and 'A forest is also: A wild uncultivated waste, a wilderness'.

For the purposes of imagery, the dictionary definition may not be important, for if the psyche wants to lead the client to a pasture while exploring the woods, so be it. I have included the definitions so that you may have some pictures in your own mind.[2]

Many clients, when given the choice, as they are in the first session, of which theme to explore, instinctively leave the wood until much later. Woods represent the depths of the unconscious, in a similar way to the sea or ocean. The principal difference is that the sea explores the below-ground level, and the primeval, essence of life, while woods represent the growth of the unconscious. The sea, at least on the surface, is light, while the wood is mostly dark. The sea is a reservoir, collecting from many sources and containing millions of different life forms; the wood represents upward striving to reach the light. The roots of the trees burrow into the unconscious; the trunk pierces the conscious and the branches are in the element of air, where they support the life of birds and tree-living creatures.

So much for a survey of the general symbolism; now to the use of the woods theme. I would rarely direct the client into the woods as that could precipitate acute anxiety. The woods theme is deeply buried in our collective unconscious, through myths, legends and fairy tales, which often feature frightening archetypal figures. Woods, however large, have a boundary, a perimeter, an edge, and this is often an appropriate place to start the exploration.

2   See also entries on 'forest' and 'wood' in Stewart 1996.

Some clients, bold enough in exploring the other themes, are overcome with timidity when they approach the woods. So, rather than rush in, I would ask, 'How would you describe the wood? Does it have a hedge or fence? Are there any paths? Can you see any animals? I would ask similar questions as for the meadow or the house. The lack of paths may indicate an unwillingness to explore just yet. Animals often represent archetypal figures, and may be fearsome or friendly.

An invitation to explore the boundary usually helps to allay fears, and where a path was not visible, such an exploration often shows a path in to the woods.

Peter's journey into the wood illustrates a different theme. He didn't want to 'waste time' by looking at the exterior, and there was a ready-made path waiting for him. As he went deeper into the wood, it became more dense and dark and then he was confronted with a wood within the wood, and he felt he could go no further. 'There's something in there I don't like the feel of.' I suggested that he walk round this part and pay attention to what he saw. He did this and imagined a pathway which he sensed led right through to the other side. 'Could you go down that path?' I asked. 'I could if I had a light,' he replied, as he equipped himself with a lantern. 'You feel safer now?' I inquired. He nodded.

His journey through the woods led him on a strange journey to end up in a cave, near the sea, in which he found an old chest containing twelve empty green bottles. We never did discover the significance to him of those bottles, but possibly they represented a past life, or perhaps they represented his present inner life which he felt was not very productive. This journey would have felt very negative, but I encouraged him to look around to see if there was anything else. A door in the cave led him down into another cave and a lake of the most beautifully blue water, in which he bathed and was refreshed.

In the Preface, I introduced Jane and recounted how she confronted her fears of the tree by befriending it. Fears can take many forms, not just those of animals or people. Just as Peter needed a lantern (some form of light is an image often used when exploring the unconscious), so other people may need the presence of another person or an animal, or some other form of talisman. This is not silly, for the psyche is preparing the person for what lies ahead, particularly if the fears take the form of fearsome creatures.

Some therapists use the technique of 'calling out' whatever is lurking in the woods. Although I don't often do this, Karen was one client with whom I did use it. She was terrified of going into the wood, and to my question, 'What is it you're most afraid of?' she replied, 'I wouldn't be able to cope with whatever is in there. It must be something really horrible.'

'What's the most horrible creature you could imagine?' I asked, basing this on the principle that if we can imagine the worst, then anything else would seem manageable. 'One of those three-headed dragons I've seen in picture books,' she replied, with a shudder.

Her reply is an indication of the level at which she was functioning. The word 'picture books' suggested she was at quite a young age, and possibly reliving some lurid fairy tale. I said, 'Before we go on, I suggest you provide yourself with some sort of protection against what's in there. What would it be?' Quick as a flash, she said, 'A sword.' 'So you are Saint George, ready to slay the dragon?' I deliberately made a joke of it, and she smiled.

A sword, as we shall see in the next Journey, represents the masculine principle, and it was interesting that Karen recognised that the masculine part of her needed to be acknowledged, and put to use. I asked her to describe the sword, and again I thought the psyche was enjoying a joke. 'It's large, one of those two-handed swords, with a beautifully carved handle.' The reason for my comment about the 'joke' was that Karen was a petite five foot in height, and yet the sword she described was large and would have been heavy to wield. The more I thought about it, and since, the more I realised that this was more than a joke. Karen had a high-powered, demanding, competitive job in research, where feelings took a low priority. So her masculine principle was certainly very strong.

'So you now feel equipped to tackle whatever might come out of the wood when you command it to?' I asked. She nodded. After a few minutes, as she stood some distance from the edge of the wood and called, 'I command you to come out, whatever you are that's making me afraid', and started giggling. Humour in counselling is a joy, and this was one of those infectious moments. 'Do you know what's emerged? A rabbit, a soft, furry, white rabbit. I don't believe it! I've been frightened of a rabbit.'

In one of those moments of inspiration, I said, 'No, not of the rabbit, you've been frightened of the fear.' She looked at me, taking in what I'd said, then nodded. 'Yes, that's exactly right. There never was anything to be frightened of at all, just a picture in a book.'

There was no need for Karen to do any further exploration of that particular theme, at that time. While the client certainly needs to be protected from undue exposure, it is often difficult to achieve a balance between realistic protection and over-protection. Karen brought the fear 'into the open', into the meadow, from the unconscious into the conscious. Karen's rabbit may also represent a part of her personality she was reluctant to admit to – as scared as a rabbit, would be an appropriate interpretation.

Theme Six – The Rosebush

The rose, like the lotus, is often used to represent the mystic Centre (the core of one's being), and the opening rose, the unfolding of the psyche. If this sounds poetical, then it is; working with imagery often enters the realm of the poetic; it certainly uses the language of the poet or the mystic.

The image of the rosebush can be carried out as an exercise in imagery, but it is an exercise that holds great significance. Rather than deal with this by description, I will recount what happened with June. June came to me at the close of a workshop, asking if she could have a session with me. June was a nurse, of around forty years of age, who had recently divorced after eighteen years of marriage.

I will stop here and talk a little about method. For me it is unnecessary to ask details about a client or her life; my firm belief is that all that is necessary will be revealed as and when it becomes pertinent. If at the end of the session there are areas I don't know about, then so be it. Counselling is not an investigation and it is not answering a series of questions which are often for the benefit of the counsellor rather than the client.

June volunteered that amount of information in the workshop, that much I knew. That she was unhappy was obvious, as she talked about her recent divorce and the years of sexual abuse that had led to her making the break. I said, 'June, it seems that what you are desperately seeking now is healing; to have the pain and trauma eased'. She nodded. We had already established in the workshop that she could work with imagery, so I suggested we build on the workshop experience.

As is my custom, I introduced a deep state of relaxation, then proceeded with the imagery. I then introduced the meadow theme, and moved on from there. These are more or less my words. 'You decide to take a walk through the meadow and come upon a beautiful garden. Please describe it to me.' She described a typical 'country cottage' garden, and the time of year was as it was then, July. 'Take a walk around the garden and tell me what you imagine.' She found a seat under a large chestnut tree, and she could hear the hum of bees searching for nectar in the lavender bushes near her. Her whole demeanour had changed, as she relaxed into the imagery. I felt that now was the time to introduce a definite image. It had been my experience that roses exert a healing aura; their oil is used in the most expensive perfumes, and the essential oil is used in aromatherapy.

WILLIAM: I would like you to imagine that in the garden near to you is a beautiful rose. Can you imagine that?

When she nodded, I went on.

WILLIAM: What colour is it?

JUNE: It's a beautiful dark red, with a heavenly perfume. I can smell it from where I'm sitting.

WILLIAM: I would like you to go closer to the rosebush, and see if there is anything about it that has a special meaning for you.

After a few seconds, she wiped her eyes with her fingers.

JUNE: There's a broken branch, and the flower on it has withered. Oh, I feel so sad.

WILLIAM: What does that seem to be telling you?

JUNE: That's my marriage, broken, withered.

WILLIAM: Anything else?

This question is based on the belief that very often there is more than one meaning attached to a symbol.

After another pause, during which she started to weep softly.

JUNE: It's me, all the abuse has broken me and I feel I'm withered and of no use.

WILLIAM: You've lost all your perfume?

JUNE: *Nodding through her tears.*

WILLIAM: June, I want you to look closely at the rosebush, and visualise a new bud. See it in its infancy, touch it, feel how firm it is. It is green, yet you know that underneath there is colour and perfume, not yet revealed. But if you look again, you will see that just at the top is a slight showing of colour. Continue watching as the bud slowly begins to open, the green starts to separate and the red colour is now clearly visible, but still the bud is closed. Now one by one the petals start to unfold, and there on the undamaged branch is a perfect red rose. Smell again the delicious perfume. Imagine you are walking barefoot through a pathway of rose petals. Feel the softness of the petals, inhale the perfume as your feet gently crush the petals. Now go back to the rosebush, hold the rose between your hands, bend down and let the rose brush your face.

June had entered into the imagery so well that the expression on her face was of the utmost tranquillity.

WILLIAM: I now want you to imagine that the perfume is not only entering your nostrils, it is becoming a part of you. Visualise the perfume as it travels to every part of your body; to the lungs, then through the bloodstream to the muscles, right to the finger tips, to the brain, and the muscles of the head and face, to the internal organs. And as the perfume touches these various parts of the body, it is bathing them in the same beautiful perfume. I now want you to imagine that the perfume is going even deeper, right into your spirit, bringing healing where you most need it. Tell me what's happening.

JUNE: I can see the perfume touching every part of me, it's warm and soothing. It's not red like the rose, it's pure white, and I just know it's healing all the hurt and abuse. It's like it's centred somewhere in the middle of my abdomen and radiating out from there.

Discussion of June

June and I had participated in a deeply profound experience that I am quite certain has remained with her as it has with me. There may be some questions you would like to ask, so I will anticipate what I think they might be.

I chose to use this one theme because I knew that time was limited, and that June and I would probably not meet again. So I wanted to get the maximum effect in the time available. I had used the rose before, but never in this way, so it was a matter of going with my intuition.

June absorbed (introjected) the perfume. Assagiloi (1965) talks about introjecting the rosebush, my instinct told me that this would not have been appropriate, particularly as part of it represented her broken marriage. I also think that introjecting a whole bush requires a massive leap of imagination, and would not be suitable for a one-off session. A point to bear in mind is that the perfume *is* the rose, and the rose is the bush, so by absorbing the perfume, June is taking in the bush. This is similar to one drop of water represents all water; one drop of the sea represents the ocean. June had absorbed the vital essence of the rose.

June and I did not discuss the broken marriage, or the events leading up to it. If June had been coming for regular sessions, then such discussion would have been appropriate and probably necessary.

It might be necessary to point out that themes are not presented to be applied as if they had come off a mould or a conveyor belt. They are guides to be adapted according to the situation and the client, not to be applied with rigidity, according to the book. Therapeutic imagery does have a structure, but it also has a spontaneity. We cannot put the psyche in a straitjacket of preconceived ideas.

Summary

This Journey has taken us into six interesting and thought-provoking themes, but has also introduced many linking ideas. What I hope has happened is that you, too, have explored the six themes for yourself that you have not been left untouched by what you have read; that this has been more than an intellectual exercise. Therapeutic imagery, in my opinion, deals with the whole person. This may be nothing more than a hackneyed phrase, that is true, however, I hope that everything you have read so far has found an echo within you somewhere.

In all the six themes, it is only possible to give limited information, for each theme could fill a book on its own. What I have tried to do is to bring the 'theory' alive by talking about clients and some of the images they had, and how they explored the various themes.

In the first theme – the meadow – we saw that although this is the introductory theme, it may be full of emotional meaning to the client. As an introduction, the Meadow Theme is an excellent preparation for all the others, in this level and the two to follow.

In the second theme – the stream – we explored the principles of tracing the stream to its source or to its destination, the sea, and the different psychological meanings of these two different routes. Tracing the origin is generally uphill, and quite often the journey does involve much uphill work. Tracing the origin can be exhausting work, emotionally, and this must be taken into account. Indeed, the goal may take several sessions before it is reached.

Tracing the route to the sea, although considered to be downhill, can be equally taxing and can be more exciting than tracing the origin. One is backward-looking, and not everyone wants to do this, while the other is looking into the future. Another point about tracing the destination is that instinctively the client is drawn towards the as yet unspoken thought of merging with the great waters of the ocean, and the treasures that are often waiting to be found.

In the third theme – the mountain – we set the theme within the wider theme of landscape. We saw that the associated theme of the valley should not be divorced from the mountain theme. Valleys and mountain are figurative language for the downs and ups in life; we need them both, for how would we appreciate the mountain if there were no valleys, and vice versa. Valleys are places of fertility, but are often associated with death, and what is sombre, while mountains are thought of as the ultimate challenge. Travelling through the valley is usually a preliminary for climbing the mountain, from where we may view the way ahead.

In the fourth theme – the house – we saw that this is symbolic of the person, and, like the three foregoing themes, is an indicator of what is happening within the client's inner world. The house was set within the wider context of what is around it, and although we only touched on the garden as a sub-theme, this short exploration gives a reliable indication of how this theme, and others, can be extended. The house may be set in wide open, landscaped parks, wherein run herds of deer, and where other wild life abound. Some clients discover the woods within the boundaries of the house, and therein lies another interesting development, not explored here.

The house comprises many different rooms, each with its own function and symbolism. As with all six themes, the house may need to be explored several times. Indeed, it could be safely said that however many times it was explored there would always be fresh things to discover. This is analogous to counselling in general – where and when does one stop?

One of the features of the house theme that wasn't explored in depth was the presence of other people. This will be covered in Third Level themes.

In the fifth theme – the woods – we saw that this can be approached in two ways: exploring the edge of the wood, and exploring the interior. In general it is advisable to invite the client to take a good look at the edge of the wood, before venturing in to the interior. As with all the themes, exploring the woods can be done at a superficial level or at a deeper level, and which one depends on the confidence of the client and on the competence of the counsellor, in being able to come to the client's aid if confronted by fearsome creatures emerging from the woods.

The sixth theme – the rosebush – is a demonstration of how one symbol can be used in a one-off session. If the rosebush is taken as a representation of the person, it makes it easier to see how the theme can be used, and how it was used with June. A rosebush in full bloom says one thing, a rose in winter says another, while a bush with all the blooms fading and dropping says something else. With all themes and symbols, the thrill is discovering something else, some new meaning that has eluded you until now.

The idea of introjecting the perfume of the rose may sound strange, but it is offered with sincerity as a way of making sense of the symbol. This was one way of dealing with a problem; a different problem, under different circumstances may have generated a different way of working. For example, the client could pick a rose, and then be asked what he or she would like to do with it. Would it be placed in a vase on a desk, or would it grace the dress of some loved one?

Finally, it is worth repeating that themes and symbols are not cut out of metal and stamped on the client; they are cast in sand, or written on water, seldom to be repeated exactly as before.

Exploring Second-Level Themes

Theme Seven – The Book

What I do not want to imply is that there is a set progression through the various themes; nor is it necessary to use them to the fullest extent. The first-level themes show the way, the second-level themes take you a little deeper further along the road. This does not mean that the first-level themes are less important or less potent; it is how they are worked and developed that will lead the client towards healing.

The book theme symbolises inside and outside; potential and reality. A book may be closed or open. We speak of a 'closed book', a person who doesn't give anything away; or being able to read someone like a book, referring to openness. A book's cover is in contact with the outside world, keeping the contents secure from prying eyes. When the book is open, its secrets are available.

A closed book speaks of unwillingness; an open book speaks of willingness. Opening a book symbolises the start of something; closing, of ending something. The type of book changes the meaning: a notebook may speak of memories; a ledger may speak of striving for balance. The book's title influences the symbolism: *The Tales of Frankenstein* will generate different feelings from, *Tales of Love and Romance*. The *Holy Bible* would evoke different feelings from the *Satanic Verses*.

A book can be an analogy of a person, with a number of chapters, each representing a stage in the person's life. Some chapters are closed; others remain open. Unclosed chapters represent unfinished business. Counselling may need to help clients re-open chapters in order to close them properly: chapters that remain open create 'holes' in our emotional life, which draw energy into themselves and hamper us moving on properly to the other stages.

We have seen one example of the 'book' in Beverley's diary. When Roy worked with the House theme, he imagined one of the walls of the sitting room covered in books. Now follows his exploration of the book theme.

WILLIAM: Roy, have a good look round the shelves. Somewhere you will find a book which you know is your life story. When you find it, take it down.

It took Roy some considerable time to find it, for it was hidden away behind some other books. He blew the dust off it.

	Has it got a title on it?
ROY:	It has, but it's so faint I can't read it.
WILLIAM:	How do you feel about it being all dusty and not being able to read the title?
ROY:	A bit sad really, as if my life hasn't been worth much.
WILLIAM:	Now open it and read the title page.

He put his head in his hands and cried, then he said.

ROY:	It says, Roy...the account of an insignificant man.
WILLIAM:	Is that a fair description?
ROY:	I suppose so. Not much to my credit.
WILLIAM:	What would you like the title to read?
ROY:	(*After several moments thought*) Roy...a man who overcame.
WILLIAM:	You have the power to rewrite that book, so let's look at what's in it, what pictures do you imagine?
ROY:	(*Starting to open the book*) The first chapter reads, 'How it all began' and all the pages are stuck together. What does that mean?
WILLIAM:	Maybe it's telling you that this chapter is closed. What about the next chapter?
ROY:	That's headed, 'Relationships', but it's only one page, with lots of blank pages.
WILLIAM:	Looking at that chapter, with all those blank pages, how do you feel?
ROY:	Bloody sad again. You know and I know that relationships and me...
WILLIAM:	So that's an area we could look at. Any other chapters that are open?
ROY:	There's one here, entitled 'Sexuality'. That's a long chapter.

He read through a few pages, and his face turned white.

I don't want to read that stuff; it's disgusting.

WILLIAM:	So what's there really gets at you, does it? And it's not true?

Roy looked at me (we hadn't previously explored his sexuality), and said,

ROY:	True enough, but I don't have to like it, do I?
WILLIAM:	No, I guess you don't. Neither do you have to talk about it. The choice is yours. But if that's in the book, and if that chapter is still open, then if you don't read it now, you'll have to one day.
ROY:	I'd be ashamed to tell you what's there.

WILLIAM: People who feel ashamed often feel they would be judged for what they feel they want to talk about. Perhaps that's something how you feel.

ROY: I do think that. I suppose I'll have to, some day.

WILLIAM: Any other unfinished business, open chapters?

ROY: Aye, there's this one, Father. He was a bastard, and I hate him. Funny, though, there's a photo of him before he died, and he's got his arm around my shoulder. Now how did that get there. It certainly wasn't real; that never happened.

WILLIAM: Your voice had a lot of longing in it, Roy, as if you wish it could have happened.

ROY: Rubbish! He didn't want to, it neither did I.

He looked at me, obviously no longer using his imagination, and I had a mental image of him snapping the book shut.

I don't know what you're trying to do to me, prying me open like that. I don't want to do any more of this imagery stuff. I think I've had enough for today.

WILLIAM: Roy, it's not a good idea to bring a session to a close like this, and I feel pretty bad, that you feel I've pushed you too far.

ROY: It wasn't you, William, it's me. I just can't get into this book, it's too painful just now. Maybe in the future I'll come back to it. I'd rather call it a day now.

Discussion of Roy

This is one of those occasions where, with hindsight, I might have done it differently. My self-examination of the session led me to question why I had chosen to direct the imagery, rather than let it develop. I thought that Roy could handle the 'personal book' rather than, as Beverley did, find it if it was 'right'. Perhaps there was too much all at once. Was he right, that I was prying? Certainly that's what he felt. Perhaps that explained the book being hidden away and covered in dust, and had I 'forced' him to expose it?

I would like to say that Roy returned and worked through to closing each chapter, but he didn't. He cancelled further counselling. And I? I was left with the feeling of trampling over someone's life story with my size twelve, mountain-climbing boots, yet having learned a valuable lesson.

An important variation of the book is the video or audio tape. So often our behaviour seems to be influenced by old tapes that switch on in our minds. One of the ways we can help clients to become aware of the content of these tapes is while they are using imagery, asking them to imagine they are sitting listening to the radio, or watching the TV; suddenly the programme is interrupted, and they are listening to or watching something of their own life. 'What are you hearing (seeing)?' This can be very revealing, particularly when a related question is asked, 'Who is it speaking, what are they doing?'

When I encouraged Jenny to do this, she could hear her mother storming at her, 'You are useless, Jenny, useless, you'll never make anything of yourself. If you were like your sister, she's bright... She's got a man, no man would ever want you'. Vera struggled to contain her tears of anger as she relayed this to me.

What we did was to get her to play the tape again, and then to operate the 'Stop' button. 'It sounds so easy, William, why didn't I think of that before.' Her face lit up as she said, 'That puts me in control, doesn't it?'

We did the same thing with a video tape. Jenny was in a disastrous relationship with a man who ill-treated her, beat her, demeaned her in every way, yet she couldn't break free from him. I encouraged her to imagine picking up one of the tapes for her video player, it was marked ' Jenny'. 'As you play it, what do you see?' As with the tape of her mother, this was a thoroughly demoralising scene, in which the man belittled her, called her useless, ugly, and as sexy as a cold fish. This session came towards the end of a period of eighteen months in which Jenny had vacillated between leaving him, and had been hospitalised for attempted suicide. By now she had made some progress towards breaking from him, but there were still bits that were 'hooked into her' (her words). 'What I suggest, Jenny, is that this tape needs to be destroyed, it doesn't deserve house room. How would you like to destroy it?' She thought for several minutes, then said, 'I'm going to tear it out of the case and burn the tape'. I watched as, in her imagination, she did just that. When she'd finished, she wiped her hands together in a gesture of dismissal, or of cleaning her hands of unwanted material. 'That's better, I feel clean now.'

It was several more months before Jenny finally made the break from the man whose only purpose seemed to be to confirm her mother's prediction. About two years after this, I had a letter from Jenny. She had taken a job in Saudi Arabia, and was doing well.

Theme Eight – The Cave

Caves were thought to be the symbols of the womb of Mother Earth, and, as such, were worshipped by the ancients. Indeed, they were the places where all religious rites were carried out before temples were built. Caves are still used for religious purposes, as in Lourdes. Caves feature in many legends, where they have given protection to people being pursued by enemies.

In a general sense, the meaning of the cave relates to containment, of the enclosed or the concealed. In mediaeval language the cave represents the heart, the spiritual centre. It also stands for the security of the unconscious. In pictures of myths the cave is a meeting place for deities, forebears and Archetypes, and as such is an image of Hades, as well as the unconscious. The cave is also used in literature. In Part V of *The Furies* by Aeschylus, Athena leads the procession downwards into the Cave of the Furies, under Areopagus.

In Grimm's *The Valiant Little Tailor*, the giant says to the valiant little tailor 'If thou art such a valiant fellow, come with me into our cavern and spend the night with us'. The little fellow is willing, and follows him. When they went into the cave, other giants were sitting there by the fire, and each of them had a roasted sheep in his hand and was eating it.

The cave is connected with the interior of the earth, and as such is said to represent the female genitals, in that there is the mouth and the cave itself, the uterus. The cave is often the place where some wise person dwells, such as Merlin of the Arthurian Legend, and equally often, the cave can only be reached after a stiff climb, symbolising that the way to wisdom is not lightly gained.

In Islamic writings, the cave features as the place of the mystery of rebirth; the secret cavity in which one is shut up in order to be incubated and renewed. Thus the cave becomes a symbol of transformation. When we enter the cave within us, the unconscious, we find ourselves involved in transformation. By daring to enter the cave we start to make contact with the contents of the unconscious.

Caves are generally dark, yet that darkness often hides great beauty, such as stalagmites and stalactites, waiting to be discovered. Caves often contain underground lakes and rivers, which symbolically mean that there are further depths to be discovered in the process of descent. In mythology and legend, caves are often the place to discover treasure; once again an allusion to the treasure of the unconscious. Sometimes the entrance to the cave lies under water, which symbolises entering one element to gain access to another, and to the cave itself. The theme of the cave is similar to the wood: the cave can be viewed from a distance and then entered and explored. As with diving into the sea, it is wise to err on the side of caution when working with the cave symbol. These various symbolic interpretations of the care are not, of course, the only ones. The cave also has associations with the container, the next theme.

As with the symbol of the edge of the woods, the client can be instructed to 'call out' who or what is in the cave. It is not unusual for fabulous or mythological creatures to emerge, for these are common in myths and legends, so they are archetypal figures. They are often representations of distorted feelings or repressed conflicts. The images are usually highly charged with emotion, and keeping them in the cave drains a lot of emotional energy. So calling them out is a way of bringing them into the light of the consciousness.

Before the client is encouraged to explore the interior of the cave there should be adequate preparation; the most obvious aid is some form of light. Light also represents the spirit, although the light of the spirit often seems to come from nowhere and yet everywhere. In this instance, because the client *decides* to take a light, it is more appropriate to think of it is Ego consciousness. Preparation should not be drawn out, otherwise the impetus may be lost. I think it is better to let things happen, and then find ways of overcoming whatever hurdles or dangers present themselves.

One way of presenting the theme is to suggest that there is a dragon in the cave, guarding something, then leave it to the client to imagine what that 'something' or 'someone' is. This is not my approach. The following extract illustrates how I used this theme with Phil. On his journey up the mountain Phil commented that he could see a cave in the distance, 'One day I want to explore that, but I want to get to the top'. Phil had climbed up to the cave, not an easy climb, for the entrance to the cave was from a narrow ledge, high up on the mountain. (This is another joke of the psyche, as if it is saying, 'If you want what is there, then you have to work for it!')

WILLIAM: You have two choices, to call out anything that might be there, or go straight in.

PHIL: You know me, straight in.

WILLIAM: Anything you want to take with you?

PHIL: Ah, yes, a light of some sorts. I'll wear a miner's helmet, that should give enough light.

WILLIAM: When you get just inside, stop, look, and listen. (I thought that this warning might be necessary, possibly because I felt Phil could be a bit impetuous).

PHIL: I'm inside, I'm moving my head round slowly and the strong light is penetrating the cave. It's huge, but it's bare. Now that's a surprise.

WILLIAM: You sound disappointed, as if you were expecting something dramatic. What's the atmosphere?

PHIL: That's funny, I've been here before, a long, long time ago, beyond my memory.

WILLIAM: What's the nearest thing you can think of?

PHIL: This is going to sound crazy, the womb?

WILLIAM: Not so crazy as you may think. What I suggest you do is sit down on the floor and get immersed in the feeling. (I was conscious of an excitement building up within me, for my intuition told me that I was about to witness a rebirth).

PHIL: I'm sitting on the floor, lotus position, staring at the mouth of the cave. Suddenly I'm being propelled down, along a tunnel on a sort of toboggan, but it's on water, and the sides of the tunnel are all pink and red. I'm being pushed from side to side, and I can see at the end some huge hands. Now I'm being squeezed all round, I want to scream but can't. I can hear water swishing all around me, like some huge waterfall. Now I'm out in the open, at the bottom of the mountain, and I'm gulping in air. I hear crying, a woman, it's my mother, and she's holding me in her arms and rocking me.

So profound was this experience that I was already in tears. When Phil had finished, and as he realised the significance of that experience, we cried together. It is a rare experience to witness someone's rebirthing, a tremendous privilege, of which Phil's was only one of two I've ever shared.

Discussion of Phil

Neither Phil nor I had the slightest idea that this was to be the outcome of that particular journey. On looking back, however, there had been indications. Phil was an Australian whose relationship with his mother had been very strained, partly because she was dominant and possessive on the one hand, yet dismissive of him on the other, mainly because he did not conform to the her image of what an Australian 'man' should be. He had never wanted to be anything other than a doctor, and this had alienated him from both his parents. This 'rebirth' symbolised an emotional separation, for although twelve thousand miles separated them physically, he still felt tied to her.

Although caves and caverns are often portrayed as the evil places, wherein dwell giants, evil spirits and the Devil, they are also places where the most glorious treasure is discovered.

A tale of a cave

This is part of the story of *The Alhambra: The Enchanted Soldier* by Washington Irving.

> The Cave of St. Cyprian at Salamanca, where in old times dark and damnable arts were secretly taught by the devil himself, disguised as the church. The cave has long been shut up and the very site of it forgotten. A wandering minstrel stopped by the Cross of St. Cyprian, where he found a ring with a symbol of Solomon's Seal on it. He took this as a sign from the Saint that he would be provided for.

> The minstrel meets a soldier who had been bewitched three hundred years before, who tells him that once every hundred years, on the festival of St. John, the enchantment ceases to have control. Then he is permitted to go and stand on the bridge of the Darro, where the minstrel met him, waiting for someone to come who may have power to break the magic spell. Twice before he had mounted guard on the bridge in vain. The soldier walks as in a cloud, concealed from human sight. The minstrel was the first to speak to the soldier in three hundred years. He looked at the minstrel's finger and saw the seal-ring of Solomon the wise, said to be proof against all enchantment. He tells the minstrel that unless he can deliver him, he will stay trapped for another hundred years.

> What he had guarded for three centuries was the treasure of a Moorish priest in a secret vault, of the Alhambra, tales which the minstrel had often heard. After a tortuous journey, the minstrel and the soldier arrive at the vault; the minstrel felt comforted by the talisman of Solomon's Seal.

> The soldier pointed to a large iron coffer, secured by locks inscribed with Arabic characters. He tells the minstrel that it contains countless treasure in gold and jewels, and precious stones. If the minstrel can break the magic spell by which the soldier is enchained, half of the treasure would be his.

The minstrel was instructed to seek the aid of a priest, and a Christian maid. The priest to exorcise the powers of darkness; the damsel to touch this chest with the seal of Solomon. This was to be done at night and before three days was up, for that was all the time the soldier was permitted, or he would have to guard for another century. The one condition was that the priest should be virtuous.

At a late hour on the third the night the minstrel, priest and maiden groped their to the vault by the light of a lantern. The priest carried a basket with provisions to satisfy his voracious appetite, after his work of exorcising had been carried out.

They found the soldier seated on the enchanted strong-box, awaiting their arrival. The exorcism was performed, the maiden touched the locks of the coffer with the seal of Solomon. The lid flew open, to reveal wondrous treasures of gold and jewels and precious stones. While the minstrel and the soldier were preoccupied deciding how to get the treasure out, the priest gorged himself on the food and drink he had brought, and, by way of thanksgiving, he kissed the maiden who waited on him. Although it was quietly done in a corner, the tell-tale walls told the whole world what had happened. Never was a kiss more awful in its effects. At the sound of the kiss, the soldier gave a great cry of despair; the coffer, which was half raised, fell back in its place and was locked once more. Priest, minstrel, and maiden, found themselves outside, the magic wall closed with a thundering jar behind them.

In her haste, the maiden dropped Solomon's Seal in the vault, so the soldier was doomed to an eternity of guarding the vault, and the treasure remained where it was. 'Ah father! father!' said the minstrel, shaking his head ruefully, 'I fear there was less of the saint than the sinner in that kiss!'

There is a tradition that the minstrel had stuffed enough of the treasure in his pocket to set him up in the world. He prospered in his affairs, took the maiden in marriage. The maiden proved a pattern for wives, and bore her husband numerous children.

Discussion

I have included this legend because of its abundant imagery and symbolism and also because it does not end on a totally positive note, mainly because of someone's fallibility. The whole legend is worth reading, for it could be used to great effect as a theme in imagery. One of the sub-themes is the promise of treasure in the cave, which can only be retrieved by priestly intercession and the feminine principle. Only the feminine can unlock the treasure that lies within the chest. This could be symbolic of the heart, the emotions that are locked up until opened by the 'maiden'.

The spell put upon the soldier could only be broken by absolute obedience and truthfulness, and only as the minstrel was prepared to face danger would he have the opportunity to reach the treasure. The priest's kiss may have been innocent, but what this story seems to be saying is that the psyche reads the motives of the heart. The priest had to be honourable and chaste, and the fact that he put satisfying his appetite before the task in hand highlights that the psyche does not like to be trifled with. It seems that the priest stood accused of the two vices of gluttony and lust, both sins of the flesh.

Solomon, king of ancient Israel was the second son of David, king of Judah and Israel. In later Jewish and Muslim literature Solomon appears not only as the wisest of sages but as one gifted with the power to control the spirits of the invisible world. The Seal of Solomon represents the two elements fire and water, and beyond that the Seal represents the wisdom of Solomon and the power over the forces of darkness.

The minstrel used the Seal as a talisman, and it was this that opened the chest and revealed the treasure. It is highly doubtful if there is any inherent power in a talisman; its power lies in what the person invests in it. That is why talismans are useful objects for clients to carry, and why one should always at least suggest that the client looks for something that will aid them on their journey.

Theme Nine – The Chalice

There are many symbols that relate to the container theme. In symbolism, the container is universally accepted as representing the female, the feminine principle. The ultimate container of course is the womb, from which we are all born.

If we take it that the above assumption is correct, that the container represents the feminine, then we can extend that and say that it represents the feeling function, whether of male or female. As the function of the container is to hold, then we could say that the container holds the contents of life. Some containers hold ingredients and transform them into something else; saucepans in the kitchen, the pestle and mortar in the pharmacy. While the pestle and mortar are sexual symbols, they are also symbolic if the transformation and the union of opposites.

Taking the container on a much wider basis, the body is the most marvellous container, which hold matter together and transforms different elements for the purpose of maintaining life. The womb represents the positive aspect of the container; the witches cauldron is the negative aspect. Holding something within a container represents holding the flowing forces of nature. Putting a lid on a container ensures what is inside is kept secure, but this can also be a trap. Imagine a delicate, beautifully coloured butterfly, resting on the rim of a vase; it starts to explore the inside of the vase, drawn by the lingering perfume left over from dried rose petals. At that stage the butterfly is an explorer. Now imagine someone coming and putting a lid on the vase; the butterfly is now a prisoner, trapped by a smell. Taking the lid off symbolises escape, freedom, liberation. A closed vessel may also represent the unconscious, and the inability to explore it.

In the Bible story of Noah's Ark, his 'container' saved mankind. A similar story is told of Deucalion in Greek mythology. The son of the Titan Prometheus, Deucalion was king of Phthia in Thessaly when the god Zeus, because of the wicked ways of the human race, destroyed them by flood. For nine days and nights Zeus sent torrents of rain. Only Deucalion and his wife, Pyrrha, survived drowning. They were saved because they were the only people who had led good lives and remained faithful to the laws of the gods. Having been warned by his father, Prometheus, of the approaching disaster, Deucalion built a boat, which carried him and Pyrrha safely to rest on top of Mount Parnassus. The oracle at Delphi commanded them to cast the bones of their mother over their shoulders. Understanding this to mean the stones of the earth, they obeyed, and from the stones sprang a new race of people.

The above is the positive side of the symbol of the container; the negative would be Pandora, who, because of her disobedience, was held responsible in Greek myth for all the illnesses that have plagued the human race.

This general introduction paves the way for an exploration of one symbol, the chalice. The chalice features as the Holy Grail in the Arthurian Legend and it is used in the sacrament of Holy Communion. During the Middle Ages, it became common for chalices to be wrought out of silver or gold. They were often ornamented with precious stones, elaborate carvings, and embossed decoration. They may also be made from crystal, when they have associations with hydromancy (divination by means of signs derived from water, its tides and ebbs, or the pretended appearance of spirits therein).

A chalice with a lid represents the human heart, and it then becomes similar to the chest or coffer as container. Because of its spiritual association, the chalice is also is linked with the mystic Centre (here, the allegorical centre of earth). The symbolism of the chalice is influenced by what it contains, or its purpose. A chalice used for the Sacrament, although representing the Communion, the Lord's Supper, also signifies the Last Supper, and the Communion of Saints. Although some of this is mysterious, it does have a certain sense of the 'down to earth', whereas the Holy Grail is so shrouded in mystery and myth that it has been invested with a totally different meaning.

In the French romance of Parceval, the lance is that which pierced Christ's side and the Grail or basin is that in which Joseph of Arimathea caught the divine blood. This miraculous vase procures all the good things of heaven and earth; it heals wounds, and is filled at the owner's pleasure with the most exquisite food. To approach it one must be in a state of grace; only a priest can tell of its marvels. Celtic mythology tells of a mysterious vase (also called a cauldron) which inspires poetic genius, gives wisdom, reveals the future, and unveils the secrets of the world.

The chalice and imagery

'Finding the chalice' may be a significant stage in our personal quest. Some therapists believe that it is essential for the male client to discover the chalice, and for the female client to discover her sword (lance or spear, which will be discussed next). This is possibly based on Jung's influential work on the Anima and Animus. While there are undoubtedly times when it is appropriate to distinguish male from female, I prefer to work with both, and leave the choice to the client. The next theme will now be considered, then we will look at both chalice and sword.

Theme Ten – The Sword

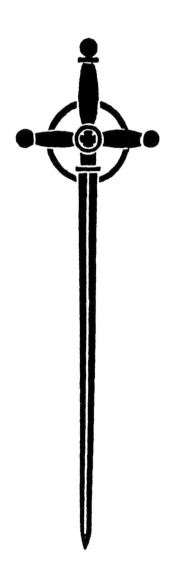

Figure 1 Sword

I hope that as you work through these various themes you are finding images springing up, triggered off by what you read. Take note of these images, write them down, and try to work them through, to increase your awareness and understanding.

Although the theme here is the sword, I will also include the related symbol of the lance.

The sword, composed of a blade and a guard, symbolises conjunction, especially when it takes on the form of a cross. The sword was an object of veneration; the Romans believed that it had the power to ward off evil spirits, because it was made of iron, the metal of Mars, the god of war.

The sword has the power to wound, and it symbolises liberty and strength. It has been contrasted with the distaff, which is the feminine symbol of the continuity of life; thus the sword and the distaff represent, respectively, death and fertility. The sword is used on ceremonial occasions as a symbol of honour or authority.

The sword is the instrument or symbol of penal justice; hence, the authority of a ruler or magistrate to punish offenders; more generally, power of government, executive power, authority, jurisdiction; also, the office of an executive governor or magistrate.

In Norse mythology, Frey (or Freyr) was the god of fertility, peace, and prosperity. He was one of the Vanir gods, who were responsible for wealth, and the brother of Freya. Among his magical possessions was a sword that he gave to Skirnir, who in return obtained him Gerda, the most beautiful woman in the world, as his wife.

In Greek mythology, Thanatos was the god of death. He dwelt with his brother Hypnos (Sleep) in the underworld and is portrayed as winged, bearded, and holding a sword. He was said to be the only god who shunned sacrificial offerings.

In Biblical symbolism, the sword is synonymous with spiritual warfare. The 'sword of the mouth' is pernicious talk, false accusation, slander, and misrepresentation (Psalm 57:4). 'Many have fallen by the edge of the sword: but not so many as have fallen by the tongue (Ecclesiastes 28:18). The 'word of God', that is delivered with grace or judgment, is likened to a two-edged sword.

When the sword is associated with fire and flames, it symbolises purification, whereas the whip and the lash are associated with punishment. The golden sword is a symbol for supreme spiritualisation. The Western type sword, on account of its shape, is masculine; whereas the Oriental, curved sword, is lunar and feminine.

The knight's sword represents conscious intellect that has won the mastery over brute passions. Forging the sword is symbolic of the human spirit at work transforming base material into something worthy. In the story of King Arthur and Excalibur, Arthur pulls the sword out of the stone and is acknowledged as the long-awaited king. This is sexual symbolism for the freeing of the phallus from the female. On a spiritual level, it represents the freeing of the spirit from the constraints of the lower nature.

The Lance symbolises war and the phallus. While the sword symbolises the spirit, in contrast, the lance symbolises the earth. The lance and the chalice (Grail) are often paired, representing masculine and feminine.

In the eleventh century it became an acceptable battle technique to charge with the lance couched, that is, held under the right armpit. The left, or shield, side of the knight was always turned to the enemy. The former oval-shaped shield was, therefore, modified to an elongated form with a sharp lower point, to protect the horseman from eyes to knee.

The chalice and the sword

It should be the client who chooses to search for either the chalice or the sword or both of them, for both are necessary, which ever gender we may be.

Case illustration – Glenn

Towards the end of his time with me, Glenn, as part of his journey, found both the chalice and the sword. Outwardly Glenn had no difficulty with the feminine part of himself; he was a caring medical student who showed every promise of continuing this caring into his career as a doctor. Inwardly, however, there was a struggle as to how to balance the opposite, for he saw them very much as opposed rather than complementary, parts of himself.

He had developed his 'masculine' part very well, in that he was an logical thinker, yet at times he felt the other part, his heart, struggled for control. There was no conscious decision as to which symbol he would seek first. When he was relaxed he found himself on a pathway that led to a church. The whole scene exuded tranquillity, peace and security. He could hear the organ playing, and he could see brilliant stained-glass windows. He found a small door on the side of the church that led down into a room smelling of aromatic oils. I asked him if he had any idea what lay behind the door. He knew that it would lead to light, and wanted to go through. He found himself in a brilliant place of green grass. I suggested that there was a path somewhere, which he saw stretching into the distance. He didn't want to explore what lay ahead. I suggested that a wise person would come along who would guide him.

This was one of those rare moments when I felt envious of what was happening, but dared not interrupt. The expression on his face clearly showed that whoever he had met was someone special. I waited and watched. Now follows what he said when the journey was over.

> 'Just after you said to look for a wise person to be a guide to me, I saw this figure coming towards me; he wasn't walking, and he was brilliantly radiant, and his expression was so kind and gentle. He spoke, but I won't tell you what he said, not yet, but I knew I had to follow him. He led me to a cave, where I found an old, brown, wooden chest, all covered in cobwebs. There weren't any locks that I could see. I knew it had to be opened. Now that's funny, the cave should have been dark, but it wasn't. He lit it up. The chest intrigued me, so I tried to open it, but the hinges must have been too stiff; with rust, I suppose. I got down on my knees, thought that would give me more leverage. My, what an effort it was, but the lid lifted. I was shocked, I can tell you; for all there was were some old rags. It seems like some cruel joke. I looked at my guide, he only smiled, and I started to feel annoyed. Then I thought, what do old clothes mean? They mean something outgrown, unused, not wanted. Then it really hit me; they meant me, my old life, and if that was so, then perhaps there was something else in the chest. I rummaged, and right at the bottom guess what I found? A beautiful cup, like the Sacrament cup, but decorated with jewels, and inlaid with gold.
>
> I held it up, and that's when I started to cry. I knew you wouldn't mind. It was so wonderful. It was like finding the Holy Grail. All I wanted to do was have people with me, and fill it with wine and share Communion. It was the most wonderful moment in my life.
>
> Just then, a shaft of light burst through the wall of the cave and lighted up a corner I hadn't noticed. I put the cup down on the chest, and went over to the corner, to a huge stone that looked as if it was covering an opening. How I found the strength to move it, I don't know, but I did, to see a flight of steps going up. I wasn't going to leave the cup there, so I took it and climbed the steps. Then there was a really funny thing. The guide was in front of me, although I hadn't seen him leave. Now you're going to think this really weird, but the steps led up to the top of the mountain I'd been to before, right into that same cave, where I found the scroll.
>
> Hanging on the wall was a sword, my it was spectacular! The sword and the cup could have been made by the same person; it was jewelled in the same way as the cup. They made a wonderful pair, and so complemented each other. I took it off the wall and held it in my right hand, and did I feel strong! In a flash things changed, I was being led into the exam room by my guide, and he was the one who was going to judge me on my work. I've never felt so secure and at peace.'

Discussion of Glenn

I don't think that interpretation is needed of Glenn's two finds. I think it is worth drawing attention to the fact that he had to go down first of all, then he had to go through. 'Going through' often symbolises a breaking out of something. Then he had to trust himself to someone, and that is not always easy, even in imagery. If I had been directing Glenn, the obvious place to find the chalice is in a cave, and probably in some sort of chest, for it represents treasure. It is also interesting that only when he had found the chalice, did the light shine on to the next stage of the journey.

Again, the sword (spear, lance) is often found 'in the heights', and often after a hard climb. Glenn finally realised that the chalice and the sword (feminine and masculine) are complementary. When we discussed his journey, he would not tell me what his 'guide' had said to him, and he never did. Perhaps whatever he said was so special that to have shared it would have tarnished it. Glenn never said who he thought his guide was, but there was little doubt in my mind that this was spiritual experience of the most profound kind. Glenn retook his exam and passed with flying colours, so the 'scroll' of his imagination became a reality.

Theme Eleven – The Dragon

Figure 2 Dragon

The dragon is associated with the worm, the snake a winged crocodile with a serpent's tail, thus the words dragon and serpent often mean the same thing. It is credited with having acute eyesight. In the sacred writings of the ancient Hebrews, the dragon frequently represents death and evil. Christianity inherited the Hebraic idea of the dragon, which figures in all the important prophetic literature of the Bible, notably in Revelation: 'And he laid hold on the dragon, that old serpent, which is the Devil, and Satan, and bound him a thousand years' (Revelation 20:2). It also appears in later Christian traditions. In Christian art, the dragon is a symbol of sin. It is often represented as crushed under the feet of saints and martyrs, symbolising the triumph of Christianity over paganism.

The ancient Greeks and Romans believed that dragons had the ability to understand and to convey to mortals the secrets of the earth. Partly as a result of this conception of the monster as a benign, protective influence, and partly because of its fearsome qualities, it was employed as a military emblem. The Roman legions adopted it in the first century AD, inscribing the figure of a dragon on the standards carried into battle by the cohorts. The ancient Norsemen adorned the prows of their vessels with carved likenesses of dragons. Among the Celtic conquerors of Britain, the dragon was a symbol of sovereignty. The legendary monster was also depicted on the shields of the Teutonic tribes that later invaded Britain, and it appeared on the battle standards of the English kings as late as the sixteenth century. Beginning in the early twentieth century, it was inscribed on the armorial bearings of the prince of Wales. King Arthur and his father, Uther Pendragon, were kings of the red dragon.

In China, the dragon symbolises imperial power and the mastering of wickedness. It is associated with the 'rhythm of life' in China, and with lightening, rain and fertility, thus it becomes the connecting link between the Upper Waters (the heavens) and earth. The dragon is said to have the strength and speed of the horse, to be vigilant, and to have exceptionally keen eyesight. In Chinese symbolism the red dragon is the guardian of heights, and the white dragon represents the moon.

Possible psychological interpretation

The dragon is the enemy of the hero. In feudal castles, ladies were kept in the most secure part, guarded by a dragon, or dragons. There is a sexual symbolism here: the castle wall representing the hymen, the dragon guarding the treasure which only the valiant knight might secure.

In the Middle Ages, the dragon is depicted with the throat and legs of an eagle, the body of a huge serpent, the wings of a bat and with a tail ending in an arrow twisted back upon itself. The eagle stands for the celestial potential of the dragon, the serpent for its secret and subterranean characteristics, the wings for intellectual ascent, and the tail, associated with the zodiacal sign for Leo, for submission to reason. Dragons, and also bulls, are fought by sun-heroes such as Mithras, Siegfried, Hercules, Jason, Horus, Apollo.

The dragon which inhabits caves or lives in the depths of the sea symbolises the underworld, and the unconscious that threatens to destroy the Ego if it dares to challenge it. In the Bible, the final battle (Revelation 12) is between the red dragon, (Satan) and Michael; Satan and his angels are defeated. There are many stories of dragons being slain: Apollo, Cadmus, Perseus, Siegfried, but probably the most well-known is that of St. George.

St George and the dragon

St George, Christian martyr and patron saint of England, was born in Cappadocia (eastern Asia Minor). His life is obscured by legend, but his martyrdom at Lydda, Palestine, is generally considered a matter of historical fact. The most popular of the legends that have grown up around him relates his encounter with the dragon. A pagan town in Libya was victimised by a dragon which the inhabitants first attempted to placate by offerings of sheep, and then by the sacrifice of various members of their community. The daughter of the king was chosen by lot and was taken out to await the coming of the monster, but George arrived, killed the dragon, and converted the community to Christianity.

POSSIBLE PSYCHOLOGICAL INTERPRETATION

The legend is an allegory to express the triumph of good over evil. The dragon, representing the devil; St. George, representing Christ; the virgin representing the church. At a deeper level, the dragon is the enemy not only of the hero, but also of the quest for truth and freedom. The dragon's dwelling is in caves, or the depths of the sea, thus it represents the underworld, the unconscious, the land of the dead or of sleep; of unconscious motivations and compulsions. Dragons are often associated with one of the four elements: water, earth, air, fire, or which are related to the four functions of intuition, sensation, thinking, feeling, so where the dragon resides gives an important clue as to the particular function which is under attack. In some legends, the dragon guards treasure, and in order to reach the treasure the dragon has to be subdued, either by being killed or subdued by befriending.

In Part XXXVIII *Beowulf*[1] there is a story of a noble, last of his race, who hides all his wealth within a barrow (an ancient grave-mound or tumulus) and there 'chants his farewell to life's glories'. After his death the dragon takes possession of the hoard and watches over it. A condemned and desperate man hides in the barrow, discovers the treasure, and while the dragon sleeps, makes off with it, and carries it to his master who pardons him. The dragon discovers the loss and exacts fearful penalty from the people round about. Eventually the dragon is killed by a warrior with a sword.

The above story from Beowulf is a good example of the discovery of the treasure guarded by a dragon. The barrow is an excellent example of the Collective Unconscious, and far more potent than a cave, but like the cave, and the forest, or any other representation of the unconscious, great care should be exercised in using it.

Many legends and myths surround the ancient burial grounds, similar to those connected with the Egyptian tombs. The old burial ground of Avebury in Wiltshire, England (very close to Stonehenge) was once so regarded as so holy a place that no

---

1   *Beowulf*, an Anglo-Saxon epic poem, is generally considered the work of an eighth century Anglian poet who fused Scandinavian history and pagan mythology with Christian elements. The sombre story is rich in metaphor; a famous example is 'whale-road' for sea. It tells of a hero, a Scandinavian prince named Beowulf, who rids the Danes of the monster Grendel, half man and half fiend. Fifty years later, Beowulf succeeds in repeating these exploits, freeing his own land from devastation.

reptile could live there. There is an old temple there, and from the centre of Avebury spring five rivers, and the whole district is scattered with tumuli and dew ponds. Its two main barrows stretch in serpentine form from the Temple.

Theme Twelve – The Mentor

Some therapists speak of the 'wise person' (man or woman), the 'helper', or 'guide'. All these are perfectly acceptable terms, however, I prefer to use the term 'Mentor'.

Mentor, in Greek mythology, was friend of the hero Odysseus and tutor of his son Telemachus. In the Homer's *Odyssey*, the goddess Athena frequently assumes the form of Mentor when she appears to Odysseus or Telemachus. In modern English the tutor's name has become a synonym for a wise, trustworthy counsellor or teacher.

I started using 'mentor' in preference to 'supervisor' in counselling development, mainly because the word 'supervision' or 'supervisor' implied control and judgment and measurement by set standards.

We have already met the mentor in the form of the wise person in Glenn's work. Being able to ask a wise person what one should do is valuable in imagery. The answer may not be given in clear terms. In the Bible, the rich ruler asked Jesus how he could inherit eternal life (Luke 18: 18–24). When he was told to sell all he had and give it to the poor, he couldn't accept this and turned away full of sorrow. So, although he asked, the reply was not to his liking. In imagery, then, however wise the person, however wise the counsel, the client retains free choice.

A legend from the Alhambra (Irving 1832)

A certain Muslim prince, Ahmed, was reared in isolation by his father, who kept from him all things of the heart, and had his head stuffed with algebra and philosophy. Eventually heart drew him away from head, and he began to change. He heard the word 'love' from his friends the birds but they could not tell him the meaning, and his tutor was afraid to, terrified of the consequences. For his master had made it plain that his son was not to fall in love – ever. His tutor advised Ahmed not to listen to the seductive notes of the birds, for they would only bring disaster. The prince could not understand this, for if love is the cause of wretchedness and strife, why were not the birds drooping in solitude, or tearing each other in pieces, instead of fluttering cheerfully about the groves, or sporting with each other among flowers?

While Ahmed mused on the contradiction, a dove, chased by a hawk, fluttered through his window and found refuge in his room. The prince lovingly caressed the dove, and put it in a golden cage, and offered it, with his own hands, the whitest and finest of wheat and the purest of water. The bird, however, refused food, and sat drooping and pining, and uttering piteous moans. The prince was puzzled, and rebuked the dove for refusing all it was offered. The dove replied that he could not be happy because he was separated from his love, his partner.

Ahmed asked what love was, the dove replied, 'It is the torment of one, the felicity of two, the strife and enmity of three. It is a charm which draws two beings together, and unites them by delicious sympathies, making it happiness to be with each other, but misery to be apart'. Not being able to make sense of the dove's statement, Ahmed let the dove go free.

Ahmed's tutor was terrified at the discovery the prince had made, knowing that this was knowledge forbidden by the king, and his head would roll if the king found out. The dove returns to tell the prince that some distance off, there was a princess, whose garden was surrounded by high walls where no man was permitted to enter. Inspired by these strange feelings, Ahmed wrote a love poem and addressed his letter 'To the unknown beauty, from the captive Prince Ahmed', then, perfuming it with musk and roses, he gave it to the dove.

Day after day Ahmed watched for the return of the messenger, but he watched in vain until one evening the faithful bird fluttered into his apartment, and fell dead at his feet, having been mortally wounded by an arrow, but so full of love was the dove that it had struggled on to deliver its message. Ahmed discovered a chain of pearls round the neck of the dove, attached to which, beneath his wing, was a small enamelled picture of a lovely princess, but who was she, and where? The prince determined to go in search of his princess, and sought the aid of the owl who knew all parts of Spain. He asked the owl to be his mentor and accompany him on his quest.

So, travelling by night, and sleeping by day, Ahmed and his mentor arrived in Toledo, where he had news that his princess was called Aldegonda, and that she was the daughter of a Christian king, kept apart until she was seventeen, when her suitor would have to win the hand of the princess at tournament. But the prince knew nothing of weapons and fighting; all he knew was algebra and philosophy. The owl came to the rescue by telling him of a cave nearby where there was a suit of magic armour, and a spell-bound horse that has been there for generations, waiting for this moment.

Guided by his mentor, the prince found the cavern, A lamp of everlasting oil shed a solemn light through the place. On an iron table in the centre of the cavern lay the magic armour, against it leaned the lance, and beside it stood an Arabian horse, made ready for the field, but motionless as a statue. When Ahmed laid his hand upon the horse's neck, it pawed the ground and gave a loud neigh of joy that shook the walls of the cavern. Thus amply provided with horse and rider and weapon to wear, the prince determined to defy the field in the impending tournament.

Ahmed was Muslim, and this debarred him from taking part in the tournament, where the prize was Aldegonda. The other contestants sneered and jeered Ahmed, but spurred on by love, and carried by his magic horse, he charged and scattered his opponents, including the king who challenged him.

At noon, the magic spell wore off and the horse returned with Ahmed to the cave. Ahmed is distraught, when news was brought to him of the princess who had been struck insensible by Ahmed's disappearance. He remembered the words of his tutor, 'Care and sorrow and sleepless nights are the lot of lovers' and wondered if he had made a terrible mistake.

The prince is determined to effect a cure on the princess, so he disguises himself and gains admission to the palace, where he plays a tune on his pastoral pipe, which cause the princess to recover. The king offered Ahmed anything he wanted, but he only asked for the silken carpet that had once belonged to the Muslims, and was now stored in a wooden box in the castle.

They brought the sandalwood box and the carpet. 'This carpet,' said the prince, 'once covered the throne of Solomon the wise; it is worthy of being placed beneath the feet of beauty'. He placed it under the feet of the princess, then sat at her feet, and told the king, that he and his daughter had long loved each other in secret. 'Behold in me the Pilgrim of Love!', the words on the banner he had worn at the tournament.

Scarcely had the prince uttered the words, than the carpet lifted off and bore the prince and princess away. There was great consternation, and the king's advisers were severely trounced for their negligence, but they were ignorant of the meaning of the Arabic writing on the sandalwood box. The prince's father had died by the time the Christian king found his daughter, and he was reconciled to Ahmed. Ahmed appointed the owl, his mentor, to be his prime minister.

DISCUSSION OF THE LEGEND

I have included this story for interest's sake, but also because of the imagery and symbolism, and for the part played by a nonhuman mentor. Indeed, in this short story we have an excellent representation of the union of opposites. The saying, 'Anything is possible in imagination' is true, and the more one engages in it, and works with people who use it, the more true it becomes. Quite often, in the early days with clients, when it is suggested to them that they have a conversation with an imaginary person, they find it very strange. However, it is not so strange, for how often do we have conversations with ourselves? How many times do we talk to our pets?

In the story given above, the 'wise person' is an owl, and the owl has a reputation for wisdom, so the choice of the owl is not totally surprising. Other figures may be Jesus, or one of the prophets, Solomon himself, one of the gods or goddesses, some well-known figure from history, or even still alive. The theme will be explored further when we consider sub-personalities in the next journey.

Whoever the person (or creature) imagined by the client, they represent the psyche itself, but the psyche is a concept, an idea that is difficult to visualise. Visualising a person (animal or object) to represent the psyche is a useful way of 'objectifying' the idea. The same technique of objectifying is used when we ask a client to visualise an object to represent the feeling.

The client who says, clenching his fist, 'I've got his hard feeling right here in my head' may then be helped to explore that feeling by objectifying it, by creating an image to represent that feeling. For example, he may see a rock, a stone, or a pebble. He may, as Tony did, when he complained of piercing headaches, imagine a walnut. There is a significant difference between the symbolism of a stone and a walnut. The one is exceedingly difficult to break; the other is a shell that conceals something, protecting what is inside. So the method of working would be different.

Working with the mentor image, then, is likely to call up some interesting facts of the person's personality. Why, for instance, did Glenn, at the particular moment 'choose' the figure he did, with the strongly spiritual overtones? Why did Carole choose a cocker spaniel as her guide? These are questions which, if explored with the client, may lead to greater understanding of their inner world.

Summary

We saw that we may use a book just with text, with pictures or the modern form of book, the audio or video tape. It is worth mentioning that some people find it easier to 'hear' what they are imagining, while others 'see' quite clearly. For other people, especially in the early stages of using imagery, actually 'think' their way through the image, and only see it dimly. We saw that the book theme may reveal 'facts' about the person that creates alarm, so 'softly, softly' is the watchword.

It is worth stating that although the eighteen themes deal with separate issues, they can be combined as the need arises. For example, we saw how Carole, without guidance, combined the stream with the cave; Glenn combined the mountain with the sword; Roy combined the house with the book. The needs of the moment should be a guide to what is used, rather than a rigid sticking to the 'rules'.

The theme of the cave, as representing the unconscious, is one that occurs frequently, in legend and mythology, as well as in the client's own journey. It would appear that the symbolism of the cave is almost universal, and appears in all cultures. Within the (natural) cave there is such symbolism as dark versus light, descent and ascent, creatures that inhabit the dark, the origins or rivers, underground lakes and so on. It is only possible in a book such as this to introduce a topic, but there is so much to this particular theme that it must be left to you, the reader, to explore your own caves.

The chalice and the sword are linked symbols, and are often considered together, representing, as they do, the feminine and the masculine principles. However, that would be limiting the symbols if we only considered the sexual aspect. The chalice is one of the broad range of 'container' symbols, and this is one of its meanings. The chalice is mostly associated with that which is spiritual, and around it has grown up a wealth of myth and legend. The quest of the Holy Grail, is probably the most widely known legend, which, by itself, contains so much symbolism.

William Blake (1993) contrasted the sword with the sickle (masculine versus feminine, or possibly Mars (God of War) versus Demeter (Goddess of Harvest)).

The sword sung on the barren heath
The sickle in the fruitful field
The sword he sung a song of death,
But could not make the sickle yield.

Shakespeare, in *The Merry Wives of Windsor*, uses the sword in what could be interpreted sexual symbolism. 'Why, then the world's mine oyster, Which I with sword will open.' (2:ii, 1–2)

The dragon (and its variation, the serpent) is deeply embedded in the Collective Unconscious, through fairy tales, legends and myths. One of the classical features of the dragon is that it is the guardian of treasure of some sort, often a princess who needs to be rescued. While the sexual symbolism should not be ignored, neither should be overstated; it is one theme among many. What is of equal importance is what the dragon represents. Very often it represents what is feared or held in contempt or disgust. If the idea of the dragon is related to the shadow, it makes sense; that part of us we would rather not own.

The dragon as guardian. What is it guarding, and why? If it is treasure, what is the treasure? If it is a princess, what part of us is that princess? If a man imagines a dragon guarding a princess, it is very possible that the princess represents his Anima, being held captive. The symbolism may also be that he is being driven by a desire to be a rescuer. If a woman works with a similar image, she could feel that *she* is the prisoner; then the question must be asked, imprisoned by whom? Is it a tyrannical Animus? Someone from the past? Held prisoner by some moral or social restraint? Who does she want to rescue her? What will she do when she is rescued?

Finally, the dragon is often reduced to size, to something less frightening. This transformation is a most effective way of dealing with the dragon (or other wild creatures), using the principles of confrontation, feeding, and reconciliation.

This particular Journey, exploring the second level of symbols, closed with a discussion of the mentor, the wise person, the helper, the guide. The mentor figure appears in many of the accounts of the 'quest', and usually at a point in the story where the traveller has reached an impasse, or needs help.

The mentor may only listen to the client, he or she may give advice, or practical help or instruction. 'Look up to the right, on that ledge, you may find something to get you of this difficulty.' Or more positive, when the client is really struggling, and afraid, 'If you move down there a bit, you will see a tree fallen across the river'. It is as well to remember that one of the functions of the psyche is to assist the person to move forward in the quest.

The counsellor's own psyche works in partnership with the client's mentor, and when this partnership is fully exploited, it can prove immensely rewarding for both client and counsellor. It might seem obvious to say that it would be difficult to attempt to go with a client on his or her journey, if we, ourselves, have not trod a similar pathway. This applies to all counselling, and although we do not need to have trodden an identical pathway, possibly of death of a spouse, we do need to have explored the pain that lies within. When the client experiences blockages that he or she cannot overcome (as in the case of Roy's book), the counsellor may need to take a hard look to see if there is a similar block with his or her inner life.

On that note I will end this Journey, for it was only after Roy's experience, and my own meditation on it, that I was forced to acknowledge that I had 'chosen' the direction of Roy's exploration because *I* needed to work on a particular chapter in my book, so that I could close it; unfinished business related to the death of my father. Thinking about the 'partnership of the psyches', whose psyche, Roy's or mine, was directing that particular journey?

Exploring Third-Level Themes

Theme Thirteen – The Lion

Although the male lion is called the king of beasts, it is the less heavy and less majestic female lion that does most of the stalking and killing of prey and is the centre of the lion pride. The male lion's mane makes him appear bigger without adding expensive weight. In the event of an attack, the mane also serves to snag or cushion the impact of an opponent's claws and teeth.

Possible psychological interpretation

The lion corresponds to gold and to the sun, hence it is found as a symbol of sun gods, such as Mithras. In Egypt it was believed that the lion presided over the annual floods of the Nile, because they coincided with the entry of the sun into the zodiacal sign of Leo. The lion is the king of beasts; gold is also know as the lion of metals. The lion is the earthly equivalent of the eagle: the possessor of strength and of the masculine principle. The young lion corresponds to the rising sun; the old or infirm lion to the setting sun. The lion victorious represents the exaltation of virility; the lion tamed is symbolic of power subdued.

In the Bible, David killed a lion that had come to terrorise his flock of sheep. This could not have been done without a struggle. Symbolically, this represents the struggle of one figure with the opposite side of his nature. In Biblical symbolism, the lion represents kingship, royalty, courage, boldness.

The spontaneous appearance of a lion, from the woods, for example, or as an obstacle on the client's journey, could be an indication of hidden aggressive tendencies. The lion may appear caged, or tamed, possibly part of a circus act; it may not be alive, but a statue. It should not be assumed that the lion always represents aggressive tendencies; it is known to be the mentor, certainly a protector.

Androcles was a Roman slave, the hero of a first-century story by Aulus Gellius. One day he saw a lion in pain and removed the thorn embedded in its paw. When Androcles was later sentenced to die in the arena, the lion recognised him and refused to harm him. This story symbolises the importance of *befriending* the fearsome parts of the personality that threaten to destroy us.

Theme Fourteen – The Sub-personalities

The concept of sub-personalities is related to that of Archetypes, and comes from Assagioli's (1965) *Psychosynthesis*. The subject was previously dealt with by William James, as 'the various selves'. Sub-personalities are distinct, miniature personalities, living together within the personality, each with its own cluster of feelings, words, habits, beliefs and behaviours. They are often in conflict with one another and engaged in a constant jockeying for position.

They are remnants of helpful and unhelpful influences left over from a time when they were needed for survival to meet lower level needs. For example, a policeman sub-personality is helpful in keeping one on the right side of the law, but becomes tyrannical when it always pushes the person into punishing other people for minor breaches of his or her self-imposed standards.

Examples of sub-personalities

Boffin	Policeman	Executioner	Professor
Gaoler	Rebel	Granite	Saboteur
Monk/Nun	Seducer	Nurse	Spider
Playboy	Tiger	Victim	Persecutor
Rescuer	Judge		

An analogy from astronomy helps to fix the idea of sub personalities as Archetypes. The centre of our solar system is the sun, which has three main qualities: energy, warmth, and light. Around the sun, and totally dependent on it, and influenced by it, a number of major and minor planets revolve. When considering the psyche, the analogy is continued thus:

1. The sun is the psyche.

2. The revolving planets are different part of our self – our sub-personalities.

3. Each sub-personality is made up of three parts: body, emotions, and mind.

Just as the earth (to take one of the planets) rotates on his own axis, and at the same time revolves around the sun, so each sub-personality 'planet' constantly rotates around *its* own axis, and revolves around the psyche. This brings every one of the three parts of each sub-personality within the focus of the psyche, there to exert the three main qualities of energy on the body, warmth on the emotions, and light on the mind.

This beautiful picture, regrettably, is marred by the undeniable fact that very often the sub-personalities strongly resist the influence exerted by the psyche. At the same time, however, just as each of us is made up of many sub-personalities, so each sub-personality is acted upon in a different way by the psyche. But nothing is ever static. Change produced in one area often necessitates change in another. There is not such state as total conflict replaced instantly by total harmony: there is always a dawn. Gradually, however (and it may take a lifetime), the conflicting areas can be brought into harmony with the psyche as we continue the quest for wholeness and integration.

The psyche can also be thought of as a powerful communications satellite, receiving, decoding, and transmitting signals to and from all the sub-personalities. For just as the planets in the solar system influence one another, so each of the sub-personalities is related: they have to be, for together they make up the personality. So each needs to know what is happening with the others. Some may not like what is happening in another, particularly when change produces a threat, and will send strong signals expressing their resistance. The result is conflict and confusion. Conflict if left solely to the conscious is likely to lead to only partial resolution. This is because the warring factions have no mediator. When the psyche acts as mediator, every sub-personality is allowed a proper hearing. They are then influenced by the psyche and mediation results in resolution. When this process is repeated many times over, integration is greatly enhanced.

In this sense, possibly more than in any other way of working, the counsellor is a guide, one who accompanies the client.

A 'guide' can mean someone who knows the route so intimately that he can lead his party to the goal with safety; such a guide on a journey through the Alps would be invaluable and necessary. In this sense I refer to a guide in counselling; someone who walks alongside, who, if necessary, holds an imaginary hand, who succours, who encourages, who may say, 'Hold on a minute', 'Take a breather', 'What do you see at your left hand?', 'What sounds do you hear?' The guide thus enters into the world of the client and is an active partner who experiences the frustration of the client who, when climbing a mountain pass, is suddenly confronted by a landslide that blocks the way. The guide may say something like, 'How long has it been there?', 'Where did it come from?', 'Who caused it?', 'What do you want to do with it?' The client may feel like giving up and walking away; the guide may struggle with that feeling of disappointment, resignation, despair, as the blockage seems too difficult to overcome. As they walk away from the landslide, and the counsellor asks, 'What feelings and thoughts are you experiencing right now?' The client has to confront what it is like when she or he walks away from difficulties in the real life.

Case illustration – Jim

I think the best way to handle this subject is to illustrate it with two cases studies – Jim and Joan. Jim you have already met in The Third Journey (The Meadow). After the first session when we discussed Jungian personality types, we agreed that he had very well-developed thinking and sensing functions, and I expressed the opinion that probably his intuition and feeling functions had been trapped by his drive to achieve, and to be an engineer to please his father. Jim was a thinker, an analyst, and organiser, and we agreed that as he continued his journey he would start to make more use of his intuition and feeling functions. He thought the emphasis on thinking was a compensation for having his feelings trampled on by a bullying and hyper-critical teacher at primary school who nicknamed him 'Mental Jimmy'.

When I asked him to visualise an object to represent himself, he was startled at the image which appeared almost immediately – a very nice-looking brass vase, but empty. This caused him great distress. To have left it there would have been destructive, so I asked him to create another image, of how he would like it to be. He saw the same vase but filled with flowers that drooped gracefully over the edge. From our discussion so far in this book, it will be seen that a possible interpretation is that outwardly Jim was presentable, but that is all. A vase is something to be used, mainly for flowers, and that the fact that his vase was empty suggested that this was how he felt. Adding the flowers provided beauty and fruitfulness.

On another level, the vase could represent his feminine principle, that was empty, and needed the addition of flowers (representing the masculine principle) to complete the picture. The addition of the flowers represents the union of opposites.

This image paved the way for several interesting sessions exploring his sub-personalities. The setting for his 'drama', as he called it, took place in a gaol house in the middle of a desert, surrounded by a massive wall. He identified the following 'actors':

1. The 'Major', something like a KGB officer, or a policeman.

2. The 'Boffin', sitting at his desk, shuffling his papers.

3. The 'Executioner', with his mask and axe, whose job was to keep all others out.

4. The 'Martyr', dressed in white, bowed, carrying a cross.

5. The 'Playboy'.

6. The 'Maiden'.

The Playboy and the Maiden were in separate cells in the dungeon, and all were being kept in control by the Executioner. Jim was both intrigued and startled by the appearance of the executioner, for without much input from me, he recognised this as representing his angry and potentially violent side. He interpreted the axe as his tendency to use his intellect to win an argument by the use of cutting comments that had the effect of putting the other person down.

Over a period of time we discussed his various characters, and one of the early discussions was about the Playboy. Jim thought he probably symbolised his underdeveloped, demanding, pleasure-principle child (he was reading Freud at the time). The Maiden, he thought, was the innocent, defenceless child within him. He said that his child felt worthless and empty, and that whatever the child did he could never be certain of his parents' love. 'That's why I still feel I have to earn someone's love in a relationship.'

As we ended that session, he said, 'I really want to work on my sub-personalities next week'. I asked him just to take a look and see how they responded to that statement. He pulled a face, then said, 'The Executioner doesn't like that, he's not at all happy, and looks apprehensive at the challenge to his position'.

The following week he found that the Executioner had been replaced by an aggressive South African soldier who befriended Jim and left him in charge of the 'prisoners'. He felt more comfortable with the new-style Executioner. He linked this change in character to a dream in which he broke out of a room by bursting through the window. I commented that it seemed like there was a similarity between a repressive regime and repression, and then a breaking out, an asserting of his authority, a 'breakthrough'.

This transformation, however gradual, often happens, as the client receives insight. It also points to another significant principle; how important it is to take note of what happens in the life of the client away from counselling, in this case, what happened in his dream.

Having made the 'breakthrough' in his dream, following on from his previous imagery of the change to the principal character, Jim was eager to 'get on with it'. I suggested he try to befriend the Executioner, but he remained very aloof, arms folded across his camouflage battle-dress. He didn't want Jim to go into the dungeon, but I encouraged him to persist, and to assert his authority. He found this difficult, but eventually won that round of the battle. (Much of the language assumed military type terminology.) The Executioner insisted on going with him, down 20 steps, to a small landing, then down another five, to where the Major sat. He wouldn't make a decision to let Jim speak to the two prisoners; he needed to confer with the Martyr and the Boffin, and get their support.

Eventually there was reluctant consensus, and Jim went to talk to the Maiden. She told him, yes, she wanted to be free but that she said she would lose her position. I asked Jim what the position was that she would lose. 'Well, she's the innocent, she only has to flutter her eyelashes and people do as she wants.' As he said this, Jim's face coloured, and I sensed he was on the verge of tears. I said, 'So, she's in a conflict, if she comes out, she gives up some of her power'. He nodded, then said, 'She's come out and is hanging on to the Executioner for support. He's putting his arms around her and they've made friends'.

The tears he had been struggling to control now started to flow. This was the twentieth session, and it was the first time he had permitted his control over his feelings to relax enough to cry. The Executioner needed softness of the Maiden; she needed the his strength. Jim watched them as the climbed the stairs and waved Jim farewell.

That was a thrilling and moving session for both of us, and although we knew there was more to do, that 'breakthrough' was surely significant. As Jim left, I said, 'May I give you a hug?' He nearly strangled me! I feel it was essential to ask clients this, and on the rare occasions when I do, it is usually right. That is one gesture one should never take for granted.

DISCUSSION OF JIM

The description of the two sets of steps remained unclear, other than the fact that they went down a long way. Bearing in mind that 'descent' represents going into the unconscious, then his sub-personalities were deeply rooted. The two sets of stairs deserves further thought. It is possible that the first twenty steps brought Jim in sight of the cells, and then there was a small landing, where he could take a breather. The remaining five steps represented the final bit of the descent, one fifth of the total. I also think that the 25 was part of Jim's mathematical mind, although we never did discuss its possible significance.

It is interesting to note that although the other sub-personalities remained, the two principal characters – the Executioner and the Maiden – had made friends, and that's what seemed important. The feminine principle was being kept prisoner, yet exercising power by manipulation.

Case illustration – Joan

Joan, who had come to me as part of her personal development as a counsellor was in her early 50s, a married lady with children. One of the ways in which the sub-personalities may be contacted is by using the house, although at a separate time from exploring the house theme. Joan already knew that the house represented her, and she had come across a 'wise woman' hidden away in an attic room, working away at a tapestry, with one tiny bit uncompleted. (The symbolism of tapestry may be of one's life, or of a particular part of life).

I suggested to Joan that she stand outside the fence of her house, and call out to the 'people' within to come out. She said, 'I had to say it several times before anything happened. It was as if they weren't going to obey me, but then I got really determined. You probably heard me giggle, that was when a policeman came out, and started to walk around, making notes in his notebook, and saying, "Tut-Tut, that will never do. I'll have to report that." The next one to come out was a monk, so solemn he was, and I felt quite intimidated, as he walked round with his had bowed. The next was a nurse in a very old-fashioned uniform, and so bossy!'

Joan paused in her account, and I asked her if there were any more. 'I'm not sure.' 'Then call again,' I suggested.

Joan started giggling. 'Do you know what! Out rolled one of those stone mushrooms that oast-houses (where hops are dried) stand on. I was dumbstruck, and could only stare at it. The policeman was sitting on it.'

Again there was a pause, and it became obvious that something profound was happening, for tears were starting to break and roll down her face. I waited, knowing she would tell me in her own time. 'I don't like this person,' she eventually said, as her tears stopped. 'Do you want to tell me about it?' 'Oh, I'm so ashamed. She's dressed in a very short scarlet dress, with heavy make-up, leaning on the doorpost, with cigarette smoke curling around her face. She's now walking out and she goes up the to monk, who turns his back on her. The policeman is tut-tutting again, and the nurse is looking down her nose.'

Joan started sobbing as she reached this point. Her eyes remained closed, as if wanting to keep the image, and possibly not wanting me to see the depths of her suffering. 'They obviously don't like this lady...' I said. 'Lady! She's no lady, she's a whore.'

As she spat out the word, she opened her eyes, and said, 'I've never used that word in my life. Does that mean I'm a...one of those?' 'That would be the last thing you would want to be, wouldn't it? Where do you think she came from?' 'When I was about fourteen, and staying at my grandparents for a holiday, I came into the living room, smartly dressed, as I thought, for I'd spent a long time doing my face. Grandfather took one look at me and said, 'Joan get that muck off your face, you look like a street-walker'. I could have killed him, and him supposed to be a Christian. My father told him off, but I never really liked him after that.'

Rather than break into the imagery, I delayed any discussion on that issue. 'What do the sub-personalities want to say to one another? I asked. 'They don't want to say anything. They're just walking round, not looking at one another.' I advised Joan, 'Now you take control. They might not like it, but you have to do it. What will you do?' This is what Joan said, aloud. 'Right, you lot, you are living in my house, and we have all got to get on together. I won't have squabbling or this stupid not talking. You've all got your part to play, so let's start talking.'

I had never heard Joan sound so determined, as she then described what happened. 'The Policeman was the first to do anything. He put his notebook away and went up to the Nurse and started talking about her family. The 'Temptress' (that's what I've decided to call her) narrowed her eyes and looked at the Monk, and winked. She was really giving him the "come-on". He started swinging the cord around his waist, but it took ages for him to move across towards her. She moved away from the doorpost, stubbed her cigarette out, and put her arm through his, and they walked away in silence.

'Then the strangest thing happened. That stone mushroom suddenly changed into my grandfather. It all became clear then. We'd often said he was as hard as stone. That left me with a problem. All the others had "made up", what was I to do?

'But it was him who made the first move. He said, "Sorry, Joan. Forgive me?" Joan started to cry. 'He's been dead 10 years, and I've had this lump of stone in my heart for about 40 years. We linked arms and joined the others as they walked. What do I do now, William?' 'When sub-personalities 'come out' they must go back, but why not all enjoy yourselves in some way. Ask them what they would like to do.' 'They said they'd like to have a picnic.'

That is what they did, and when it was time for the session to close, I suggested that Joan tell them that for the time being they were to go back inside. She stood at the door and kissed every one of them, ending with her grandfather.

DISCUSSION OF JOAN

The Policeman. Joan recognised this character. 'He's the one who is judgmental, always right, always getting me and others to toe the line. He can be quite useful in keeping me on the straight and narrow, but at times he oversteps the mark. Like the other day, I passed a car parked partly on the kerb. My Policeman nearly had me knocking on the door and telling the person off. I hadn't realised until now why that was, just thought I was being "public-spirited".'

The Nurse. This was not a surprising sub-personality for Joan, for that had been her background, but Joan recognised in this character one of the deputy matrons who had influenced her in the early days of her training: a stiff and starchy woman, who always looked down her nose at anyone of lesser rank. 'I'd no idea she was lurking there. Heavens! have I been giving that impression?'

The Monk. Joan said, 'He's easily explained – my Catholic background. I still need that, but I'm glad that he could unbend a bit with 'Temptress'. I felt overjoyed when they made it up. I think I've still got some work to do on her, and my grandfather. Does it mean that I'm like her?' I explained, 'You seem to have taken in (introjected) grandfather's injunctions and prejudices against women who wear make-up and dress unconventionally. When he said that, at that moment, you *were* a prostitute, a temptress, and she took residence in your house. Tell me, thinking about her now, how has she made herself known?'

Joan sat for quite some time, deep in thought. 'When I became a Catholic, just before I married, I began to dress very conventionally – like I am now and although I've always worn some make-up, it was always discreet, not enough to offend my husband! Just listen to what I've said! Whenever I read of prostitutes being charged for soliciting, I'd say to my husband, 'Serves them right'. Wasn't I horrid? But you know, William, it wasn't the Monk who had to make peace with her, it was me. I've decided to change her name. My middle name is Alice, so that's how I'll think of her.'

I hope that these two illustrations of sub-personalities will open the doorway to some interesting and fruitful work on your own sub-personalities and when you work with clients.

Theme Fifteen – Sleeping Beauty or Briar Rose

This is one of the stories by the Grimm Brothers, which can be used in imagery either spontaneously or (and this is more likely) as directed imagery.

> A wicked fairy causes Beauty to prick her finger on the needle of the spinning wheel. Instead of dying, a kindly fairy turns the wicked spell into a sleep of one hundred years. A briar hedge springs up around the castle. All the people in the castle sleep with her, so that she, Beauty, will not be alone when she awakes from sleep. Many brave men perish in their attempt to break the spell, and the briar is festooned with their skulls. The king's son, without effort, penetrates the briar hedge and wakens Beauty with a kiss.

When a client is suddenly confronted by a hedge, particularly a briar, or sees a castle behind a hedge, or has an image of someone asleep, then may be an appropriate time to introduce the fairy story, and see how it relates to the client's journey. For the purpose of this theme, I will use it in a directed way, first for a male client, then for a female client.

It is worth pointing out that this theme may not be applicable for everyone; for it has much to do with sexuality that is unawakened or is trapped. I will relate the first part to the story of Antonio.

Case study – Antonio

Antonio was twenty-eight years of age, unmarried, and, on his own admission, 'quite promiscuous'. That was not why he was in counselling; he had come because he wanted to work through his acute attacks of panic. We had done some behavioural work on reducing his stress levels, when he said, 'I've told you about all these birds I've been out with, but I've never settled down; I think it's about time I did'.

What I had learned was that he was dominated by his mother, an Italian lady who had brought Antonio, her only child, up on her own, since his father died when Antonio was 10 years old. They had no financial worries, his mother came from a well-to-do family, and had many relatives living in this country. She still expected Antonio to live at home, and every time he tried to break away, she made his life a misery by becoming ill.

I introduced him to the meadow scene, and when I thought he could handle that I asked him if he knew the story of Sleeping Beauty. He didn't, so I gave him an outline. Then I invited him to become a knight on a white horse, carrying a lance and a shield, and a sword at his side. I simply said, 'You have heard a call to go on a journey to break this spell. Off you go'.

At first he galloped round and round the meadow, until I said, 'You seem to be going round and round and getting nowhere, as if you're not sure what to do. Look for a path, a road, that will take you somewhere'. He found a track that led him over hills and streams. (The meadow seemed to represent the confines and constraints put upon him by his mother, and he needed my encouragement (permission) to break out.)

When he gone some distance, over 'really beautiful country', he said, 'Why have I never done this before?' I told him, 'In the distance you can see just the tip of a flagpole on the turrets of a castle, but it is surrounded by a thick briar hedge. In the castle, asleep in an upstairs room, is the princess who has been bewitched and has been asleep for one hundred years. Now she is waiting for you to set her free. That is your task, to awaken the Sleeping Beauty.'

When he arrived at the hedge, he prepared to use his sword, but didn't need to, for the hedge parted before him. He found all the courtiers and servants slumbering, and I told him to climb the stairs and find the princess's room. I told him to be courteous and gentle as he wakens her; that she has waited one hundred years for this moment. Antonio said, 'I've knocked on the door, and am walking cautiously in. My sword clanks a bit, so I hold it so as not to alarm her. She *is* beautiful. I stoop and gently kiss her on the lips. She looks up at me, with eyes as bright as stars, and a smile that melts my heart. I take her hand and lift her to her feet. I kneel before her and am completely smitten.

'She takes my hand and leads me on a tour of the castle, where now everyone is awake and doing things. I say to her, "I want you to come with me and meet my mother. I will tell her we are to be married"'.

I said to Antonio, 'Ask the princess for a token of her love for you.' 'She gives me one of her rings and I offer her my sword for it seems it's the most precious thing I have.' When it was time to leave that scene, I suggested that this was probably his special place, which he could return to and no one could invade. 'I don't want to leave, William, I still have to face mother.'

Awakening of Beauty represents the feminine side of life which is lost in unconsciousness, where life then seems nothing but thorns. On the one hand Beauty may be regarded as a symbol of the Anima; on the other she symbolises the archetypal images that lie dormant in the unconscious, waiting to be stimulated into action. Sleeping princesses usually symbolise to passive or undeveloped potential.

Anything spiky, such as thorns, may represent the penetrating penis and be a symbol of the masculine side of life. Beauty's negative Animus, the wicked fairy, put Beauty to sleep, effectively taking her out of circulation just as she reaches puberty, and discouraging young men.

The whole castle sleeping represents a state of stagnation, of sterility, because the masculine and feminine parts cannot relate. This fairy tale can be interpreted on the wider scale of society; for to be truly functional, society must blend both masculine and feminine attitudes.

The 'chosen one' who awakens Beauty on a personal level symbolises the consummation of marriage. On a broader scale it represents the forces of life and death; there is little we can do to control either.

The whole trouble arose in the first place because the wicked fairy had been left out of the feast. It is always the neglected part of our unconscious that causes us most misery.

DISCUSSION OF ANTONIO

When we finished that imaginary journey, we discussed what had taken place. First I asked him about the meadow and he said, 'When you said I seemed to be going round in circle, that came as a surprise, for I thought I was doing well, making real progress. Why was that?'

Rather than give my interpretation about his mother, I said, 'What does it remind you of, this 'getting nowhere'?' 'Something in my life, I suppose; that's what it's all about, isn't it?'

I said, 'What part of your life is like that, riding furiously, but only going round in circles?' He became quite cross, as he said, 'I don't know. You tell me.' 'I wondered if it was something to do with relationships. Is there a relationship that's like that?' 'I don't have relationships, I only have flirtations. You know that.' 'Not one relationship a bit like that?' I sensed the penny dropping by the expression on his face. 'My mother? Hang on a bit. If that was something to do with her, this going round in circles... Yes, that is it, and I couldn't see it because it would mean leaving her. Is this what it's all about. You cunning...' He chuckled. 'And all that about the princess, who was *she?*'

To have given a psychological interpretation could have spoiled things for Antonio; he had to discover that for himself. What I did say was, 'Now you've made the connection between the journey, the fairy story, and your mother. How can you work it out?'

He said, 'I know one thing, William, that was more than a fairy story for me. Okay, mother is in there somewhere, and I've got her to deal with, but it was also to do with me. You know how I've treated women, but just seeing the princess lying there, so beautiful and innocent, I felt something happening here [pointing to the region of his heart] and I knew that I wanted to love and be loved. Sounds wet, doesn't it? In a funny way, I feel liberated from something.'

Antonio took many months before he could make the break from his mother, and only achieved this when he moved into another city, although he still had to cope with her telephone calls saying how ill she was, and how sad and empty life was without him.

There are other ways this story can be used. It applies when working with a female client who is tied to her father. She *is* Beauty, who pricks her finger and sleeps for one hundred years. During this long sleep, the client could imagine what is going through her mind. What does she feel and think as she hears the door being opened? What does she want to happen?

The male client can swap places, and imagine what it is like to be the princess; the princess can swap and become the knight, and imagine how he feels. However the story is used, it should be tailored to meet the needs of the particular client; then it becomes a personal journey, not just an exercise.

Theme Sixteen – The Volcano

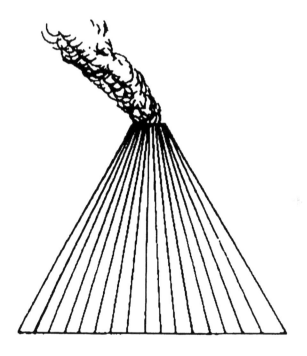

Figure 3 Volcano

The word 'volcano' comes from the Latin volcano god, Vulcan, or Vulcanus. The Greek counterpart is Hephaestus. In mythology, the volcano is invested with powers of opposites: on the one hand, volcanic earth is incredibly fertile; on the other hand the destructive fire of the volcano is linked with the idea of evil.

Possible psychological interpretation

As a psychological symbol, the volcano represents the passions which become the sole source of our spiritual energy once we have managed to master and transform them. In dreams, the volcano points to subterranean forces, repressed passions and impulses erupting to the surface.

There is an obvious psychological difference between imagining an active volcano and one that has exhausted itself. There is a difference, too, between climbing up to the rim, standing on the rim looking into the volcano, and walking around in the floor of an exhausted volcano. That is one good reason for not stopping with the first image, but exploring it in its many aspects.

One of the pleasant images to remember about volcanoes is that they often become places of beauty. For example, the Serengeti National Park, a wildlife refuge in northern Tanzania, East Africa, was once an enormous volcano, extending to around 6000 square miles. It is now home to many species of animal. This image by itself is worthy of exploration.

Case study – Gareth

I had been working with Gareth, a man of about forty, for several sessions, on the problems in his marriage. He was describing his response to an argument which, he said, had got out of hand, and was still fairly steamed up. I said, 'It sounds as if you're both living on the edge of a volcano.' He stared into the distance, then said, 'That's it! you've broken my dream a few nights ago. Funny it was. I'll tell you'.

'I was climbing Snowdon, carrying something very heavy. When I reached the top you took it from me. It was a witch's cauldron filled with gold. Even in my dream I thought that was funny. You cut off the top of the mountain with your hand, and put the cauldron on what was now a volcano. When the gold started to bubble, you said, 'Now it's time for the refining, Gareth'. You lifted me and held me over the bubbling gold. I screamed and struggled, but there was no escape. You dropped me in. But I felt no pain. I woke up sweating and shaking, and it was *ages* before I got back to sleep again.

'The dream continued, or was it a dream? I'm not sure now. I saw the flames being put out by a spring, deeper than the volcano, and the crater was filled with crystal clear water, which looked so inviting and refreshing that I wanted to swim in it. One of the eagles of Snowdonia flew over my shoulder and plunged into the waters, but when it emerged, its plumage had changed. It was now radiant reds, golds, blues and greens. From somewhere I heard these words, 'The waters of transformation are available to all, But not all will be transformed.' 'I took the plunge, and when I woke, I felt clean, and I had a deep sense of peace. What do you think of that, William?'

'It sounds like your dream was leading you into refinement, like gold that has to go through the fire. Perhaps that has something to do with your marriage; perhaps it was both you and your marriage that was "in the pot". It also seems to be something to do with beauty hiding that which is ugly; peace neutralising passion. Passions serve a purpose, but when they get out of hand, like the volcano, and spew out fire and brimstone, then they are destructive. Maybe that's the goal, to transform your inner world into a more peaceful place. The cauldron you carried with difficulty was the very thing that brought you peace, even though you fought so hard against what was happening. I wonder if this was the treasure, the pot of gold.'

This account illustrates an important principle in all counselling, but more so in imagery, whereby often what takes place in the session is carried on and developed within the client's unconscious. It is for that reason that I frequently work with dreams, particularly when the client says something like, 'I had this dream recently and it bothers me'. The relationship between dreams and imagery is so close that I am certain they influence each other, and to ignore the client's dreams is to ignore a potentially fruitful exploration.

Theme Seventeen – The Wilderness

The wilderness and/or desert is an image that frequently arises spontaneously in the personal quest, and I have included wilderness, desert and quicksand, because in many ways they are related.

A wilderness is a wild or uncultivated region or tract of land, uninhabited, or inhabited only by wild animals; a tract of solitude and savageness, a waste or desolate region of any kind in which one may wander or lose one's way. A desert denotes an uninhabitable and uncultivable region, and implies entire lack of vegetation.

We saw it in the case of Jim, who pictured his 'prison' in the middle of a sandy desert. In my own experience it arose spontaneously when, during a training session, my guide suggested I visualise my birth. The picture that arose quite spontaneously was of a cold desert, with a windmill with its sails perfectly still. It was a picture of utter desolation. I wept then and many times since as I have struggled to make sense of it.

Years later, when writing of the life of my parents, that earlier scene started to make sense. I was born in Australia, 14 months after my parents' second son was killed in house fire. As I wrote, grief engulfed me as I relived their story. I have slowly come to the conclusion that the 'desert' was the feelings I was picking up from my parents, still caught up in their grief. Almost 60 years afterwards, I was re-experiencing some of the grief they felt and, somehow, had communicated to me, either in the womb or afterwards, but it has taken me almost a lifetime to understand this.

In religious symbolism, wilderness is applied to the present world or life as contrasted with heaven or the future life. In Bunyan *Pilgrim's Progress*, we read 'As I walked through the wilderness of this world'. And in the Bible, 'He (God) found him (Jacob) in a desert land, and in the waste howling wilderness; he led him about, he instructed him, he kept him as the apple of his eye' (Deuteronomy 32:10). John the Baptist was the 'voice crying in the wilderness,' (Deuteronomy 32:10) living on wild honey and locusts. The wilderness is associated with temptation : Jesus spent his time of temptation alone in the wilderness; and in Psalm 95:4, we read, 'To-day if ye will hear his voice, harden not your hearts: as in the provocation, and as in the day of temptation in the wilderness'. The Scapegoat was released into the wilderness bearing the sins of the Children of Israel; in the Biblical parable of the Lost Sheep, Jesus refers to leaving the ninety and nine in the wilderness to seek for the one that is lost (Luke 15:4).

Ishmael and his mother, Hagar, were cast out into the wilderness by Abraham, who had sired Ishmael. Ishmael was the ancestor of the nomadic Arabian Ishmaelites, arranged, like the Israelites, into twelve tribes. Because Islam traces its lineage from Abraham through Ishmael, and Judaism and Christianity traces its lineages through Isaac, Muslims, Jews, and Christians are all spiritual 'children of Abraham'. Jews and Muslims are Archetypes of the conflict between brothers.

The wilderness is a place of entrapment: 'In this so vast wilderness, full of snares and dangers' (St Augustine, 1838). Dante in his *Divine Comedy* speaks of 'this savage wilderness'. Sir Percival, in his search for the Holy Grail, found himself wandering in a wilderness, fearful that he would die there. By inference, the wilderness is a place without direction, where one could easily become lost: 'Behold, I will do a new thing; I will even make a way in the wilderness' (Isaiah 43:19).

The wilderness is a place of contemplation: 'Lying in the wilderness, and looking at the stars, I was led to contemplate on the condition of our first parents when they were sent forth from the garden; how the Almighty, though they had been disobedient, continued to be a father to them, and showed them what tended to their felicity as intelligent creatures, and was acceptable to him' (Journal Of John Woolman 1772).

The wilderness can refer to water, as in: 'So that finding ourselves, in the midst of the greatest wilderness of waters in the world, without victuals, we gave ourselves for lost men and prepared for death' (The New Atlantis, Sir Francis Bacon, 1627), or frozen water: the polar regions are vast frozen wildernesses.

The wilderness represents all that is evil:

> Now, lady of honour, where's your honour now?
> No man can fit your palate but the prince.
> Thou most ill-shrouded rottenness, thou piece
> Made by a painter and a 'pothecary,
> Thou troubled sea of lust, thou wilderness
> Inhabited by wild thoughts, thou swollen cloud
> Of infection, thou ripe mine of all diseases,
> Thou all-sin, all-hell, and last all-devils... (Francis Beaumont, c1610)

The wilderness is also symbolic of death: 'Now at the end of this Valley was another, called the Valley of the Shadow of Death, and Christian must needs go through it, because the way to the Celestial City lay through the midst of it. Now, this Valley is a very solitary place. The Prophet Jeremiah thus describes it: A wilderness, a land of deserts and of pits, a land of drought, and of the shadow of death, a land that no man (but a Christian) passeth through, and where no man dwelt.' (John Bunyan, *Pilgrim's Progress*)

The wilderness is the habitation of the Devil:

> Indeed, though in a Wilderness, a man is never alone, not only because he is with himself and his own thoughts, but because he is with the Devil, who ever consorts with our solitude, and is that unruly rebel that musters up those disordered motions which accompany our sequestered imaginations. (Sir Thomas Browne (1643))

As part of their initiation, North American Indian youths took part in the 'vision quest', in which the youth went into the wilderness alone, without food or water, in search of a personal guardian spirit, usually revealed to him in a dream. Very often it is helpful to link the wilderness with the desert.

Wandering in the desert or wasteland is a poignant symbol for the human condition of questioning despair, of the search for meaning in a world which seems to be devoid of life and feeling. It symbolises the place of revelation and preparation. The desert is the place of the sun, but the sun in all its intensity, without relief; yet when the sun goes down, the desert is cold. This can be likened to a painful experience, in which the way ahead seems to go on unremittingly through blistering heat and cold lonely nights. Water, symbolic, of physical and spiritual nourishment, is markedly absent in the desert, which becomes a place of emotional and spiritual emptiness and starvation, of longing and of grief. Yet within that there is a paradox, for the intense sun also stands for purification, through the burning up of what is undesirable. The desert, or wilderness, is the domain of the goddess Artemis, and 'going into the wilderness' means getting in touch with the feminine principle. People who deliberately choose the wilderness way as a means of increasing self-awareness find themselves becoming more reflective. They find that their dreams are more vivid, which contributes capacity to look within themselves.

Very often in myth and legend the questing hero is forced to go through the desert to find that which he is seeking, whereas, one usually goes into the wilderness for a purpose. Yet within the desert fulfilment is attained. The whole of Isaiah Chapter 35 speaks of opposites. The desert (wilderness) will blossom as the rose, the inhabitants will rejoice, there will be joy and singing, waters and streams shall break forth. There will be oases full of vegetation, and there will be peace and tranquillity. The chapter ends with, '…and sorrow and sighing shall flee away'. This chapter was written as a prophecy for the exiled children of Israel, but it is also a symbolic writing for the personal quest, and hold great promise for the desert experience.

The image of quicksand may helpfully be related to those of the desert and the wilderness. Quicksand is a state in which saturated sand loses its capability to support, and acquires the characteristics of liquid. Although struggling may cause a person to lose balance and drown, contrary to superstition, quicksand does not have the ability to 'suck' people under.

In spite of the 'truth' about quicksand, it is a powerful image that is deeply embedded in the psyche. The quicksand is symbolic of the unconscious, and to deliberately get into quicksand speaks of foolishness; so deliberately immersing oneself in the unconscious may hold terror of death. At a related level, the quicksand can also symbolise immersing oneself in the inferior function[1] – intuition, for example – or in one's Anima or Animus. It is said that to dream of quicksand signifies loss and deceit. If one is unable to get out of the quicksand, this heralds overwhelming misfortune. It can also mean that there is a hidden desire to be rescued.

Case illustration – Carole

When Carole was about half-way through her forty sessions, she reached a point of having to confront her desert. Since the beginning of counselling, two parts of her personality had brought her into conflict; she had a desperate need to achieve, yet, as she said, 'I have this in-built programme that says I will fail'. (She was training to be a nurse.) This conflict used up a great deal of energy, and she either failed to get her assignments in on time, or she left them so late that she didn't get grades that satisfied her.

She visualised these two conflicting aspects of her personality as a twin-peaked mountain in the distance, which she named as 'Rejection' and 'Abandonment', but in between her and them was a desert, through which she had to pass. 'I'm not looking forward to that one little bit, in fact, I'm quite scared.' She then went back several sessions to when she went into the hill to find the origin of the stream. 'Then I had to learn to trust my feelings; now I've got to do the same. But it's more than that; I think it's taken me all this time to feel that I can trust you, William.' I thanked her for her for being so candid.

One of her struggles had been with the rejection she felt she had experienced from both parents who had divorced when she was five years of age. It was very possible, therefore, that in addition to the two parts of her personality, the twin peaks represented her parents, particularly related to the names she gave the mountains.

What is interesting is that twin-peaked mountains represent duality: positive and negative; male and female; thesis and antithesis; paradise and inferno; love and hate; peace and war; birth and death; praise and insult; clarity and obscurity; scorching rocks and swamps. Twin-peaked mountains appear in many myths, and are sacred symbols; as in the Paps ('Paps' meaning breasts) of Jura, in the Hebrides.

In the next session she started across the desert. She found a dried out riverbed, that headed in the general direction of the mountain. She was finding the going wearisome, hot and lonely. When she was about a quarter of the way across, I suggested that she find someone to travel with her; she imagined a Red Indian Chief on horseback. He said to her, 'My daughter, you have travelled a long hard road to get here, there is more to travel yet, but keep your eyes fixed on the peaks, and I will meet you there. Take this with you'.

Carole said, 'He's telling me I'll make, isn't he? Gosh! that feels good. He gave me a strong staff. I guess it's for me to lean on'. As she travelled, I suggested that she would come across an obstacle. I frequently do this when it seems that the client

---

1   Most people feel more comfortable working with sensation or intuition: feeling or thinking. The dominant or superior function is often used in preference to the other of the pair, which remains underdeveloped, or inferior.

is either having too easy a journey, or, in this case, when the dreariness of the desert, with no variation, could wear her down.

'There's a large crack in the riverbed, and I feel very sad.' 'So, you have a dried up riverbed and a crack in it. What does that tell you?' I asked. 'That I feel lifeless, and that I'm going to crack, or have cracked?' She sounded as if she was searching for an answer rather than believing that she had cracked. 'It sounds to me as if you've been dry for such a long time, that the riverbed just can't take it any more. Maybe the crack is something to do with reaching down into the depths.' She thought about this, then started to cry. 'It's my emotions that have been dammed up, somewhere between the mountain and here. I've got to find that dam.' 'What I suggest is that this crack is not all bad, there's something precious in there, waiting for you to find it' I told her.

I find this is helpful when clients have come through a rough patch, to let them find something that compensates. In addition, a symbol such as a crack means an opening, and very often this refers to an opening up of something which was previously closed. If the riverbed symbolised Carole's emotional life, then she had allowed this crack to appear, so she 'deserved' a reward. Perhaps the 'crack' was her admission that she had found it difficult to trust me.

'I'm putting my hand the crack, and find a little white mouse. I love mice. I'll call him "Little One". He can travel with me. I've found some crumbs in my pocket, and he's eating them out of my hand.' 'That's nice, Carole. Could you extend that a bit. *Who* is eating out of your hand?' She laughed. 'My husband, naturally.' 'And you feed him all good things?' I joked. 'I try to.' 'How do you feel about continuing the journey?' 'It's getting too hot. I'll take a rest under a rock I can see'

As she continued her journey, the ground rose quite steeply, and she all but shouted for joy, 'There's a trickle of water. I'm really getting somewhere at last'. The river bent round, then, 'I'm now on the top of a dam, and pear-shaped lake. I feel so excited'. I asked her to examine the dam closely and to determine what had caused the blockage; was it intentionally made, like a reservoir? 'No, it's blocked with trees and branches and stuff. I know, it's a beaver dam. I can see them splashing about.'

There were several possible interpretations to this image of beavers. 'You've been working like a beaver', was my first suggestion. She agreed, then said, 'Beavers – the Indian Chief; there has to be a connection,' and I had to agree. We looked more closely at the symbolism. What did the beavers represent to Carole? Being aquatic creatures they represented something in her unconscious that was working to 'dam up' her emotions. My 'working like a beaver' helped her to look at one possibility, that all the expectations of her were that she would 'achieve', like her elder sister. She had a private education, but, on her own admission, was 'more interested in having a good time than in doing well'. 'University was too much like hard work, then I really would have to beaver away.' She grinned.

Carole now felt caught on the horns of a dilemma: 'If I release the water, the beavers will suffer, and if I don't, will I suffer?' I acknowledged the conflict, but pointed out that the beavers were representations, and in imagery, anything is possible. However, I urged caution, and suggested that she first explore the lake and find its origin. This cautionary note is based on the principle that time is usually

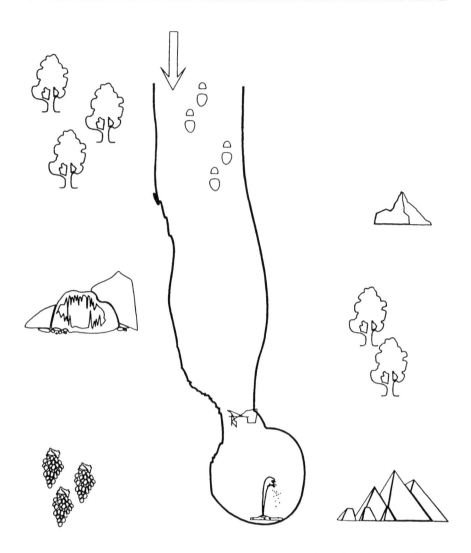

This was one of two big rocks Carole imagined; one on either side of the riverbed.
The sketch shows how she described the scene.

Figure 4 sketch of riverbed

needed before any sort of transformation can take place; time for the unconscious
to work, the more so as the beavers, as aquatic creatures, relate more to the
unconscious than to the conscious.

The mountains could be seen more clearly from the lake, and it would have been
'logical' to expect that the lake would have been fed from it. But this was not so;
'At the far end of the lake I see there is a fountain, coming from a spring. I know
that doesn't sound logical, but it doesn't have to, does it?' 'So, once again, Carole,
you've traced the source. Congratulations!'

'About the beavers, I think I'll build a shelter and sleep the night here. I'll be comfortable here until morning. Then I'll think what to do about the dam.'

That was all we could do in that session, and when she returned the following week, she said, 'It's happened! I had a really lovely dream. I was asleep in the shelter when the Chief came to see me. 'My daughter, you have no need to go to the mountain, for you have found all you need here. Come with me.'

'He took me by the hand and led me to the lakeside. There was a big hole in the dam, and the water was starting to run through. I'm sure he could see I was anxious about the beavers, for he told me to look, and he pointed across the dam. I saw a beautiful vine, with clusters of black grapes on it, and I just knew that the vine and that somehow the beavers been transformed. I looked round to speak to the Chief, but he'd gone. I made sure I wrote all that down in my journal; I didn't want to miss any of it.'

Carole and I worked together for another six months, and although the dam had been breached, she still found it difficult to show her feelings. 'But I'm learning that it's okay to do so, and that's important.' Several times, when she was talking about her lack of feelings, I encouraged her to look again at the riverbed.

Had it been necessary, and this is what I thought of in the week between her sessions I might have encouraged, Carole to explore under the dam, and go into the lodge, to talk with the beavers, to find out why they had chosen to build there. In the event, that wasn't necessary, for transformation had taken place.

Theme Eighteen – The Witch

Figure 5 Witch

The witch is the Archetype of the evil mother. She is the destructive, negative side of the Mother Archetype. The fear of the Devil and witches has its origin in ancient times. Much of the superstition surrounding witches comes from Christian persecution of those who refused to abandon their pagan beliefs, particularly their worship of the Earth Mother. The witch features in many fairy tales and legends.

In Grimm's *Hansel and Gretel*, Grimm says of the witch, 'When a child fell into her power, she killed it, cooked and ate it, and that was a feast day with her'. In myth and legend witches have red eyes, and cannot see far, but they have a keen scent like the beasts, and are aware when human beings draw near. In *The Tinder-Box*, Hans Andersen describes the old witch thus: 'She was very hideous, and her under lip hung down upon her breast.' In Shakespeare's *Macbeth*, the three witches prophesy his rise, then his downfall.

In Grimm's *The Frog-King*, the beautiful princess was playing with her golden ball when it ran into a well. An ugly frog promised to get it for her if she would promise to '…love me and let me be your companion and play-fellow, and sit by you at your little table, and eat off your little golden plate, and drink out of your little cup, and sleep in thy little bed – if you will promise me this I will go down below, and bring you your golden ball up again'. The princess readily agreed, but when the frog retrieved her ball, she ran off. Next day, while at dinner, the frog appeared, reminding her of her promise. Despite her reluctance, the king said that what she had promised she must fulfil. So the frog ate from her golden plate and drank from her cup. She was repulsed by him sleeping in her silken-sheeted bed, so she threw him against the wall. Instantly he was transformed into a prince, who had been turned into frog by a witch.

This story symbolises the transformation of the contents of the unconscious by befriending. It also draws attention to the importance of honouring an agreement with the psyche.

In the Bible, King Saul seeks help from the *Witch of Endor* (called a 'familiar spirit'). He wants to know from the spirit of the dead Samuel how he should regain the favour of God, who has deserted him and given his kingdom to David. Samuel, through the witch, foretells of the downfall of Saul.

In *The Poetry Of The Celtic Races* by Ernest Renan, circa 1856, we read,

> One day as Bran the Blessed was hunting in Ireland upon the shore of a lake, he saw come forth from it a black man bearing upon his back an enormous cauldron, followed by a witch and a dwarf. This cauldron was the instrument of the supernatural power of a family of giants. It cured all ills, and gave back life to the dead.

In *Faust*, the witch dips her skimming-ladle into the cauldron and throws flames at Faust, Mephistopheles and the Monkeys. The Monkeys whimper. The Witch, with extraordinary gestures, describes a circle, and places strange things within it. The glasses meanwhile begin to ring, the cauldron sounds and makes music. Last, she brings a great book and places the Monkeys in the circle to serve her as a desk and to hold the torches. She beckons Faust to approach, and hands him the rejuvenating potion.

The witch symbolises the resistance of the unconscious material being brought into the light of the conscious Ego, and the rational will. Witches prefer the night world, the depths of the forests; they inhabit the borderland between the conscious and the unconscious, the threshold that leads to the unconscious. As the archetypal Bad Mother, they represent the repressive Anima of man.

Case illustration – Tracy

Tracy was coming to towards the end of almost three years' personal development counselling. She was a senior nurse who, at the start of the counselling relationship, had been under severe stress over too much responsibility and not enough support. One of her patients had died, and this had caused her great concern and conflict; she felt she had been criticised.

On this particular occasion, the subject was raised again, and explored at a different level. Prompted by her 'I know I'm judging myself', I said, 'Visualise a court scene: what does it look like? See the dock, the judge, and prosecutor, the defence. What are the feelings?'

I put myself into the scene and read out the 'charge'. 'You, Tracy Negligent, are herewith charged, that on the fifteenth day of November, 1987, you did wilfully neglect a patient in your care and failed to give her the proper supervision so that she died. How do you plead, guilty or not guilty?'

Taking part in the action in this way is risky, and one has to be sure of the client to do so, for it is a profound way of working. Tracy started to cry, for obviously I had struck a emotional chord. I repeated, 'How do you plead, guilty or not guilty?' I wanted Tracy to hear herself say, 'Not guilty', which she did, through her tears.

I then asked her to look more closely at her judge. 'She's a horrible witch, one of my school teachers, standing there with her white face, and long pointed stick. She's pointing to some writing on the board, which says, "Tracy...is guilty of malicious neglect."'

'And what do you say?'

'I yell out, "No I am not, you witch."'

'Who else does she remind you of?'

'Death. I thought of a witch and of a clergyman. He gave me instruction for Confirmation, there was something creepy about him.'

The association with judgment and the witch may need a little explanation. The clergyman represents the Church; the Church represents God, and God represents ultimate judgment. The witch is normally depicted dressed in black, seated on a broomstick, or holding one. The school teacher holds a long blackboard stick associated with a broomstick. The writing on the board was stated in 'black and white', for all to see.

'You've heard the charge, Who is the defence?' What does the defence say?' 'It's my little girl.' Tracy was sobbing by now. Very early on in our relationship, Tracy imagined herself as an ugly little girl whom nobody (including Tracy herself) wanted to know. As time went on, this image changed, and she became 'almost pretty'. Then Tracy named her, something she could not bring herself to do until then. She called her Queenie. Now Queenie had come to her defence in the court room.

There was no need to for Tracy to hear what Queenie said, for as she started to speak, Queenie moved across and stood side by side with Tracy, and slowly they merged to become one. This was a peak experience for both of us.

Summary

The final six themes have taken us into different images and landscapes; I hope you have enjoyed the journeys. As with all the themes, I feel it is necessary, once again, to state that nothing is absolute; I have assiduously tried to avoid creating the impression that even when 'principles' are talked about, they are not carved in stone, but are fluid principles.

The lion theme may not often appear, indeed some of the other themes may not appear either, although they can be used effectively in directed imagery where that is considered to be therapeutic. There is little doubt that the lion conjures up pictures of majesty, strength and power, and superiority; in that sense the theme is a useful one. The creatures which different people imagine is often a reliable indicator to the fears that lie within them. To be stalked by a lion would be a frightening experience; just so in one's inner world, where people feel they are stalked by such a creature (their fears). Bringing their worst fears into consciousness is often enough to rob the fears of their power.

The theme of sub-personalities is closely related to the Collective Unconscious and to Archetypes. I have associated the idea of sub-personalities, for the association is too close to ignore. Just as we may be ruled by an Archetype, so we may be governed by a tyrannical sub-personality, that dictates what we do, think and feel. As we work on our own Archetypes and sub-personalities, we will be able to help clients to recognise theirs for what they are – figures of the past that no longer have any relevance in the present.

An analogy was drawn between the idea of sub-personalities and astronomy, with the various planets circling the sun, the psyche. In the case illustrations, we had an account of how Jim worked through some of his six sub-personalities. The principal lesson from his experience was the freeing of the feminine principle then the integration of two opposites, represented by the Executioner and the Maiden.

A second point is that the various sub-personalities often exert a great deal of pressure against change. I never cease to be astonished at just how accurate the psyche is in the characters portrayed in imagery, as we saw with Joan. Joan was forced to acknowledge that there was at least one 'unsavoury' character in her house, and she upset quite a few of the others, who didn't like what she symbolised.

Joan, too, had to do some work on reconciliation, as she was confronted by her grandfather, whom she imagined as a stone. A stone mushroom, as she imagined, is an extremely useful object; for on it stands the oast-house, and the rats cannot get into the building. But in Joan's case, she had turned that part of her heart into stone.

The fairy story of Sleeping Beauty took a different slant, for this is one of the rare occasions where the imagery was directed, although I would hasten to point out the difference between 'directed' and 'controlled'. This particular theme is full of sexual symbolism, although once again I think it necessary to say that symbols often have more than one possible meaning, and one should not immediately latch on to one and possibly limit the exploration.

The volcano theme touches on the difference between an active and an exhausted volcano. If the volcano represents passions, then an active volcano, spitting out fire and lava, is a powerful image of the tremendous force and the potential destruction. But, although a volcanic eruption does wreak havoc, it can also create fertility. So in imagery it is always a sound principle to look for something positive within the negative. This applies to exhausted volcanoes, such as the Serengeti in Africa, which now provide thousands of miles of rich haven for wildlife.

We traced the wilderness theme through the eyes of Carole, as she moved through the desert to find a dried-up riverbed, and her dammed-up lake. Although Carole didn't complete her journey to the mountain, in later sessions she was able to use the strength from the transformation to help her work through her feelings of rejection and to deal with her mother, and to work towards asserting her individuality.

In the final theme, the witch, we saw how images often become blurred or mixed, and when this happens it is essential to find the common thread. In the case of Tracy, the common thread was the feeling of being judged. In the final scene, Queenie, whom Tracy had judged for years, was finally accepted as she became Tracy's advocate, and integration took place. These 18 themes have taken us into many fascinating areas of the inner world. I know I have been excited as I have dipped into my case book, and into my own Collective Unconscious, and as I have encountered some of my own Archetypes and met again some of my sub-personalities.

Exploring Creative Imagination

Introduction

Having explored some of the essentials of using imagery in counselling, and looked at some terms, principles and themes, it is now time to move on to a study of imagination and creativity, and how these can be developed.

At one time the term 'imagination' encompassed the reviving or 'recollecting' processes (memory), as well as the process of creating mental images (imagination). The present, stricter, definition of imagination excludes and contrasts with that of memory, as the concept of forming something new contrasts with that of reviving something old.

Events and objects that are perceived in dreams are examples of imaginative exercises that are neither verifiable nor repeatable. The 'imaginative' person is sometimes viewed with suspicion or scepticism, and children are sometimes criticised as being 'over-imaginative'; as a consequence, the use of imagination is looked on as one of the less useful processes.

Why Use Imagination?

Possibly the answer should be, 'Why not use imagination?' or 'Can we avoid using imagination?' I would go as far as to say that we cannot enter into someone's world in empathy unless we use imagination to understand their feelings or plight. So, developing imagery is a valuable aid for any counsellor. What clients speak in imagery and symbols is often nearer the emotional truth than when they speak through the Ego. A word may trigger an image, and an image may arouse a word, and the more specific the word, the more easily the image will be triggered. Abstract words do not easily trigger images, although this is entirely dependent on the word and the client's experience. Peace is an abstract word, yet when Julie was asked to imagine an image to represent what she was experiencing, she immediately imagined a red heart with a white dove hovering above it. This was a significant step forward in her therapy, as we explored what those two symbols meant to her. As we shared her feelings in this way, we moved closer together in understanding each other.

Our minds cannot tell the difference between real experience and one that is vividly and repeatedly imagined. That is a salutary statement, for if we constantly imagine what is negative, our unconscious mind will absorb that. Conversely, if we constantly imagine what is positive, our mind will absorb that. So, working with imagination in counselling can help to reverse negative to positive. I make no apologies for such a statement, for I have seen it work in the lives of too many people to attribute the change to chance. People become clients usually because they are experiencing some conflict, in which neither side is prepared to concede. The role of the counsellor is to help the client reconcile the two sides of that conflict, so that she or he can move forward.

Glenn failed the practical part of his final medical degree. So much hung on his next attempt, but he was in a constant state of anxiety. Over the twelve weeks before his resit, we worked to establish a positive image of his taking the exam and being successful. He was instructed that whenever he was 'tempted' to think negatively, to take six deep breaths, and replace the negative image with the positive one. In this way he was able to keep his anxiety under control on the day of the successful exam.

Sandra had never passed an exam in her life, and failed her mock hospital nursing finals. Over six weeks she constructed a positive image of going to bed, having a good sleep, getting up in time for breakfast and a leisurely walk to the exam hall, walking up the stairs, entering the room, getting herself organised, all in a calm frame of mind. While she waited for the start time, she was to close her eyes and breathe deeply, and repeat, 'I am calm', 'I can do this.' She sailed through the exam.

Later I shall take you through some more detailed imagery sessions. Meanwhile, in the Appendix you will find suggestions that will help you improve your imagination.

Creative Thought and Innovative Action

We are born with the ability to be creative, yet not everyone uses that potential. Conformity thwarts the developing child's creative expression. The spark of creativity will be extinguished if it is not given expression. Increasing personal effectiveness requires creativity and unlearning non-productive and self-defeating behaviours.

Characteristics of creative people

Creative people are open to experience, flexible in thinking, and able to deal with conflicting information. Creativity develops within a psychologically safe environment in which there is acceptance, a non-judgmental attitude and freedom to think and feel, where we are not unduly swayed by criticism or praise.

Barriers to creativity

Being creative is bedevilled by barriers, mental fogs that prevent us from perceiving a problem correctly, or conceiving possible solutions.

PERCEPTUAL BARRIERS TO CREATIVITY: HOW WE SEE THINGS

We may fail to use all the senses in observing, and fail to investigate the obvious. We may be unable to define terms, or have difficulty in seeing abstract relationships. We may fail to distinguish between cause and effect. We may find difficulty using the unconscious, for example not using visualisation or fantasy. At the same time we may have difficulty using the conscious mind to organise data.

CULTURAL BARRIERS TO CREATIVITY: HOW WE OUGHT TO DO THINGS

Our culture may emphasise a need to conform; the onus may be on competition or on co-operation; a drive to be practical and economical at all costs may dominate. Different cultures have different beliefs about fantasy; some see it as time-wasting, while others place great faith in reason and logic. Many cultures are work-orientated and stress the need to keep trying and to be always prepared, which does not fit easily with the use of imagery.

EMOTIONAL BARRIERS TO CREATIVITY: HOW WE FEEL ABOUT THINGS

Fear of making mistakes is a potent anti-imagery barrier, as is fear and distrust of other people's ideas. This may lead us into grabbing the first idea that comes to mind. People who are plagued by personal feelings of insecurity, such as low self-esteem, anxiety, fear of criticism, fear of failure, or lack of curiosity, may find imagery too threatening because it does not provide structure. The need for security, which may make a person fearful of risk-taking, or of trying new things, also gets in the way of using imagery.

What is Creative Thought?

Creativity is a state of mind, an attitude that has an interest, as well as an investment, in exploring ideas. It is a breaking with the accepted, traditional approach in order to see things from different perspectives; speculations and similarities are encouraged. Creative play in children makes use of unlikely objects and transforms them into items necessary to complete the fantasy. Creativity is the ability to hear old ideas in new ways, and to find new connections to old solutions.

We all possess creativity, but how far do we use our own creative potential? How far do we facilitate creative potential in others? Creative thought may not be our accustomed mode of thinking, but everything is there, already created and to hand. All we have to do is use it. Avoid blocking creativity by asking: what can be used from this idea? What are the principal concerns about this idea? How can I turn the difficulties in into stepping stones?

Creative techniques

Avoiding and overcoming the common barriers to creativity is best achieved by altering the way we think, feel and behave. Brainstorming, a group activity where people let fly with ideas and possible solutions, without stopping to evaluate is one way of being creative; it can also be done alone easily. Other ways of stretching ourselves are by the use of analogy, analysis, questions, imagery, fantasy, metaphors, and symbols, which will now be considered.

1. **Analogy:** Analogy is a process of arguing from similarity in something that is known to similarity, or apparent similarity, in something unknown. Using analogy based on personal experience is one way of tapping into the subconscious. For example; on planning an aeroplane flight to Australia, I can draw on the experience of a previous flight to Cyprus, and in this way start to 'feel' what it may be like. On the other hand, if I have never flown before, I can use my imagination to 'feel' what it may be like.

2. **Analysis:** In analysis, we may break down something complex into familiar and recognisable components. In this we list as many alternatives as possible for each component. Then we put some of them together to create something new.

3. **Fantasy:** Imaginary activities that are produced spontaneously (as in daydreams) or as a direct response to inkblots or ambiguous pictures. Understanding the fantasy means working with its symbols.

4. **Imagery:** The inner representation of objects and events created at will by the conscious mind.

5. **Metaphors:** A metaphor is a figure of speech, an indirect method of communication, by which two distinctly separate elements are brought together in comparison to form a new meaning. Metaphors abound in everyday conversation: the arms of a chair; the legs of a table; a sparkling personality; rivers of blood. The ability to use metaphors is a right-brain activity.

6. **Paradox:** A paradox expresses truths about the existence of opposites, in an apparently illogical and self-contradictory manner. The purpose of a paradox is to arrest attention and provoke fresh thought. Paradoxical statements are often used for ironic or satirical purpose. In George Orwell's *Animal Farm*, the first commandment of the animal's commune is a remake of a previous paradox, 'All animals are equal, but some animals are more equal than others.'

Taking a paradox as the union of opposites, or two apparently irreconcilable ideas, statements or principles, we can think of this as the union of the conscious and the unconscious. The intellect does not like a paradox, because it cannot be reasoned, and to try to *explain* a paradox robs it of its pleasure. The more we integrate the unconscious, the more we are able to work with the unknown, the more comfortable we will be with paradoxes, because they connect with a part of us that does not need to explain them: the inherent truth is recognised.

Health may be regarded as a paradox; precious, yet cheap enough to throw away by abuse and misuse. A Biblical paradox is that we are created in the image and likeness of God, yet we are as grass that withers in the field. We can only reach the light through the dark, the hidden part, the unconscious, the shadow. Jesus could only be reunited with the creator by going through death and the darkness of the tomb. Believers only receive their reward *after* death.

In myth and legend symbols of paradox are found in the way everything changes into its opposite. The son turns into the father; the daughter into the mother. Beauty turns into ugliness, and out of it comes the prince, the rescuer.

7. **Questions:** Probing and questioning generate alternatives and the possibility of discovering creative solutions. Most of us can remember the time in our life when we besieged our parents, or teachers, with many questions, some of which were so difficult to answer that we were told, 'Don't keep asking questions'. For many children, the inquiring mind has been locked in a dungeon. In later life, when such questions would be a creative asset, we seem to have lost the art of enquiry.

8. **Symbols:** Symbols are objects or activities that represent, and stand as substitutes for, or are thought to typify, something else. Material objects may be used to represent something invisible such as ideas. For example, the dove is a symbol of peace. Symbols are products of feeling and intuition and erupt spontaneously from the imagination. The development of language, and its use, hinges on the ability to work with symbols.

Left-Brain and Right-Brain Creativity

A small boy stopped and spoke to a man hitting a rock, and asked him why he was doing it. Michelangelo looked up and replied, 'Because there's an angel inside who wants to come out'.

Creativity involves conscious thinking and ideas, but also tapping into the sub-conscious – the angel imprisoned within. Powers of imagination and insight exist in the deepest regions of our minds, often unrecognised, and frequently ignored.

The left and right hemispheres of the brain specialise in different activities. The left, 'logical', systematic brain controls movements on the right side of the body. It is more concerned with 'active doing'. The right, 'intuitive' brain controls movements on the left side of the body, and is more concerned with the whole, not parts.

Left-brain thinking

Left-brain thinking is predominantly concerned with:

Processing	Rationality
Analysis and deduction	Reducing problems to workable parts
Convergent thinking	Science and technology
Facts, data, figures	A step-by-step precision
The end product	Using a highly sequential approach
Structure	Verbal, literal, concrete language
The logical and the sequential	Working to well-defined plans
The mathematics mode	Order

Left-brain behaviours

The person using the left brain creates endless lists, puts everything down in strict time order, spends much time on detail and must get one point clear before moving on.

Right-brain thinking

Right-brain thinking is predominantly concerned with:

Abstract topics	Perception
Artistic expression	Prayer, meditation, mysticism
Body-image	Problem-solving
Constructive tasks	Remembering faces
Ideas and feelings	Spontaneity
Creative crafts	The visual
Divergent, global thinking	Working symbols and fantasy, dreams
Emotions	Working with metaphors and imagery
Process, not outcome	Working with opposites
Using experience	Working with the unknown
Knowledge through images	

Right-brain behaviours

When we use the right brain, we use a lot of visual aids, and tend to become agitated over data and too much fine detail. The sort of thing the right brain will say is, 'I know the answer, but how?' When we use the right brain, we often appear to be disorganised. The right brain tends to 'think' with the eyes, and likes to see the problem displayed graphically.

For the Mojave Indians, the left hand is the passive, maternal side of the person; the right, the active father and in Jungian typology, the left brain is more associated with sensing and thinking, while the right brain is more associated with intuition and feeling. For left-handed people the specialisation is not so consistent. Even in right-handed people it is not an 'either or'.

Damage to the left hemisphere often interferes with language ability; damage to the right hemisphere is likely to cause disturbance to spatial awareness of one's own body. Damage to the left brain may prove disastrous to an author, scientist, mathematician, but may not prove so damaging to a musician, craftsman or artist.

The hemispheres have a partnership function. A poet, using deep feelings, imagery and metaphor, draws on the right brain for these, and on the left for the words to express what the right side creates. The hemispheres may also be antagonistic: when, for example, the left hemisphere becomes too aggressive, trying to solve everything with logic and analysis, intuition and feelings are subdued.

Using both hemispheres

Profoundly creative people are reported to be comfortable using both hemispheres. Einstein, it is said, relied on geometric mental images rather than language for his analyses.

Creative people are exceptional only in that they have learned to pay attention to, rather than ignore, their insights, visions and altered states of consciousness. At the same time, they subject their visions, insights and intuitions to the most rigorous testing and evaluation. The key to true creativity lies in a balance between the two hemispheres, rather than dominance by one over the other.

The traditional mode of learning and problem-solving is rational, which involves reasoning – a left-brain function. It should be emphasised, however, that many brilliant plans fail because they do not take account of the non-rational, emotional components of the plan.

While it is comparatively easy to teach a rational, logical approach (provided the pupil is temperamentally suited), we can only *develop* and *train* the right-brain functions.

Most of us face decisions and actions. Many of us have been conditioned to believe in the superiority of the logical and analytical process, and do not trust emotional, intuitive, or value-based processing of information.

The left-brain problem solver

- Defines the objectives of the decision to be made.
- Classifies the objectives according to their importance.
- Identifies alternative courses of action.
- Evaluates alternative courses of actions by the objectives.
- Selects the alternative with the best outcome.
- Identifies and assesses possible consequences of alternatives.
- Implements the decision with careful monitoring and follow-up of possible negative consequences.

The right-brain problem solver

- Moderates rational thought with emotional-intuitive preferences.

- Uses various techniques to bring 'out-of-conscious' material into awareness.

- Avoids censorship of ideas during their 'incubation'.

- Views divergent, even contradictory, ideas with respect rather than with scepticism or defensiveness.

- Tries not to ignore internal warnings that something is wrong.

- Checks any rational problem-solving method to see whether it feels intuitively good in process and in the final decision.

- Tries to remain constantly self-aware.

Yin-Yang and creative thought

The ancient Chinese believed that a life-force flows through all things. In ourselves, it flows along meridians or pathways (which are used in acupuncture) that correspond to different organs of the body. The energy that flows between the two opposite poles of Yin and Yang is known as 'chi'. These opposite poles equate roughly with masculine/feminine, and positive/negative.

Yin and Yang are the two complementary principles that make up all aspects of life. Yin is conceived of as a dark square (depicting Earth, and earthly forces) female, passive, cool, moist, contracting and absorbing. It is present in even numbers, in valleys and streams and is represented by the tiger, the colour orange, and a broken line. Within our bodies, the Yin organs are those that are hollow, and involved in absorption and discharge, such as the stomach and bladder.

Yang is conceived of as Heaven, a white circle (depicting Heaven and celestial forces), male, light, hot, dry, active, expanding, and penetrating. It is present in odd numbers, in mountains, and is represented by the dragon, the colour azure, and an unbroken line. The Yang organs in the human body are the dense, bloodfilled organs, such as the heart and lungs.

The interaction between the Yin and the Yang is represented by the famous symbol of the circle divided into two equal sections by a sigmoid line across the diameter. The white (Yang) section has a black spot in it, and the black (Yin) section has a white spot in it, to symbolise that everything living, and all that we do, must contain within it the seed of its opposite. The sigmoid line is a symbol of the movement of communication and serves the purpose of implying the idea of rotation, of perpetual motion, metamorphosis, and continuity in situations that are characterised by contradictions: life and death, is an example.

The two forces are said to proceed from the Supreme Ultimate (T'ai Chi), and their interplay with one another is a description of the processes of the universe. As Yin increases, Yang decreases, and vice versa.

The concept of Yin-Yang is linked with the five elements of fire, water, metal, earth, and wood. Yin-Yang and the five elements support the Chinese belief in a cyclical theory of becoming and dissolution, and an interdependence between the world of nature and the events of man.

In the human body, a proper balance of Yin and Yang is seen as being necessary for complete health. If one or the other predominates, mental or physical problems will arise. Probably the most eloquent description of the interplay of yin-yang energy is in the ancient writings of the *I Ching*, or *Book of Changes* (Chetwynd 1986). There the concept of change is applied to individual lives, groups and organisations. The *I Ching* proposes a cyclical theory of change; change as movement that returns to its starting point.

Change is orderly, as in the seasons, but its orderliness is not always perceptible. Change in human lives is often very complex.

The eight polarities of I Ching

1. **Heaven:** Creative power; associated with energy, strength and excitement.

2. **Earth:** Yielding, docile, receptive; associated with the womb, nourishment, the great wagon of the earth that carries all life.

3. **Thunder:** Arousing and confronting; associated with movement, speed, expansion and anger.

4. **Sun:** Support; associated with gentle persuasion, quiet decision-making and problem-solving.

5. **Water:** Body and feeling; associated with toil, hard work, danger, perseverance, and melancholy.

6. **Fire:** Intellect and thought; associated with dependency, but also with clarity and perception.

7. **Mountain:** Reflective silence; associated with fidelity, meditation, watchfulness.

8. **Lake:** Joyful interaction; associated with the pleasure of eating, talking, singing.

The eight polarities are arranged in a circle of opposites known as the 'primal arrangement', or the 'mandala of earlier heaven.'

Yin-Yang and creativity

The concept of Yin-Yang has been introduced to show that there is another way of awareness. Although many people in Western cultures are familiar with Yin-Yang, it may be quite new to others. In order to be creative, we often have to move out of the familiar into the unknown. For you, then, Yin-Yang may prove to be the key that unlocks the door of creativity.

A second reason for introducing Yin-Yang is that it touches on symbols and symbolism. Trying to understand symbols will take us away from the 'natural' into the exciting world of intuition and imagination.

Develop your Intuition

Intuition is an awareness that arises from within or beneath consciousness, rather than arising from teaching, reason or logic.

Intuition is often associated with the feminine principle, the Yin of Oriental psychology. Creativity, lateral thinking, core construct and gut reaction are related to intuition. Intuition indicates where something came from and where it is going.

Ten keys are now offered to help you develop your intuition. Related exercises are to be found in the Appendix.

1. **Mandala:**[1] A mandala depicts the basic patterns of the psyche which spins from itself the web of life. The circle and the square depict, respectively, the inner and outer aspects of life; the watery fluid, the inner realm, is round while the earthy world of substance is square.

   The term 'mandala' is a Hindu term for 'circle', instrument, ritual, or emblem; mandalas are found all over the Orient. In the form of geometric diagrams, they are used to aid contemplation and concentration. A mandala may be produced in sand in coloured threads or dust, painted on paper, or created in three dimensions. A mandala is a mental image built up in the imagination. No one mandala is the same as another, because each is a projected image of the inner world of the creator.

   The basic components of a mandala are geometric figures, counter-balanced and concentric, formed around the 'centre', which is suggested but never visually depicted. Everyday examples of mandalas are a snow flake and the human eye, with the pupil surrounded by the iris. Others are:

   - wheel of the universe
   - Mexican 'Great Calendar Stone'
   - lotus flower
   - mythic flower of gold
   - the rose
   - labyrinth
   - temples and cathedrals
   - mosaic floors.

   Jung believed that the spontaneous production of a mandala in dream work is a significant step in the person's journey toward individuation, the integration of hitherto unconscious (personal and archetypal) material by the conscious self. Mandalas are useful to induce relaxation and to get in touch with the right-brain functions.

---

1   Further examples of mandalas and exercises are to be found in the Appendix.

2. **Biofeedback:** Literally, this is information fed back about bodily functions. Most feedback is through sensory channels. Feedback can help us control heart rate, blood pressure and blood flow in the limbs. Although biofeedback often relies on special machines, it is possible to become so aware of, say, the heart beat, that by using this awareness, plus imagery, it is possible to reduce the rate.

3. **Imagery:** Imagery is the visual picture your mind creates in reverie and in dreams. Imagery is more powerful than daydreaming and more controllable than dreams.

4. **Treasured objects:** Many children become attached to a particular toy or a blanket. Recall opens the door to reliving past events and associated feelings.

5. **Other-hand writing:** Trying to recall events and their feelings may be aided by writing with the non-dominant hand. This releases the control of the left brain.

6. **Sensory:** The senses are often the gateway to enhanced creativity. Sight, hearing, taste, touch and smell all evoke powerful images and feelings.

7. **Fantasy stimulation:** Many of us fear admitting to 'indulging' in fantasy. If we discourage a person from dreaming, we deprive that person of something precious. In fantasy we can be liberated from the frailty of our bodies, and the limitations of our knowledge.

8. **Dreams:** Keeping a log or dream journal is a most effective way to develop your dream life. It does mean being very disciplined, however, and recording the dream immediately you wake, before you do anything else. Dreams have a frustrating habit of slipping back whence they came, the very second we cross the threshold into consciousness. But they can be 'tamed' by creating the habit of instant recording, even though it means writing them in your journal, under the bedclothes by the light of a torch!

9. **Free Association:** Free association, developed by Jung and then by Freud, refers to a sequence of ideas which seems to come without logical connection. Something triggers something else, and we can be engaged in a long chain of events and experiences.

10. **Affirmations:** Affirmations counteract negative self-talk. Examples of affirmations can be found in the Appendix.

Summary

Creative thought may be something we are born with; it may be encouraged by early learning style and experience – discovery learning, for example – and it may be encouraged in later life by virtue of our chosen work. It does seem that certain people are more creative than others, but that does not mean the rest of us should hide our creativity away, never to show it the light of day. Creative thinking can be encouraged, and several techniques are discussed. If there is one that stands out, although this could be simply a personal preference, is the use of imagination: learning to work with what could be, rather than with what is.

It is a sad reflection, although true, that so often creative ideas have ice-cold water poured on them by people who, themselves, operate from a non-creative base. It is also unfortunate that many of these people maybe in positions of significant influence – parents, teachers, managers and friends. When this happens as adult, we can normally rise above the remark; children are more vulnerable, and it is at this vulnerable stage of development, when creativity is at its height, that so much creative potential is killed by, usually, unthinking remarks and put-downs.

An exciting development over recent years is the work done on right/left brain creativity. For so long, many of us have been programmed into left-brain thinking – logical and analytical, and the acquisition of knowledge. In the process, our right – creative – hemisphere has been relegated to the fourth division. It is salutary that many geniuses testify to using both hemispheres in their great works. If they need to, so must we!

Right-brain thinking and creativity go hand-in-hand, and the techniques are applicable in both. The Chinese knew this centuries ago and what they say about the balancing forces of Yin and Yang is very relevant in our discussion on creative thought. To our Western minds, the concept of Yin and Yang may sound strange, but what it does is to take us out of what we know, to what might be. If we reflect on the symbolism of the eight polarities of the *I-Ching* our imagination will certainly be expanded.

Exploring Symbolism

Alchemy

The first significant milestone on this particular journey is alchemy. Alchemy is an ancient art dating back to the first centuries AD which was practised especially in the Middle Ages. It was devoted chiefly to discovering a substance that would transmute the more common metals into gold or silver, and to finding a means of discovering the elixir of life, indefinitely prolonging the human life span. Gold was regarded as the symbol of illumination and salvation. Although its purposes and techniques were dubious and often illusory, alchemy was in many ways the predecessor of modern science, especially the science of chemistry.

Jung thought that alchemy, looked at through symbolic rather than scientific eyes, could be regarded as one of the forerunners of a study of the unconscious, particularly of the analytical interest in the transformation of the personality. The alchemists of four hundred years ago had two linked goals:

1. To alter or transform base material into something more valuable, sometimes referred to as 'gold' or a universal elixir, or the philosopher's stone.

2. To transform base matter into spirit; in other words, to free the soul.

The various goals of the alchemists are also metaphors for psychological growth and development.

The alchemical process made use of elements that were opposites, so that what was produced would be totally different from the original substances, and would be pure. Male and female, with their biological similarities and differences, represented a living example of the process, as a new life is created. The alchemist worked in relation to another person, referred to as his mystical sister. Thus we see how a relationship with another person promotes internal growth, and also how what transpires within one can benefit the relationship. Perhaps nowhere is this seen more pointedly than between counsellor and client. The first four stages detailed below relate to the alchemical process of the ancients. In psychological alchemy there are three more stages, and already we are starting to work with symbols, such as colours and metals.

1. **Calcination** (black; guilt; origin; latent forces). Calcination masks with primary matter a symbol of the soul in its original condition. The symbolic meaning is the 'death of the profane', or the extinction of all interest in life, and in the material world.

2. **Putrefaction** (white; minor work; first transmutation; quicksilver). The symbolic meaning is the separation of the destroyed remains.

3. **Solution** (red; sulphur; passion). The symbolic meaning is the purification of matter.

4. **Distillation** (gold). The symbolic meaning is the rain of purified matter, standing for the elements of salvation isolated in the operations that have gone before.

5. **Conjunction:** symbolises the union of opposites, identified by Jung as the close union of the male principle of the conscious with the female principle of the unconscious.

6. **Sublimation:** symbolises the suffering resulting from the mystic detachment from the world and the dedication to spiritual striving. The emblematic designs of this stage are depicted by a wingless creature borne away by a winged being, and also by the Prometheus myth.

7. **Philosophic fusion:** the binding together of the two principles.

The seven metals in alchemy, with their Deities, are as follows:

1. Gold   Apollo
2. Silver   Artemis (Diana) the Moon
3. Quicksilver   Hermes (Mercury)
4. Copper   Aphrodite (Venus)
5. Iron   Ares (Mars)
6. Tin   Zeus (Jupiter)
7. Lead   Saturn.

Personal alchemy goes through the first six stages outlined above, and can be summed up in the advice: analyse all the elements in yourself and dissolve all that is inferior in you, even though you may break in doing so. Then with the strength gained from the process, allow fusion of the two principles to take place. This sounds an awesome task, and not to be undertaken lightly, or hurriedly. Indeed, it is the work of a lifetime, and involves high level imagination.

Imagination, as we saw earlier, expresses repressed parts of personality. Imagery has an *obvious* and a *hidden* meaning:

- the obvious is conscious and concrete
- the hidden is unconscious and implied.

The hidden content takes the form of symbols. Understanding the content means working with the symbols.

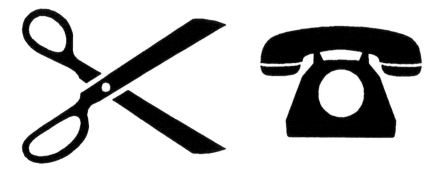

Figure 6 Scissors   *Figure 7 Telephone*

The Role of Symbols

Symbols are all around us, part of everyday life, so working with symbols is not something mysterious, although it is a bit like learning a new language: the more one practises, the more skilled and fluent one becomes.

In psychoanalytic theory, a symbol maybe:

1. An unconscious representation of something not directly connected with it.

2. A representation of conflict within the psyche.

3. An expression of repressed, sexual material.

4. The only way the unconscious may be reached.

The real meaning is not normally available to the conscious mind and only makes itself known through dreams. Dream symbolism is important in the process of concealing unconscious wishes or conflicts through displacement and condensation or revealing them through interpretation.

The use of symbols, and the transfer of interest from one thing to another, is an important step in children's development. The development of language and its use hinges on the ability to work with symbols. We use symbols in everyday life when we work with diagrams, maps, pictures and words.

In Analytical (Jungian) Psychology, symbols are:

- Dreams that express themselves as images.

- Captivating pictorial statements.

- Obscure, metaphoric and mysterious portrayals of a person's inner world.

- Individual representations of universal phenomena.

- Archetypal in quality.

Working with symbols is a way of by-passing ego-control and intellectual filtering, and of getting in touch with the urges, feelings, ideas and impulses that would not be tolerated in the conscious. Symbols may appear in dreams, fairy tales, icons, folk tales, mythology, legends, allusions and proverbs.

Dreams

Before going on to look more closely at myths and legends, and their place in working with imagery, it is necessary to examine a related topic, that of *dreams*. These wild, stimulating images, tangled metaphors, and complex scripts are the products of the right-brain hemisphere at work. An Australian aboriginal expression says, 'He who has no dreaming is lost'.

The differing views of the two 'greats' in this field – Freud and Jung – are now summarised.

Psychoanalytic theory of dreams

Freud (1990) referred to dreams as 'the royal road to the unconscious'. He believed that dreams reflect waking experience, and developed a highly systematised approach for interpreting and using dreams in therapy. He thought that thinking during sleep is primitive and dips into repressed material, and that dreaming is a mechanism for maintaining sleep and fulfilling wishes.

In dreams, wishes and desires are disguised to keep us from waking and being confronted by repressed material which is too difficult to handle. This is all the more important if a frank expression of those wishes would be in conflict with our moral or social values and standards.

The original wish or desire corresponds directly to the dream's latent content. The meaning of any dream lies in the latent content. The transformation of 'latent' into 'manifest' content is done by 'dream-work', initiated by the 'dream-censor'. The latent material has been suppressed because of its sexual, aggressive or otherwise frightening nature.

We employ various mechanisms of symbolic imagery to deal with *repressed* material:

1. **Condensation** in which we combine certain elements within the dream into a single image.

2. **Displacement** in which we shift an impulse from one object to another.

3. **Secondary elaboration** in which we impose structure to increase the coherence and logic of the dream.

Therapy aims to retrace the dream-work and understand it by interpretation. The analyst does not interpret by referring to a dream guide in the manner of the ancients, but by understanding the general principles of transformation on which we all create our own highly personalised dream language.

Analytical theory of dreams

Jung's theories are different from those of Freud: for Jung, dreams are forward-looking, creative, instructive and, to some extent, prophetic. He believed that dreams draw on the Collective Unconscious; that Archetypes are the common symbols, which enshrine universal, even mystical, perceptions and images; and that dreams serve to enlarge our insight into our own resources, and contain hints on how to solve our own problems.

Although there are also similarities, between the two theories – both make extensive use of symbols – the principal differences lie in the interpretation of those symbols, and in central constructs. For Freud, dreams represent an element of the unconscious process of repression of unwanted, undesirable material from the conscious mind. For Jung, the dream is much wider than the individual, and is not a rigid interpretation of a symbol. While all dreams certainly have a personal element, Jungian theory would include an element of the Collective Unconscious and a much broader meaning and interpretation.

Understanding dreams and their meanings has an important parallel when working with imagery, and a study of both Freud's and Jung's theories would be fruitful. In both dream work and imagery, it is essential to consider the individual, and not to fit the person into some predetermined model. At the same time, if Jung is correct, then dreams and images, go far beyond the knowledge and experience of the person, as the client taps into the Collective Unconscious. One important similarity between dreams and imagery is that one works with the feelings aroused by the content, and this is where the individual or personal element comes in. One client confronted a dog in imagery and was terrified, even though dogs did not normally frighten her. On exploration, she related an incident of being terrified by the story of *Red Riding Hood*, and linked that memory with her fear of dark woods. She had never been able to think why she was so afraid of woods.

Research into dreaming and cognitive functioning shows that:

- Sleep may be **dreamless** or **dream sleep**.

- Dreams are likely to occur in all extended periods of sleep and their function seems to be to process sensory inputs which have been gained during periods of wakefulness.

- People with right-brain orientation whose strengths are divergence and creativity often find it easy to recall their dreams.

- People with left-brain orientation whose strengths are verbal and analytical recall dreams less easily.

Problem-solving and creative dreams occur because one's habitual thought patterns are relaxed in sleep. Dreams may be attempts to clear pathways and resolve cognitive conflicts due to blockages and dissonances within the system.

Mythology and Symbolism

Mythology is a collective term for a particular kind of communication that uses symbols. It is the study and interpretation of myth and the body of myths of a particular culture. Myths are basic to human nature and occur in the history of all traditions and communities. Myths help make sense out of some overwhelming aspects of human existence. They convey serious but not literal truth by means of a story and influence behaviours within a culture. The truth in myths is implied rather than stated.

In general, a myth is a narrative that describes and portrays in symbolic language the fundamentals of a culture: for example, how the world began, how humans and animals were created, and how certain customs, gestures, or forms of human activities originated. Almost all cultures possess or at one time possessed and lived in terms of myths. The reality represented by a myth relates to some basic aspect of human experience. Myths usually begin with 'In the beginning' and are related to tales of the origins of things; fairy tales and folk tales; fables; sagas and epics and legends.

Myths differ from fairy tales in that they refer to a time that is different from ordinary time. Because myths refer to an extraordinary time and place and to gods and other supernatural beings and processes, they have usually been seen as part of religion. Because of the all-encompassing nature of myth, however, it can illuminate many aspects of individual and cultural life.

A myth is a traditional narrative, usually involving supernatural or imaginary persons and embodying popular ideas on natural or social phenomena, events or situations. It is pure imagination, unlike legend which has a basis in fact and freely amplifies, abridges or modifies those facts. At a deeper level, the myth is a metaphor for the workings of the Archetype and myths are statements by the psyche about itself. Myths make use of symbols to describe typical patterns and sequences of the forces at work within the person or within the world. They may be considered as universal or individual.

Universal myths

Myths are products of creative imagination and, as such, mirror the unconscious. Therein lies a conflict, for the Ego, which embraces logic and reason, rejects and ignores that which it cannot explain. Facts are of no interest to the mind concerned with a myth. When we work with myths, we plumb depths that take us beyond knowledge and beyond the conscious.

Individual myths

The individual myth exists in part from one's own heritage and in part from being part of the stream of humankind. The individual myth is our own unique pattern or mandala, as unique as our fingerprints, yet there are a myriad of links with other people. We can never explain our individual myth; we can only express it through creative imagination – from the inside. The excitement is in discovering our individual myth, the pattern of our lives – a pattern that is not set in stone, but is gradually evolving. It changes and evolves the deeper we immerse ourselves in it. If this immersion is self-centred, it is sterile; it must change us, as integration takes place. Coming face to face with our inner pattern gives us a sense of direction and purpose.

Confronting one's individual myth is a bit like doing a jigsaw when one does not have a picture to work to. Yet if we heed our dreams, for example, although we may not understand them, they will often provide the missing bit of the puzzle. We may have other experiences, such as flashes of insight, words that crop up out of nowhere, or 'out-of-body experiences'. These may sound alarming; the phrase does not in fact mean 'paranormal' experiences, but the ordinary experiences. Although they go under the rather magnificent name of 'hypnagogic hallucinations', they are not a form of mental illness. These are those fleeting images and sounds that occur in the borderland between being awake and dropping off to sleep. We can seldom hold on to these long enough to make sense of them, but the fact that we open ourselves to them does help us to get in touch with things we don't understand.

Myth and psychology

Depth psychologists such as psychoanalysts found in myths a way of understanding the dynamics of both the psychic life of individuals and the Collective Unconscious of society. Sigmund Freud made use of themes from older mythological structures to represent the conflicts and dynamics of the unconscious psychic life (in, for example, his Oedipus and Electra complexes). Carl Jung, in his psychological interpretations of the large body of myths that have been collected from cultures throughout the world, saw evidence for the existence of a Collective Unconscious shared by all. He developed this theory of Archetypes – patterns of great impact, at once emotions and ideas – that are expressed in behaviour and images. Both Jung and Freud viewed dreams as expressions of the structure and dynamic of the life of the unconscious. The dream, they pointed out resembles in many of its particulars the narrative of myth in cultures in which myth still expresses the totality of life.

The most comprehensive study of myths from the perspective of depth psychology, was made by the American scholar Joseph Campbell (1904–87). In *The Masks of God* he combined insights from depth psychology (primarily Jungian), theories of historical diffusion, and linguistic analysis to formulate – from the perspective of the dynamics that are found in mythical forms of expression – a general theory of the origin, development, and unity of all human cultures. I now want to introduce some concepts that are essential if one is to understand myths.

Myth, history and reason

There has always been tension between myth, history and reason, or the rational. Some of the Greek philosophers exalted reason and made cutting criticisms of myth as a proper way of knowing reality; Judeo-Christian tradition has also been opposed to myth.

Plato used myths as allegory and also as literary devices in developing an argument. Myths and history overlap in the prologue to the Gospel of John in the New Testament; there, Jesus, the Christ, is portrayed as one who came from eternity into historical time.

Modern interest in mythology

Myth had always been part of classical and theological studies in the West – for example Greek myths were adopted and assimilated by the Romans, and furnished inspiration to such later periods as the Renaissance and the romantic era – but the concern for myth, revived with new intensity, could be detected in almost all the newer university disciplines – anthropology, history, psychology, history of religions, political science, structural linguistics. Most current theories of myth emerged from one or more of these disciplines.

Types of myth

Myths may be classified according to the dominant theme they portray.

1. **How things began (cosmogonic myths)**

   This is usually the most important myth in a culture, one that becomes the model for all other myths. It relates how the entire world came into being. In some narratives, as in the first chapter of the Book of Genesis, the creation of the world proceeds from nothing. Egyptian, Australian, Greek and Mayan myths also speak of creation from nothing. In most cases the deity in these myths is all-powerful.

   A Polynesian myth has creation coming from a coconut shell. In Africa, China, India, the South Pacific, Greece, and Japan, creation is symbolised as breaking forth from the fertile worldegg. The egg is the potential for all life, and sometimes, as in the myth of the Dogon people of West Africa, it is referred to as the 'placenta of the world.'

   Another kind of cosmogonic myth is the world-parent myth. In the Babylonian creation story *Enuma Elish*, the world parents, Apsu and Tiamat, bear offspring who later find themselves opposed to the parents. The offspring defeat the parents in a battle, and from the sacrificed body the world is created.

2. **The end of all things (eschatological myths)**

   There are myths that describe the end of the world or the coming of death into the world. Myths of the end of the world presuppose its creation by a moral divine being, who in the end destroys his creation. At this time human beings are judged and prepared for an existence in paradise, or one of eternal torments. Such myths are present among Hebrews, Christians, Muslims, and Zoroastrians.

A universal conflagration and a final battle of the gods are part of Indo-European mythology and are most fully described in Germanic branches of this mythology. In Aztec mythology several worlds were created and destroyed by the gods before the creation of the human world.

Myths of the origin of death describe how death entered the world. In these myths, death is not present in the world for a long period of time, but enters it through an accident or because someone simply forgets the message of the gods concerning human life. In Genesis, death enters when human beings overstep the proper limits of their knowledge.

3. Myths of culture heroes

Such myths describe the actions and character of beings who are responsible for the discovery of a particular cultural object or process. In Greek mythology Prometheus, who stole fire from the gods, is a prototype of this kind of figure. In the Dogon culture, the blacksmith who steals seeds for the human community from the granary of the gods is similar to Prometheus. In Ceram, in Indonesia, Hainuwele is also such a figure; from the orifices of her body she provides the community with a host of necessary and luxury goods.

4. Myths of birth and rebirth

Usually related to initiation rituals, myths of birth and rebirth tell how life can be renewed, time reversed, or humans transformed into new beings, as in reincarnation.

5. The Messiah

In myths about the coming of an ideal society (millenarian myths) or of a Saviour (messianic myths), eschatological themes are combined with themes of rebirth and renewal. Millenarian and messianic myths are found in tribal cultures in Africa, South America and Melanesia, as well as in the world religions of Judaism, Christianity and Islam.

Myths of the Messiah, the Anointed One, the Christ, occur in theology. 'Messiah' was the Hebrew name for the promised deliverer of humankind, assumed by Jesus and given to him by Christians, although Jewish belief asserts that the Messiah is yet to come.

From its theological usage, the term 'Messiah' has come to be applied more loosely to be any looked-for liberator of a country or people or to an expected saviour in any of the non-Christian religions.

6. Providence and destiny (fate)

In some myths, divine supremacy is marked by a god's mastery over fate.

7. **Remembering and forgetting**

Myths of memory can take the form of collective reminiscences. A crucial part of the celebration of the Christian Communion is remembering.

8. **High beings and celestial gods**

Thy sky is considered sacred everywhere, and is related to, or identical with, the highest god.

9. **Kings and Saints**

Myths about kings are only found in traditions that know a form of sacred kingship. Kings were believed to have union with goddesses – this was the 'sacred marriage'.

10. **Transformation**

These myths would include initiation rites and 'rites of passage' (birth, attainment of maturity, marriage, death), as well as cosmic transformation. Baptism is a transformation rite of passage.

Other well-known myths include the story of the Garden of Eden; the story of the Flood; the stories of guardian angels; the Serpent as tempter; the tree of knowledge and the tree of everlasting life; the story of the rainbow; the Valkyries. In later sections, many of the myths and legends described here will be elaborated on, as their psychological inferences are drawn.

Using dreams myths and legends in counselling

I wish there were some definite rules about how to use dreams, myths and legends, but there are not. Later on I shall deal with the broad principles of working with imagery in counselling, but myths and legends deserve a preliminary mention.

As a general principle, listen to what the client is expressing and try to link this with a story. For example, a client who is expressing that she feels lost, could be introduced to the story of Ariadne, and in imagination to start winding up the ball of string, to get back to the starting place. A client who is feeling burdened down could be introduced to the story of Atlas, and then encouraged to identify what the burden is.

While there may be some general interpretations of dreams, dreams should not be approached in a mechanical way, like turning up the meaning in a dream book. In working with any image that appears from the unconscious, it is always wise to ask oneself, 'What *could* this mean?' First, what does it mean to you, the counsellor? Then, what could it mean to the client? If the client is nonplussed, a follow-up question, 'What does it remind you of?' may be sufficient to get the client travelling along the road towards discovery. A second question may help to focus the mind, 'What feelings do you have as you look at that? What words do you associate with it?' Later in the book we will apply the general principles of this part to working with clients.

Summary

Alchemy, although rarely studied today as a science, plays an important part in the general understanding of symbols and symbolism. Jung and his disciples have added to the base provided by the ancients. The stages in the alcehmical process are symbolic of the stages in the personal growth and development of an individual.

Jung and Freud looked at symbols in different ways. Freud used a much more structured model; Jung was less rigid, and emphasised the influence of the Collective Unconscious on the personal meaning of the symbol. Dreams use symbols, and it is essential to recognise that often the same symbols are used in dreams as in other forms of imagery.

Myths, fairy tales and legends, have a central place in the Collective Unconscious, as well as the personal consciousness, so a study of myths is really a study of symbols that have come down to us from many centuries.

It is not always easy or simple to recall a myth or legend, even though you may instinctively know one might be appropriate or would be apt at that particular time. However, if you become aware of the *symbols* being used, and work with those, that is often sufficient to encourage the client and you to continue working.

An assumption is that you are sufficiently acquainted with some of the myths to be able to tap into them. A second assumption is that the client's story awakens something you, that triggers off a particular myth. A third assumption is that you have an interest in using imagery. I could assume that as you are already reading this book that you do have such an interest. This volume could not contain all the wealth of material that is available to you. I hope that a door will have been opened to what is a very wide and exciting landscape.

Of one thing I am certain: when you start working with imagery, and using myths, fairy tales and legends, you will change. For as you work with clients, and help them to discover the myths within themselves, you, too, will discover the myths within yourself. The journeys you take with each client will be journeys of self-discovery, and your contribution to the client's discovery will be based on mutuality, for your journeys become linked. You cannot help clients discover things about themselves, unless you are also prepared for the possibility of discovering the same thing, or something similar, about yourself.

There is so much to absorb in the study of myths and legends that it would take a lifetime to take it all in; however, as you read through the various parts of this book you will be slowly immersing yourself in the language and atmosphere. What may seem strange at first will slowly start to work in your Collective Unconscious, and you will begin to make connections between your own inner world and what you are reading.

Exploring Twelve Herculean Tasks

Introduction

In our personal quest for self-discovery we encounter many challenges, and while they may not be life-threatening, they can, and often do, threaten our inner balance. Yet only as we deal with these challenges are we able to rebalance, and move on to the next challenge.

Symbols, like dreams, are a road into the unconscious. According to Dante, they may have four meanings:

1. **Literal:** the obvious, the everyday, common usage.

2. **Allegorical:** that which is concealed under the veil of fables. As when it is said that Orpheus with his lute made the wild beasts tame, and made the trees and the stones follow him; signifying the wise man or woman with the instrument of the voice who can make cruel hearts humble and gentle. The stones and trees that follow represent those that follow the teaching of the wise person.

3. **Moral:** One's personal morality influences one's interpretation of a symbol.

4. **Mystical:** that which cannot be explained by any of the five senses; that which bears reference to the spiritual, the divine. In the deities we can find parallells to our own quest.

The route is from the literal (the outward) to the mystical (the inner), for only if we fully understand what has gone before can we understand what comes after. Scissors, for example, are used to cut, shape, trim – but they also represent an emotional cutting off, a threat, possibly castration, or wounding in some other way. The significance is changed if the scissors are open rather than closed. When we stop at the literal meaning, or even with the first symbolic meaning, we are in danger of only skimming the surface.

An illustration can be drawn from an exercise with a treasured object. In a workshop each person brought an object to be used in what was a fascinating session. Mary brought a glass paperweight, a beautiful, multicoloured one, in the shape of a round-topped cone. First we explored the appearance, and viewed it from many angles, and admired its beauty; felt its smoothness, and how cold it was. This exploration by the senses led into an exploration of the colours and their significance in general, and their particular importance to Mary.

To my question, 'Where does it normally sit?' she hesitated, then replied with moist eyes, 'On my desk, near a photograph'. I picked up the paperweight, held it in cupped hands, looked from it to her, then said, 'It is obviously something very precious'. This obvious statement may have seemed unnecessary, but what I was doing was acknowledging the feelings. At the same time, the open statement allowed her to choose the direction of her response. I handed the paperweight to her, and as she took it, she said, 'Yes, it was given to me by someone very precious, many years ago'. She hesitated. Aware of the delicacy, and remembering that we were in a group, I tentatively said, 'The photograph?' She nodded, as she dabbed her eyes. 'Do you want to go on, or leave it there?' I asked. She decided to leave it there.

In a one-to-one session, there is little doubt but that Mary would have continued to explore the memories evoked by her precious object. Thus we can see how it is possible to move from the literal towards a deeper meaning of a symbol; in this instance from a bit of glass to (although this is purely conjecture) exploring the pain of grief.

I have chosen to use the analogy of Hercules to demonstrate the personal quest. The Goddess, Hera, driven by hatred of Zeus who had been unfaithful to her and sired Hercules, sent a fit of madness on Hercules who killed his wife and children. She devised twelve difficult tasks, the 'Labours of Hercules', as a penance. These took him into many exciting situations, and in each 'labour' he had to overcome something that threatened to destroy him.

The following 12 tasks represent the person's journey towards wholeness and integration, which is summed up in 'balance' – the purpose of any counselling.

I will end this introduction with a quotation from Gibran's *The Prophet* (1980): 'Then said a teacher, Speak to us of Teaching, and he (The Prophet) said: No man can reveal to you aught but that which already lies half asleep in the dawning of your knowledge. If he is indeed wise he does not bid you enter the house of his wisdom, but rather leads you to the threshold of your own mind.'

I hope that as you work through this book you, too, will feel the excitement and wonder of the possibilities opening before you, as you, yourself, go through the threshold of the wisdom of your own inner world.

First Task – Exploring the Interior

The first task is to discover our 'centre', and in order to do this we must turn inwards, or back upon ourselves. The external life must be counterbalanced by an adequate inner life. In order to do this we must be prepared to give up our entrenched positions, opinions, beliefs, prejudices, drives and impulses. It is salutary to remember that the more we help others to explore their inner worlds, the more we are compelled to explore our own. The moment we refuse to do this, that is the time we stop growing. When we, the counsellors, have done our own 'inner world exploring', even though it is never complete, we will be better equipped to travel with clients on their inner journeys.

I hasten to add that the journey towards one's own centre is never on a straight line, neither is it a place one reaches and remains there. A parallel can be drawn with the Mount of Transfiguration. Jesus went up a mountain with three of his disciples where the disciples had what we would call a 'peak experience', so wonderful that they were loath to come back down, but Jesus reminded them that there is work to do 'down there'. So with our times in the centre. We may reach it, lie down and rest in it, drink in its sublime peace and tranquillity, and wish that we could stay there were everything is crystal clear, and full of light, but there is work to be done in the real world, and go we must, but knowing that we shall return.

Second Task – Exploring the Heights

The evidence of the universality of the symbolism of heights is seen in temples and monasteries that are built on mountain tops, and the many legends associated with mountains considered sacred. Jesus ascended to heaven from the Mount of Olives. The mountain top is the point nearest to heaven, the point of highest aspiration; it is the meeting place of the gods, the place where God came and spoke with Moses, and gave him the Commandments, a place of awe and mystery.

Four aspects of exploring the heights will be considered: intuition; the will; thinking; and feelings.

1. Developing intuition (refer also to the First Journey)

Intuition is the knowledge of a concept, truth, or solution to a problem, which is arrived at apparently spontaneously, without conscious steps of reasoning or inquiry. One explanation of intuition is that it is the result of a special faculty, or ability, or a special sympathy with the object known. Some philosophers and psychologists claim that human phenomena can be understood only by special intuition; many psychologists, however, attribute intuition to a thought process that occurs too fast for a person to be conscious of it. For instance, numerous minimal cues may be rapidly integrated, making possible identification of the present experience in relation to past experiences. Self-deception is possible on account of the subjectivity of intuition.

2. Developing the will

In psychology, the will is the capacity to choose from alternatives a course of action and to act on the choice made, particularly when the action is directed toward a specific goal or is governed by definite ideals and principles of conduct. Willed behaviour contrasts with behaviour stemming from instinct, impulse, reflex, or habit, none of which involves conscious choice among alternatives. Modern psychologists tend to regard the will as an aspect or quality of behaviour, rather than as a separate faculty. It is the whole person who wills.

The act of willing is manifested by:

- the fixing of attention on relatively distant goals and relatively abstract standards and principles of conduct

- the weighing of alternative courses of action and the taking of deliberate action that seems best calculated to serve specific goals and principles

- the inhibition of impulses and habits that might distract attention from, or otherwise conflict with, a goal or principle

- perseverance against obstacles and frustrations in pursuit of goals or adherence to principles.

Among the common deficiencies that may lead to infirmity of will are:

- absence of goals worth striving for or of ideals and standards of conduct worth respecting; vacillating attention

- incapacity to resist impulses or to break habits

- inability to decide among alternatives or to stick to a decision once made.

3. Developing thinking

The 'heights' are represented by the mountain-top, sky or heaven. The idea of the 'mountain top experience' has already been touched on above. Exploring the heights may mean probing the differences between base emotions and higher feelings, and accepting that they both form an essential part of our personality. It also involves the balancing of thinking between what is concrete, and the higher intellectual reasoning. Thinking is such a vital function that some time needs to be spent on it before moving on.

One aspect of thinking to be considered is *what* we think. Some of our thoughts are quite spectacular, even bizarre. Thoughts have the habit of flitting in and out of our consciousness at amazing speed. They can linger or they can become so lodged in our minds that they pester. Thoughts can be under our control or they can be like a will-o' the-wisp, leading us a merry dance into dangerous areas. They can be silent like the grave or as noisy as a bus load of chattering children on the way to school. Thoughts are such changeable things and yet they can be so persistent as to exert a powerful influence on our behaviour. They can lift us to lofty heights or to depths of despair and degradation. The thoughts that mainly occupy a person's mind declare in bold letters the sort of person he or she is. So, in our quest for self-awareness we need to be thoroughly familiar with our thought life and how our behaviour is influenced by it.

When considering sympathy, for example, in what direction do our thoughts take us? And what direction when its opposite, antipathy, is considered? It is very likely, when this exercise is carried out, that it will be almost impossible to distinguish thought from feeling. Situations and events remembered will bring feelings with them, but thought may then take us away beyond what we have actually experienced. Thought may be both historic and futuristic. Futuristic thought borders on imagination. As with emotions, thoughts may be classified as positive or negative, but once again, an emotional content has been introduced. What we think – of ourselves, of other people, of situations and circumstances – influences emotions which in turn influence our behaviour.

We may make the excuse, 'I can't help thoughts coming into my mind'. This is true, but only to a degree. We can take active steps to prevent them lodging in our minds. Dark, negative thoughts may be dispelled by light, positive ones. Racing thoughts may be slowed down by relaxation and meditation – an exercise of will – which emphasises once more the relationship between body, emotions and mind. Many people harbour hurtful memories of distant or recent origin of events or people and around these memories their thoughts often revolve.

Evoked memories often bring with them the pain of the moment, but of equal importance are the associated feelings which are brought to the surface. Two feelings which commonly surface are resentment and bitterness. Most of us indulge in negative thinking from time to time but people who dwell on negative things for long also experience feelings that are on the dark side of the emotional spectrum. Just as racing thoughts may be slowed down by relaxation and meditation, so by the use of imagination it is possible for a person to move from extreme negative feelings toward the opposite pole.

4. Developing feelings

When considering feelings as part of personality, it is necessary to identify which emotions or feelings are generally prevalent, then to discover just how, and under what circumstances, those emotions influence us. It is may not always be easy to think of particular emotions, other than some of the more obvious ones, such as love, hate, jealousy, and so on. To facilitate the study of feelings or emotions, 'The Emotional Awareness Wheel has been designed to help you explore the links between thoughts and feelings.

The 26 pairs of emotions and feelings are arranged in progressive order around the circle, divided into two groups, 'light' and 'dark'. They could also be thought of as 'positive' – those feelings that make us feel 'good' – and 'negative' – those feelings that make us feel 'bad'. If the terms 'good' and 'bad' are not acceptable, positive feelings could be thought of as those that make us feel comfortable while negative feelings are those that make us feel uncomfortable. Feelings influence behaviour, so positive feelings generally help us to get on with other people, while negative feelings have the opposite effect.

The wheel may be used in may ways; for example:

- At its basic level, to promote a straightforward awareness of words.

- By considering each emotion in turn from love through to ecstasy and thinking about the circumstances, situations, events and times in which you have experienced them.

- By considering the words in their pairs and the emotional impact they make.

The 26 pairs of words have been numbered for ease of reference and they have been so arranged that starting from number one – love – there is a gradual lessening of emotional tone through to 'innocence' which marks the end of the first quarter. The second quarter is a gradual increase of dark emotional tones to the strongest, 'hate'. The third quarter is a lessening of tone to 'optimism'. The fourth quarter is

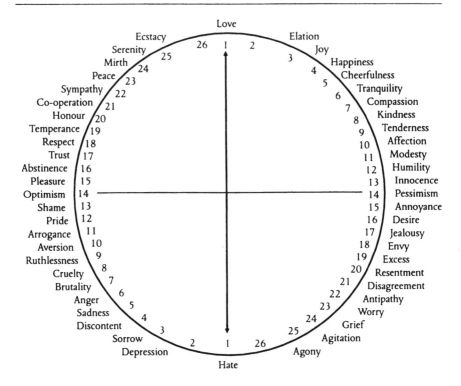

Figure 8 The Emotional Awareness Wheel

heightening of tone through 'pleasure' to 'ecstasy'. The first quarter could be thought of as 'Autumn'; the second, 'Winter'; the third, 'Spring'; and the fourth, 'Summer'. In presenting any model one runs the risk of getting some of it not quite right. It is possible that some of the pairs of words are not semantic antonyms. But what has been aimed at are emotional opposites. In practice there are many gradations between any two poles.

Imagery is a useful aid for getting in touch with emotions, by imagining a picture to represent each emotion. The inner picture may, at first, seem strange and inappropriate; however, if its every aspect is explored, its deeper meaning will surely be revealed. Every person is almost certain to have a different inner representation of the same emotion because each emotion affects people in different ways. An example may suffice.

To Andrew, the word 'serenity' evokes a scene of a calm lake (not one that he knew), upon which swim a family of swans. As he explores the scene he thinks of the meaning of the water and the feeling of being supported. As he floats on the water, his feelings float upward to the clouds that dance across the sky. He becomes one of the clouds only to realise that it represents a specific worry that has been on his mind for some time. He thinks that if he learns to relax more he will be able to rise above his difficulty. Coming back to the lake, he thinks of the water, its depth, its colour and the life contained in it. He realises that the water reflects his various moods. He also considers the bounds of the lake and how the water is contained;

he relates this to the boundaries of his own life and realises that he finds some of them irksome.

He explores the depth of the lake and there finds mud, a reminder of something that has been and is now different. Within the mud there teems wild life that provides food for the creatures that inhabit the lake. Growing in the mud are plants that would probably not be able to grow anywhere else. He discovers quite a lot of rubbish which has been deposited by picnickers (his sub-personalities), but each bit of rubbish tells him something about himself. Rising out of the lake is a tree which he climbs and he looks down on the lake, to see a different view, light and shade and breadth that had escaped him. He realises that the lake is himself and that his personality is not unattractive, that it is highly productive, but that it does have a depth that, if explored, will reveal certain facets of himself that may not always please him. On the other hand, growing out of the depths there is something wholesome. But as he continues looking, the surface of the lake is disturbed, agitated by something. There he stops. His imagination had started to take him across the dimension toward agitation. Perhaps another day Andrew will want to explore that word also.

By using the Awareness Wheel it may be revealed that there is a high tendency for the person to seek experiences that bring peak feelings – ecstasy and elation are two examples. Danger often brings a sense of elation but in the wake of peak experiences frequently comes the opposite feeling. Some of us seek a peak emotion in order to stave off its mate. As we try to evoke events and situations when these feelings have been previously experienced, we may realise that they are more frequent than we first thought. Then we need to identify how we feel when that particular feeling has passed, and what we do to adjust our emotional state.

While some people actively seek peak experiences and feelings, others seem to live on negative feelings and experiences. Helping such a person to identify situations and events which evoke negative feelings may also mean encouraging her or him to identify people who spark off these feelings. The person may need help to be able to move from the acutely negative aspect along the dimension toward the positive. The move may only be a few gradations but the change may make all the difference to his emotional balance. Deep feelings, explored within the safety of the counselling relationship, have therapeutic potential of tremendous import. Very often we are hindered from moving toward positive feelings because one or another of our sub-personalities binds us. Counselling may be the key to open the lock.

Third Task – Exploring the Depths

Exploring the depths, the descent, has been put after exploring the heights, ascent, for it is generally accepted that exploring the heights is less threatening than exploring the depths of the unconscious. When we have dealt with the challenges of the ascent, we are better equipped to deal with the challenges of the descent. However, it has to be pointed out that where the psyche is in charge, it does not always conform to man-made rules; neither does it necessarily take 'advice'. The psyche is far wiser than we are, and when we learn to trust it, it will lead us surely, if at times illogically, towards wholeness.

Descent involves becoming aware of, and incorporating, our 'shadow', the lower parts of our personality, the unconscious. Exploration of the unconscious is generally accepted as 'going down' although there is no realistic reason for this, any more than there is for thinking that heaven is 'up there'. It is analogous to exploring the dark recesses of the underworld of the Psyche. Examples of this descent can be drawn from Virgil's *Aenid*, where Aeneas descends into Hades: Easy is the way down to the Underworld: by night and by day dark Hades' door stands open; but to retrace one's steps and to make a way out to the upper air, that's the task, that is the labour. (Aeneid book. 6, l. 126) And from Dante's description in *The Divine Comedy* of his journey through Hell to Paradise. Poets, philosophers and mystics have spoken of the 'abyss' of the soul. It is no coincidence that we also speak of 'depth' psychology.

In order to explore the depths, we must have courage in our hearts, and determination, just as explorers of the darkness of underground caves need to have. The analogy of underground exploration is apt, for there the traveller will encounter many unknowns. The wise explorer will be secured with a safety line; when we explore the unconscious, we, too, must ensure that there is someone at the other end of the safety line.

If one main purpose of this exploration could be drawn out from all the others, it is the confrontation of the shadow, and its incorporation into our conscious personality. Arthur was troubled by feelings of anger towards his father. He knew he was illegitimate, and he knew his father and the circumstances of his birth, but that did not lessen the feelings of hate that frequently overtook him, although he felt there was nothing he could do, as his father had died a long time previously. In imagery he imagined himself as a knight riding on a white horse. His ride took him through a forest and into a clearing where he was confronted by a knight dressed in black, riding a black horse, who challenged him to a duel.

'Who is this knight?' I asked Arthur. 'He won't tell me. All he says is, "You know me".' They charged at each other, and Arthur's lance pierced the other knight's arm; Arthur clutched his own arm, and he winced. This happened several times, until Arthur said, 'He's stopped, and he says, "This is futile, I am you, and you are me. I am your father, your shadow."' And with that the Black Knight vanished, leaving Arthur shaken, and in tears.

As we explored this strange happening, we slowly came to the understanding that the hatred Arthur felt towards his father was not allowing him to integrate his own shadow. The lance wounds to the Black Knight were really Arthur's self-inflicted injuries, created by the black feelings he harboured towards his father. There was very little need to 'delve'; Arthur quickly made the links, and knew that the first step towards integration was to reach out in forgiveness. I would like to say that there was an instant change; there wasn't; but change did occur over quite a long period, and it was sustained. Arthur had the courage to explore the underworld, not knowing what, or whom, he would meet, and the result was a liberation of his spirit, a spiritual victory.

Fourth Task – Exploring Extension[1]

Consciousness can be enlarged or broadened so it can take in more and more impressions and facts. This happens from the centre outwards, in all directions, not just one direction, like enlarging a circle from the inside. Enlarging or expanding one's consciousness from the centre can be alarming, as the firm boundaries seem no longer to be there, and one enters a field of consciousness far beyond one's immediate grasp.

Neil had been referred because his tutors thought he was not reaching his potential. An introverted man, Neil presented as diffident and self-effacing, very unsure of himself. His intuitive function was well developed, and he elected to work mainly with imagery. In one session he followed a passage which led him to a cavern of such vastness that in his imagination he stood still in awe. He actually gasped. So immense was this cavern, full of bright light, that he hastily withdrew and ended the imagery session. He said, 'Suddenly I was confronted by the immensity of the entire universe, and felt that if I took one step forward, I'd be swallowed up and become lost in space. It was too terrifying'.

During the remainder of the three months' counselling, we talked about that experience, but at no time did he wish to return and explore what was there. The sudden removal of the boundaries had opened up a vision with which, at that time, he couldn't cope. It would have been unwise on my part to attempt to engineer the situation so that he could cope with it.

Fifth Task – Exploring Awakening

Our natural conscious state is similar to when we are asleep. In this dreamlike state we see everything and everyone through a thick veil of colouring, distortions and illusions, which derives from our emotional reactions, the effect of past psychic traumas and external influences. Too much living in illusions draws a person into mental ill-health, so the quest is to discover what is reality and what is illusion. *To awaken from this state requires courage.*

Sixth Task – Exploring Illumination

Just as normal waking is a transition from the darkness of night to the light of day, so illumination is the passage from consciousness to intuitive awareness. In a personal sense, light is symbolically piercing the darkness of the unconscious with a pencil torch; illumination is flooding the darkness with the light from a million-candle-power searchlight of intuition. There is safety in just using a small torch; not much can be hidden from what the searchlight reveals. These two illustrations are useful when a client is confronting darkness. It could be frightening suddenly to expose what is hidden in the darkness; this is what Neil experienced – too much, too soon. At the same time, that experience will stay with Neil, for it is akin to what the Buddhists speak of as 'sudden illumination', and what others call 'peak experiences'.

---

1   See Neil – The Lighthouse in Part Two

Seventh Task – Exploring Fire

The function of fire is essentially one of purification, and is one of the most comprehensive and essential tasks. Fire worship is an ancient religion, whether as actual fire or as the sun. Remnants of fire worship can be seen in the sacred flames that are kept burning on altars, such as the Olympic flame, symbol of honourable contest.

Eighth Task – Exploring Development

Development can be thought of as evolution, growth, evolvement, maturation, unfolding, increase, expansion, enlargement, advancement or progress; each one of these synonyms has different nuances. Development implies growth, a leaving behind of an outgrown phase or stage, a moving on to something different, more productive. The two principal symbols of development are the seed and the flower. The seed holds within itself the potential of new life, the acorn into the oak; the flower, which opens from the closed bud, heralds the fruit. Other symbols which have been known almost from the beginning of time are flowers such as the *Golden Flower* in China, the *lotus* in India and the *rose* in Persia and Europe. Some methods of development and meditation are based on the symbol of the lotus or the rose.

The most poignant illustration of development is the child into the adult; that is one stage. The second stage is from the state of normality to the state of enlightenment. Paradoxically, while in the natural life of humans, there is growth followed by decline; in the development of enlightenment, the growth continues, and increases, until the final breath is taken, when enlightenment is complete. The saying, 'The pleasure is not so much in the winning but in the race' applies in the process of development. The winning post is never reached, rather like in the first task, when the centre, if reached, slides away, and the quest starts again.

Ninth Task – Exploring Love

Human love is an attempt to come out of oneself, and enter into communion with another, to fuse oneself with another being. Martin Buber (*I and Thou* 1937) says, 'When I cease to regard a tree as an object, I enter into an "I–Thou" relationship' (p.20).

Buber posited a basic difference between the way people relate to an inanimate object (the I–It relationship) and the way they relate to other people (the I–Thou relationship). In the former, no genuine relationship exists because the I and the It do not interrelate. The It is regarded as an object, to be manipulated and used. Superficial human relationships tend to resemble the I–It type more than they do the I–Thou type. In the latter, a true dialogue exists because the 'I' interrelates totally with the Thou, creating a union, a bonding, between the two. The I–Thou relationship involves risks, because total involvement cannot calculate injuries that may be inflicted on the I by the Thou. Human relationships can only approximate the perfect I–Thou dialogue. When people are in a genuine dialogue with God (the only perfect Thou), the true I–Thou relationship is present.

I maintain that to do effective work with parts of our personality, we must move from the I–It to the I–Thou relationship. Only then, when we make that subtle change, will we make real headway. Only when we can move out in love to those parts of us we detest and wish we could be separated from for ever – our shadow – will we move further along the pathway of integration. Integration and reconciliation, not separation, must be our aim. For too long we have cut off the bits we don't like, repressed and denied them. When we bring them out of the closet, and accept, for good or ill, that they are a vital part of us, will we make real progress.

Gibran's *The Prophet* says of love: 'When you love, you should not say, "God is in my heart," but rather, "I am in the heart of god". And think not that you can direct the course of love, for love, if it finds you worthy, directs your course' (p.12).

Tenth Task – Exploring Transformation

Transformation, or transmutation, is a theme which Jung (1953) explores in relation to dreams and symbols. Transformation occurs through the combined actions of the previous tasks in two different, complementary ways. The first is sublimation of the energies into acceptable channels; the second is integration of the energies within the unconscious into the personality. Transformation or transmutation is possible: we can take an analogy from the world of science, where elements can be transformed by the manipulation of the atoms.

Eleventh Task – Exploring Rebirth

Transformation paves the way for regeneration, a 'new birth'. The 'new birth' is a truly spiritual process, not related to religion, although the same term is implied in religious 'conversion'. The Indian term *Dwigis*, used in reference to the Brahmins, means 'twice-born'.

The new birth implies a death of the old; in Christianity this is symbolised by baptism. In the personal quest it implies a letting go of the old, in order to take on the new. But the new cannot be taken on as one would take hold of an object; it is more a *replacing* of the old with the new, as new water replaces old in a tank. One could never say exactly when the process was complete. So it means being prepared to relinquish the old, the worn out, the outmoded, that which has served its purpose; that which was appropriate once, but no longer is applicable or desirable.

Gibran, speaking of death says, 'For what is to die but to stand naked in the wind, and to melt into the sun? And what is it to cease breathing, but to free the breath from its restless tides, that it may rise and expand and seek God unencumbered?' *The Prophet* (p.94).

Twelfth Task – Exploring Liberation

This is the elimination of encumbrances, a process of liberation from our complexes, from our illusions and from identification with the various roles we play in life, from the masks we assume and from our idols. Freedom from fear is a goal. It must be won and safeguarded every single day.

The desire for freedom is a paradox; for very often we fear what freedom means. Freedom implies commitment, self-control, courage and persistence; we must live in freedom, when there is the temptation to go back to the security of bondage. A parallel can be drawn from the story of the Children of Israel. For 400 years they were slaves in Egypt, and all that time they yearned to be free. When the time came they fled Egypt, pursued by the Egyptian army, and crossed the Red Sea in safety, and began wandering the wilderness, but they berated Moses. 'We would be better off back in Egypt than here in the wilderness.' Their pilgrimage to the Promised Land was to take them further and further away from the 'fleshpots of Egypt', yet for the forty years it took them, there were those who (metaphorically) looked back with longing.

As this is the last of the 12 tasks, I want to take this opportunity to demonstrate the process of working with images. Brainstorming this word, 'liberation', I find the following synonyms: freeing, liberating, deliverance, emancipation, enfranchisement, enfranchising, delivery, rescue, rescuing, release, releasing, loosing, unfettering, unshackling, unchaining. Every one of these words has subtle differences yet broadly means the same thing.

I then look up the antonyms of liberation, and find enslavement (servitude, bondage, indenture, serfdom, servility, slavery); imprisonment (detention, arrest, custody, confinement, incarceration); restriction (limit, bond, boundary, bridle, check, constraint, control, curb, damper, harness, leash, rein, restraint).

These synonyms and antonyms broaden my understanding of the root word, liberation. The next stage is to continue the brainstorming by thinking of ideas which some of these words trigger: I will consider only a few, and leave you to carry out your own brainstorming session.

> **Deliverance:** We have already considered one link, in the story of the Israelites and their deliverance from the Egyptians, slavery and bondage.

> **Emancipation:** Freedom from legal, social, or political restraint, as in slavery. To make a free person.

> **Enfranchisement:** I link the enfranchisement of women in gaining the vote, and the years of struggle before this was finally accomplished.

> **Liberty:** An important symbolic word. My imagination flies to the French Revolution and the liberation of the masses from a despotic monarchy, and the slogan of the people – *liberty, equality and fraternity* – symbolised in the tricolour consisting of equal vertical stripes of blue, white and red.

> **Imprisonment:** For me the associations are prison or concentration camps, deprivation, degradation and depersonalisation.

> **Restriction:** This word conjures up straitjacket, frustration, and terrible fear.

Conflict

I will end this journey with a story about Sandra, an unhappily married woman of around thirty with two children, trapped in a marriage that had become increasingly humiliating for her. Therein lay the conflict. Her whole upbringing had put upon her (or had she accepted?) being the 'good little girl' who always did what other people wanted: her mother (father was dead, but his injunctions were still around), her siblings and her work mates. Her husband and children also had the expectations of her being the perfectly compliant and servile wife and mother.

Conflict is a psychological state of indecision, where the person is faced simultaneously with two opposing forces of equal strength, that cannot be solved together.

Types of conflict

1. **Choice between positives,** both of which are desirable – for example, the choice between two attractive careers. Approach-approach[2] where chance factors determine the outcome.

2. **Choice between negatives,** where both are undesirable – for example, a man may dislike his job intensely, but fears the threat of unemployment of he resigns. Avoidance-avoidance.[3]

3. **Choice between negative and positive.** A child is dependent on her mother, and also fears her because she maybe rejecting and punitive. Approach-avoidance creates great indecision, helplessness and anxiety.

Conflicts are often unconscious, in the sense that the person cannot clearly identify the source of the distress. Many strong impulses, such as fear and hostility, are not approved of by society, so children soon learn not acknowledge them, even to themselves. When such impulses are in conflict, we are anxious without knowing why.

Conflict resolution is strongly influenced by feelings of self-worth. People with low self-worth expect to be treated badly; they expect the worst, invite it and generally get it. People who do not feel confident generally feel small and, therefore, view others as threateningly larger.

When working with conflict it is useful to be able to reduce it to two major issues, that are so evenly balanced that neither one tips the scales. The person soon learns not to acknowledge the strong impulses, even to themselves. Over recent years, Sandra had begun to be more assertive, and to take pride in what she did, but the more she did this, the less she wanted to continue to 'play the game' other people expected her to. The more she became 'herself' the more confused and angry others

---

2   Being drawn by two equally desirable goals which are mutually exclusive of one another.

3   Being repelled by two goals, neither of which appeal, but there is pressure to choose one or the other.

were, particularly her possessive and manipulative mother, and her husband who found she no longer wanted to play his kinky sex games.

This was the scenario that gradually emerged in the first three months of counselling, during which time I had said, 'You sound trapped'. She nodded, then her eyes defocused, as she looked inside herself, then said, 'Yes, and no; I think it's more caged than trapped'. The two words are similar, but have different meanings. 'You're in some sort of cage; what are you?' I find this open-ended sort of question essential so that the client is not given too much direction. She could have said that she was a big cat in a cage, pacing up and down, snarling behind bars in a zoo. She said, with moist eyes, 'I'm a canary, lying at the bottom of a cage'. She continued looking into the distance, really concentrating on this image. 'I'm lying at the bottom of the cage, with dirt all around me, and I've got wide sticky tape all over me, stopping me from moving.' 'So you feel really helpless and not able to do anything to change what's happening to you?' She nodded, her eyes filled with tears, but she struggled against them. This was another characteristic of Sandra; she had to be in control: to have cried would have revealed her vulnerability, and she had learned not to do this but to swallow her tears and bite her lip. 'What would you like to happen?' I asked. 'I'd like to be free.' 'How are you going to get free?' She shook her head. 'I'd like somebody to come along and take me out, gently take off the strapping, carefully, then look after me.' 'Then what?' I gently asked. 'Then I could fly away and sing again.'

Over the next three months, we looked at that image many times; then came the day when she looked in the cage and the canary was no longer there: it was out, flying around. But that presented other difficulties; a canary would be vulnerable in the outside world, it could not exist there. How she dealt with that is another story, but it is worth mentioning that neither her husband nor her mother could cope with the changing Sandra who was no longer prepared to play games. Eventually Sandra and her husband separated and divorced.

Change is seldom easy or straightforward. In Sandra's case, many people were hooked into her and she into them. When a person begins to change, strain is put on all the links, and inevitably some will snap. For Sandra to change, to grow and develop, other significant people would have to change in order to accommodate the changes that were taking place in her. This is similar to the changes that parents undergo: gradual changes as their children grow and develop their own personality. Parents have the opportunity to change slowly as their children develop; people, such as Sandra's husband, mother and brother, had too much vested interest in not changing, so Sandra grew away from them.

There were times during the six months of counselling when Sandra again became the bird in the cage, but she often saw the cage door open, and for much of the time, even when she was in the cage, she could hear herself singing.

Summary

The Labours of Hercules can be read as an interesting story, which they certainly are; they can also be read with an eye to the personal journey. There could be a danger of trying to draw too close a parallel between each of his 12 'labours' and the tasks I have outlined here. I chose the analogy because some of the tasks involve hardship and difficulty, and are certainly not without cost, as we saw in the case of Sandra. Sandra's story is not an isolated one, and as we saw, people often do not understand the drive another person experiences to grow, or the tremendous struggle it takes to break free from the constraints which bind us like strapping, or a straitjacket.

Summary of the tasks

1. **First task – exploring the interior:** The task is to discover our centre. The external life must be counterbalanced by an adequate inner life. The exploration of the centre is never completed, but is a lifelong quest.

2. **Second task – exploring the heights:** The exploration of the unconscious to become aware of, and incorporate one's 'shadow', the lower parts of one's personality. In order to explore, we need to develop intuition, will, thinking and feelings. As an aid to developing feelings, 'The Emotional Awareness Wheel' is offered as a guide.

3. **Third task – exploring the depths:** The third task is to accept the challenge of descent into the unconscious and incorporate what is revealed.

4. **Fourth task – exploring extension:** Consciousness can be enlarged or broadened to take in more and more.

5. **Fifth task – exploring awakening:** The natural conscious state is that of being asleep. In this dreamlike state we see everything and everyone through a thick veil of colouring and distortions, which derive from our emotional reactions, the effect of past psychic traumas and external influences. To awaken from this state requires courage.

6. **Sixth task – exploring illumination:** Illumination, the passage from consciousness to intuitive awareness. Illumination is one of life's peak experiences.

7. **Seventh task – exploring fire:** The function of fire is essentially one of purification. Passing through the fire is an allusion to the process of refinement applied to gold and silver in the stage of removing impurities.

8. **Eighth task – exploring development:** The principal symbols are the seed and the flower. A living illustration is the development of the child into adulthood.

9. **Ninth task – exploring love:** Human love is an attempt to enter into communion with another person. Only when we enter into an 'I–Thou' relationship do we establish effective communication.

10. **Tenth task – exploring transformation:** Transformation, or transmutation, is a theme which Jung explores in relation to dreams and

symbols. Transformation occurs through the combined actions of elevation and descent.

11. **Eleventh task – exploring rebirth:** Transformation paves the way for regeneration, a 'new birth'.

12. **Twelfth task – exploring liberation:** Elimination of encumbrances, a process of liberation from our complexes, from our illusions and from identification with the various roles we play in life, from the masks we assume and from our idols. Freedom from fear is a goal. It must be won and safeguarded every single day.

The journey, as I have presented it here, is full of the language of imagery, particularly as we think about the various tasks, journeys and explorations of Hercules. An explorer doesn't just set out on an expedition on the spur of the moment; the expedition is planned in great detail, and very often there has to be intense physical and mental preparation including the gathering of essentials such as map and compass.

What I have tried to do in this Journey is to provide map and compass. I would like to travel with you as you undertake each task, or as you travel with your clients in their journeys or quests. I cannot be there with you, but in way I am; for my words in this book are a part of me, and I sincerely hope that the spirit surrounding those words will somehow be conveyed to you and to your clients.

Exploring Imagery and Health

The final four journeys in this part of the book apply the principles of imagery to some issues of health. I have chosen to concentrate on three main issues: pain, anxiety, and depression, because these common conditions encompass so much of the total person; the final journey looks at the client within society with particular reference to separation and reconciliation.

I believe that we can so easily undermine our personal health by negative imagining. At the same time, it would be arrogant and totally incorrect of me if I were to suggest that it is 'all in the mind', and that positive imaging will cure all. Somehow we have to tread a path between these two extremes.

To use imagination creatively, we must be prepared to let our imaginations exercise control over our minds, albeit temporarily. I believe that being able to evoke and create images is an important function of the human psyche, both at a conscious and unconscious level. Many people find the use of spontaneous imagination easier than conscious or directed imagination. Yet it may be necessary to use both. The person who dwells on a negative memory may be helped to move toward the positive pole by a deliberate and conscious process of 'imaginary desensitisation'.

The actual situation is evoked in the client's imagination; the client then describes it in as much detail as can be recalled, including feelings at the time and afterwards. The client is then encouraged to 'replay' the scene, this time making his or her reactions more positive so that feelings become less intense. Where the event involved another person (or people) the client should be encouraged to imagine adopting a more friendly attitude. After a series of 'replays', each time adopting a more positive stance, the client is almost certain to experience a change of feeling which will indicate a move some distance away from the original feeling. The next stage is to get the client to evoke positive imaginary situations and at the same time to try to experience the feelings which they generate. The final stage is to meditate on one of the positive feelings and let spontaneous imagination take her or him into realms of thought and feeling as far distant from the negative pole as the farthest star is from the earth.

It is worth mentioning here that some people experience marked feelings of guilt if their body is ravaged by disease; or if they have to undergo surgery; or if they are the victims of trauma of some kind; or if they feel the stigma of mental illness. These feelings seem to originate in religious attitudes, but they are by no means experienced only by avowedly religious people. Such feelings possibly have their roots in the idea that man is created in the 'image and likeness of God' and any assault on the body is therefore a form of blasphemy. Some people, who are not themselves victims, feel outraged that God's creation should be rendered less than perfect, and in some cases by wilful neglect.

Pain and Imagery

We are all subject to various and varying degrees of pressure all our lives. How we learn to cope with these pressures makes a great deal of difference to our quality of life.

Physical pain

Pain is a feeling of distress, suffering or agony, caused by stimulation of specialised nerve endings. Also, pain is whatever the person experiencing it says it is, and it exists whenever the person says it does. As a result of pain, some people become so withdrawn as to exclude others from their world. Some pain is impossible to describe.

Sudden or intense pain triggers off the 'fight/flight' response. Repetitive pain, or pain of long duration, produces a 'chronic stress reaction' in which the delicate blood chemistry balance is seriously disturbed. Facial expression is a reliable indicator of inner states of pain. Movement, or lack of it, is often a reliable indicator of the site of pain.

The way we cope with pain is influenced by cultural expectations. It is generally more acceptable for children to cry with their pain than for adults to do so, at least in some societies.

We may use anger, powerlessness, fear and guilt as coping strategies. Chronic pain has been linked to depression and helplessness. Acute pain has been strongly linked to the presence of anxiety. The experience of pain has been associated with a kind of death. Pain may produce changes in body-image: 'I am no longer perfect'.

Having some idea of what we can do to relieve someone's pain, either in conjunction with pain-relief medication, or without it, helps to minimise our stress as well as the stress of the sufferer. Concentrating on peace and harmony, and creating inner pictures of peace is often enough to minimise pain.

Four principles of pain relief will now be touched on.

1. **Relate:** Believing what the person says often helps relieves their pain and its associated anxiety. Remember to help people explore what the pain is doing in them and to them. Help them to discover precisely when the pain occurs, how to describe it, its duration and its pain. We can never feel another person's pain, yet it can be very stressful watching someone else's pain. Try not to: refuse to talk about the pain (avoidance); talk about other topics when the sufferers clearly indicate that they want to talk about their pain (diversion); just listen passively (rejection).

2. **Sensory input:** Distraction is a powerful pain-relieving activity. Touch, massage (with the addition of certain aromatherapy oils), applications of heat or cold, immersing a painful limb in warm water, or the whole body in a warm bath, are all effective pain-relievers.

3. **Relaxation:** Pain interferes with rest and sleep, and lack of sleep is often a major contributor to suffering. Relaxation techniques, taught and practised *when pain is absent,* help to reduce physical and mental tension.

4. **Imagery:** Sufferers who use imaging, combining it with deep relaxation, acquire a powerful double-edged strategy to control their pain. When we produce an inner picture of the pain, thus objectifying it, then imagine how it may be transformed, we are putting to work powerful, healing forces.

Psychic pain

Psychic pain is pain of the heart, mind and spirit. It is as real and powerful as any physical pain. Suppression of psychic pain very often leads to physical disorders.

Psychic pain may be caused by such experiences as:

- bereavement
- divorce
- enforced isolation
- helplessness
- loneliness
- poverty
- loss of purpose
- loss of self-esteem.

Everyone with pain needs to have their symptoms treated seriously. To reject it as 'imaginary' is a contradiction and an affront to the person. It is fatally easy for one person to dismiss another's pain as trivial or non-existent – 'all in the mind'! Certainly pain can be 'psychogenic' – having an emotional or psychological origin – as distinct from pain which originates from an organic condition. Two personal anecdotes illustrate different aspects of this.

TWO CASE ILLUSTRATIONS

In 1946, when many servicemen were still recovering from the stress of war, I was nursing a Royal Navy officer who was suffering from an acute anxiety state. He developed severe abdominal pains and presented every indication of acute appendicitis. The pain he was experiencing was obviously severe. He was operated on but there was no internal evidence of inflammation. His 'appendicitis', and the pain associated with it, was of a psychogenic nature; his anxiety had located itself in his abdomen. But to him the pain was real; he felt it and responded to it *as if it had originated from organic change.* The reality of pain should never be dismissed.

In contrast to the naval officer was Gillian, a girl of 14 years who was suffering from leukaemia. She had been off treatment for well over a year when she began to complain of pain in her abdomen. The doctors, unable to find any accountable reason for the pain, referred her to a psychiatrist who treated her for psychogenic pain. Two months later Gillian was readmitted in severe relapse with a massive flare-up. She eventually died.

These two cases illustrate the danger of 'labelling' pain as being one type or another. In the first instance, the pain *was* of psychogenic origin, and the abdomen became the focus of the patient's feelings of anxiety. In Gillian's case, the pain had physical origins but because no physical cause could be detected, the pain was mislabelled as psychogenic.

An extract from Tony's story illustrates the use of imagery in inner healing.

> Over a period of four months I had consultation with five doctors for trigeminal neuralgia [excruciating pain of the face and forehead]. For the first time in my life I required a daily intake of drugs in a more or less vain attempt to control the agonising pain.

> When I came for therapy, full relaxation wasn't possible because of the state of my mind, the pain, depression, anger, insecurity and the overall feeling of not being a person of worth.

> I was fully conscious of my surroundings and what was said to me and also of the heat coming from the therapist's hands on my head. I was only slightly aware of time. My most vivid recollection was of being told to swallow my pain. Dark black clouds went down my throat very fast, without taste but with a sensation of swallowing a type of bile.

> Before the session was ended I was aware that the pain in my face had lessened and by the end it had disappeared completely. With it went many of my negative feelings and I was left feeling very calm.

I hoped that by relieving the pain, Tony would discover an island in the sea of his dark feelings upon which he could stand, rest, gather strength, and then start to rise out of his depression.

Elizabeth – A Case Study

Social history

Elizabeth, aged 59, has been employed for the past 12 years as an information officer in a large industrial library in the South East of England. She has a staff of six. Her basic degree at Oxford was in modern languages; her second degree, in information science, was taken at Bristol. For several years she worked in various countries in Europe.

She lives with her two cats in a spacious, detached house in a much sought-after suburb of the town. Her house is not mortgaged and she has no financial worries. Her job pays well and she enjoys a comfortable style of living. Her parents died some 30 years ago; three sisters and a brother, now in their eighties, live in various parts of England: none lives near her. Elizabeth is a devout Roman Catholic and is involved in church activities and local politics. She uses her considerable language ability as a freelance translator and interpreter, and also coaches up to A level in modern languages. She is on the editorial board of a renowned scientific journal and has written many articles and tape slide programmes and a book. She is often in demand as a speaker at national and international conferences. France is her favourite holiday country; she visits it several times a year.

Clinical history

Elizabeth is a wiry, active lady who had been very fit until the onset of the illness which led up to her having major surgery in September 1983. She dates the onset of her trouble to 1972. She had moved to her present post in the spring of that year and in the autumn had bought her house with firm plans that she and her sister (who was older by 18 years) would live together. They had barely moved in when her sister died, while Elizabeth was at work.

In 1980 her beloved cat, Topsy, died after a long illness. Elizabeth quickly took in a cat from the RSPCA. Within a week Lucy had produced four kittens. Elizabeth kept two of the four, Dandy and Rosie. When the twins were seven months old, Elizabeth came in from work one evening in November to find that Dandy had been killed by a car.

Elizabeth reacted badly to the death of her two cats. All the feelings associated with her sister's death were resurrected. She very quickly developed shingles. The doctor she attended did not seem to understand the depth of her grief reaction, and told her 'pull yourself together or you'll break down completely'. She did 'pull herself together' and very quickly became involved once more in various activities. She adopted a second cat as company for Rosie. In May 1981, while on a lecture engagement in Strasbourg, she was taken ill with abdominal pain. The pain persisted when she came back to England. It was now waking her at night. Her general practitioner (GP) told her, 'It's all in the mind. You've gone over the top about your cats. Go away for a holiday. Keep a glass of milk on your bed-side table'.

She trusted the GP, and thinking that it must be all in her mind, she went away for a holiday, but the pain went with her. She was not offered any medication. Over the weeks the pain worsened and she began to experience nausea and there was evidence of some rectal bleeding. She was suffering from lack of sleep, depression and self-doubt. 'I began to believe that I was neurotic. I just couldn't take myself in hand.'

In the early weeks of 1982 a pyloric duodenal ulcer was diagnosed. She was started on a ten week course of medication. Almost immediately she stopped the medication she had a crisis, with semi-perforation. This resulted in her being admitted to hospital and recommencing medication. From then on '...it was a miserable existence. I had to avoid every food I really enjoyed'.

In September 1983, when returning by car from a holiday in the North, she was attacked by 'agonising pain'. She completed the drive and was seen the following day by the consultant surgeon who had been involved with her case from the beginning. He arranged for an emergency operation the following day; it was to be a selective cutting of the vagus nerve and partial removal of the stomach.

Elizabeth speaks

'Questions wanted to pour from me but some of them sounded so silly and juvenile. All I asked was "What will the effect be?" He told me that I would feel much, much better; there would be no more pain; that I would be able to eat normally again. He said all that the operation involved was a snipping of some of the fibres of the vagus nerve, to control the acid secretion. I felt relieved. I had imagined it would be a truly major operation. I had never had an operation in my life. Oh, yes, I did ask him if there was any risk. What I really was asking him was, "Am I going to die?" A question I couldn't ask was, "How long will I be away from home?" There was my home, my cats, the garden and of course my staff. There were so many worries I wanted to share and there was so little time to arrange anything. As I lived alone, the surgeon said he would arrange for me to have some convalescence. I didn't realise that I would need intensive nursing care following the operation. I was so naïve.

'I thought I was dying. Something had gone wrong and I reacted quite badly to the anaesthetic. I lost three days in the intensive care unit. That was a shock, particularly as the surgeon had told me I would be back in my room in a matter of hours. Hours, certainly, but seventy-two! How did I feel? Indescribable! There is a hazy recollection of being forced to get out of bed, trying to hold my stitches with one hand and my drains and things with the other. Oh yes, I can laugh about it now, but at the time I felt humiliated and betrayed, and totally unprepared. My stomach felt like a giant football filled to bursting point with wind that would shift neither way.

'I asked the surgeon how long it would be before I felt better. He said I would be over the operation in four to six months but it might be two to three years before I felt really physically fit again. "Mentally, that's entirely up to you." I could cheerfully have hit him. I was so angry. He didn't seem to care. Neither did anyone else, or so it seemed. I was twelve days in hospital. Twelve days! and I had thought, "Oh, just snipping a few fibres, a couple of days." Is everyone so simple? I couldn't eat; swallowing was so difficult and the wind kept threatening to choke me. Frankly I was terrified. I spent a great deal of the time in tears. My days were brightened by the flowers and gifts from my colleagues and friends. I did find the nursing staff very impatient. The whole hospital affair made me feel degraded. I was not a person any more.

'Then I went to the convalescent home, where I had the doubtful "privilege" of a small flat of my own. A super view – at the top of forty-three steps! I was like the Grand Old Duke of York; when I was up I was up, and when I was down I was down! And down I certainly was. Depression overwhelmed me. This didn't exactly endear me to the staff. "What a lucky person you are. You have a nice flat, lots of visitors, et cetera. Why should you be so miserable?" I suppose I was lucky. Many of the other people there were cancer victims and went for treatment every day. But it seemed totally outside of my power to do anything about my misery.

'I was treated like a three-year-old. I loathed the convalescent home. I had been forced to become dependent. Everything was automatically taken out of my hands. An example? "Here drink this" (a nursing auxiliary). "What is it?" "Never you mind, just drink it." It was a thoroughly wretched week. It was supposed to have been two weeks, but in no way could I have stayed a second week. Yes, I suppose I was a difficult patient. There was no daily treatment. I wasn't dying (although I often wished I had) and now I was insisting on going home. There was a total lack of understanding of my physical and mental condition. Someone wanted to take me to Mass on Sunday but the staff refused to allow me to go. The priest came but I was in no state to make confession. He talked, and as he did, healing came. I think he saved my sanity.

'There was almost a stand up fight when I told them I was going home. When they saw that I was determined, the only reply was, "Can you make your own arrangements?" I said I could, and did. There was no preparation for my going home; no advice, no guidance, no indication of what I should or should not do. Rehabilitation? I don't think it ever crossed their minds.

'A friend came for me. Then my troubles really started. I was totally unprepared (it seems that I was totally unprepared for lots of things, doesn't it!) for how weak I felt. I couldn't do anything, no strength to even wash up or make my bed. Eating was difficult anyway and I suppose I just went downhill. Oh yes, I was depressed. I've never minded being on my own but the solitude, coupled with a mountain of fear, made my life quite unbearable. How did the depression affect me? I felt that I had reached the end of the line, useless; I would be forced to retire. My memory went completely, even to the stage that I couldn't remember my sister's phone number. I couldn't concentrate to read or write; I did listen to my music and did jigsaw after jigsaw. That was the level of my concentration. Emotionally I felt to be wandering in an endless desert.

'Oh yes, there was Anne, well-meaning but so undermining of my confidence. An example; one day I just fancied some wine gums. When she came back from the shop, what had she bought? boiled sweets! "I thought these might be better for you," she said. I was so deflated, having my intelligence challenged like that.

'The turning point came at my birthday, when I'd been home seven weeks. I think I'd got to rock bottom. There was a picture in my mind. I was locked in a house, staring through a window; people were going past but not taking any notice of me. The predominant colour was blue. Then my family came for the weekend. They brought me back to life. Richard encouraged me to take the car out. I had wondered if I would ever drive again. Things began to improve after that. Now I do feel so much better.

'But you know, people can be so thoughtless. When the Health Visitor came she said, "Oh you'll throw this off after a month. It's quite common with your operation". When I didn't 'throw it off' I asked her specifically what had been involved. "The vagus nerve? I haven't a clue, really." I challenged her over her previous statement. "Oh that was just to give you some sort of confidence. I'd never met your operation before." My trust in her vanished instantly. Follow up? None! Not from the hospital nor from my GP. I had a picture of the inside of my body, as if it were an electric cable that had been severed in several places; power was trying to get through, but couldn't. My lower half felt quite separate from my upper half. I just knew that I wouldn't feel right until I could feel that my parts were reunited.'

Elizabeth's told her story with a mild humour that is difficult to convey and by the time the story was told, much healing – physical and emotional – had already taken place. But what she said highlights many of the points made earlier. She had been ill-prepared for what was to happen. While it is true that her operation was something of an emergency, the surgeon had made light of the after-effects. He had not mentioned the severe discomfort or that several months would elapse before she would begin to feel well. The pain had been intense, but again this had not been mentioned as a possibility.

A few weeks after she returned to work, she was again taken ill; a doctor neighbour, knowing how little 'rehabilitation' she was receiving, and, therefore, not being afraid of treading on the toes of any other professional, diagnosed 'dumping syndrome'. His explanation, that this was something that frequently occurred in such surgery, both reassured Elizabeth and annoyed her. The reassurance came in that she was not suffering from something so dreadful that no one had dared mention it. The annoyance, mixed with a degree of resentment, came from the fact that here was a bit of information she could have been given which would have saved a great deal of worry.

If the surgeon had explained to Elizabeth that dumping syndrome was nausea, weakness, sweating, palpitation and feeling faint after a meal, and that the symptoms are similar to a mild hypoglycemia, I am quite certain she would have understood. The majority of all partial gastrectomies and allied operations can be spared the dread and discomfort of the dumping syndrome by proper post-operative management. This advice is neither new nor revolutionary; it was written about over twenty years before Elizabeth had her operation.

Elizabeth's recovery was certainly influenced by how little she was told before the operation and afterwards. The point of this case study is not to criticise the surgeon or the nursing staff or any one else but to draw attention to how stress may both influence disease, and at the same time be an accompaniment to surgery, the aim of which is to relieve distressing symptoms. Elizabeth had been subjected to three bereavements – her sister and her two furry friends. There is strong evidence that grief reactions are associated with increased illness, including myocardial infarction and other psychosomatic and physical disorders.

Elizabeth's case demonstrates just how important counselling is. That Elizabeth's recovery was as good as it has been could be attributed to a strong personality that helped her to rise above the assault on her body. Coupled with this was the support she received from her wide circle of friends and colleagues. Another person, not so fortunate, whose emotional life was less stable, and who did not have an effective support system, might well have crumbled under the weight of the stress which could have led to further physical or emotional illness.

Elizabeth came to me about the time she started going out again after the operation, and after the discovery of 'dumping'. The story as I have recorded it was given over a number of sessions. When she talked about the 'severed electric cable' and the associated image of a blue room I thought that she would respond to imagery.

Elizabeth was not an easy client to get to relax: relaxation was not her style. There were two things I wanted to do with imagery: to help relieve the pain, and to help her repair some of the damage done to her body-image. Quite often when working with pain, I will lay my hand or hands gently on the affected part. If the client is female, and if the part is in a taboo area, I will ask the client to lay her hand on the part, then rest my hand on hers. More often, for pain anywhere in the spine, I will lay my hand lightly on the client's head, just touching the hair. The 'laying on of hands' in this way has obvious religious significance, although that is not why I do it. Rather, it comes from experience, in that the head is the crown of the body, and is the focal point for all the nerves in the body.

First, with Elizabeth, after she had somewhat relaxed, with my hands laid on hers, over the area of the scar, I asked her imagine what the pain looked like. This is an example of 'objectifying the feeling' already discussed under Mentor in the Ninth Journey. Frequently, when asked to do this, clients imagine pain as something hard, like a stone, or sharp, like a ball studded with nails, and the 'object' often represents the type of pain being suffered.

Elizabeth took quite some time to imagine anything; 'Not my strong point' she muttered. 'What I do see, though, is a swirling mass of colour, like a kaleidoscope, but moving very fast, like a computer image. Not much help, sorry!' I told her that was fine, for to me it was a beautiful representation of chaos. I made no attempt to 'analyse' the colours or associate feelings to them; neither did I leave it to Elizabeth to work it out. I said, 'If you imagine you are also watching a speedometer, and relating the movement of the colours to that, what speed would they be revolving at?'

'Oh, goodness, fast, let me see. Yes, well over the speed limit, about ninety. I'm really in the fast lane.' Her linking of the inner speed to driving a car, provided a useful link. 'Right, now, keep one eye on the speedometer and the other on the colours, now slowly, ever so slowly, ease the pressure on the throttle. On every count of ten, ease back a little more. Just listen to my count.' I then started to count slowly from one to ten. 'Ease back a little more; one, two, three,' and so on, then I repeated the instruction to ease back a little more. When I had done five repetitions, I asked her what the speedometer now read. 'It's dropped to sixty.' 'And how do you feel.' 'More in control.'

We repeated the sequence until Elizabeth was able to reduce the speed to a comfortable fifty. She could not get lower, but felt comfortable with that. 'Now how do you feel?' 'All that churning has more or less stopped. I could scarcely breathe before, now I can take a deep breath, which I haven't been able to do for a long time. I was scared, I think.'

I congratulated her on her achievement, and joked that now she wouldn't be caught by the police for speeding. I then suggested we work on her damaged body-image, based on her own image of the severed cable. For this, I laid my hands gently on her head, and waited. Experience has taught me to expect that when I ask, 'What is happening?', the client will say, 'I feel heat on my head.'

There is sufficient evidence from the area of psychic healing that the hands do radiate energy, and this can often be felt several centimetres from the hands. Elizabeth said, 'I feel a tremendous heat on the crown of my head. I know your hands are there but the heat seems to be coming *through* your hands, not *from* them.' I felt it was now time to move one.

'Imagine this heat is transformed into light, pure white light, now travelling slowly down through your head, down the spine; tell me what happens when it reaches the severed cable.' Some clients need further 'instruction' as what to do next; Elizabeth didn't. 'The light has reached the broken end and I see the other end separated by a huge black gap. I ask myself, "Who can help to bring these two ends together?" I hear some words, "He will heal the broken breaches". I think they come from the Bible.' (They do: Psalm 60:2)

She continued, 'Suddenly, the light starts arcing across the space and reaching the other part. It's as if new filaments were being created.' 'Tell me when the repair job is done, please.' When she did so, I said, 'Now I want you to keep the light flowing, and let it radiate outwards to every part of your body, to your fingertips, your toes, even to the end of each hair on your head. Tell me when you feel you want to finish.' After about five minutes, during which time Elizabeth sat quite still, with eyes closed, obviously totally absorbed in what was happening within her, she said 'The light is starting to fade now. I think it's time to finish.' I said, 'I'm taking my hands away now, and when you are ready, and in your own time, return to this room.'

She smiled, opened her eyes, and said, 'That was just wonderful. I now feel whole again. Oh, I know the nerve is still cut, but that doesn't seem to matter.' I advised her that she could do either of these exercises by herself, particularly the first one, whenever she felt she was in danger of 'speeding'.

What Elizabeth appropriated was the feeling of being once more in control, and that is vitally important in healthy living. Elizabeth was not miraculously 'cured'; the vagus nerve was not rejoined. What was healed was her self-image that had been severely traumatised by surgery. She continues to experience 'dumping' problems on and off to this day, but the fear of 'something more dreadful' – cancer – has receded.

This idea of 'focused attention' is important in pain relief, and is one anyone can learn to use.

Summary

The occurrence of disease and its associated pain is, to many, a black day on a calendar, a crossroads to which they have been pushed by some unseen force over which they had no control. The painful road they now tread leads on only to a bleak land of pain which threatens to engulf them in isolating, demoralising blackness. Pain often interferes with basic activities of daily living, and many people suffer psychological disturbances such as depression, anxiety and a deterioration in personal relationships, which emphasise their isolation and withdrawal into themselves.

Pain may be easier to handle if somehow we can be prepared for it. Two cases – of Tony and Elizabeth – illustrate the use of imagery to relieve pain. It is worth pointing out here that very often there is a link between depression and the trigeminal neuralgia which afflicted Tony, although it is difficult to say with certainty which comes first. But without a doubt, prolonged, agonising pain does generate anxiety and depression.

We saw how Elizabeth was not given the answers she needed to be able to cope with the after-effects of a major operation although she asked questions. The pain she felt was certainly real, and it was possibly made worse, and made to last longer, by the anger and frustration she felt. Imagery gave her a powerful tool to control the pain through focused attention.

Exploring Anxiety

To consider anxiety and depression separately is, to some extent, an artificial approach. Sufferers of crippling disease or injury very often display a mixture of both. To avoid possible confusion, the two states will be considered separately, although it should be borne in mind that very often they do accompany each other. Anxiety and depression in their more florid states are, in themselves, crippling. Anxiety neuroses and depressive states are two emotional conditions that absorb a large proportion of psychiatric treatment. We need to be aware of how both anxiety and depression, unless dealt with, seriously interfere with recovery.

The Treadmill of Anxiety

This phrase has been chosen to indicate that anxiety is both a prison and a punishment. By this I mean that the person who experiences severe anxiety is trapped within a process over which he or she seems to have no control, in the same way that a prisoner would be subjected to the treadmill. There the pace was set by a gaoler. If he felt particularly vindictive, a turn on the control lever increased the pace at which the prisoner was forced to run. There was no respite, no escape. Exhaustion was inevitable. This is the picture and the outcome of anxiety: a state from which the victim may not escape unless some influence can be brought to bear on the gaoler to slow the rate at which the mill turns and allow the prisoner to step out onto firm ground.

Mild anxiety is a common feeling, experienced by most people at some time in life. It is a feeling of uneasiness or apprehension. Most times, normal anxiety is based on reality. Some actual event is anticipated: an interview for a new job; having to tackle a difficult assignment; an examination; giving a speech; admission to hospital. Not all events that produce feelings of anxiety are necessarily unpleasant. Getting married, or being presented with an award, are two events that could be termed 'pleasant'; yet they may also produce feelings of anxiety. When the event has passed, feelings generally return quite quickly to normal, in much the same way as the heart rate, in a healthy individual, returns to normal after exercise. Normal anxiety, in small amounts, is biologically necessary for survival. Anxiety in doses too large for the individual to handle leads to panic and panic may produce irrational behaviour. Panic is more likely to be caused by 'free-floating' anxiety: anxiety that cannot readily be attributed to any specific event or idea. It is there, constantly lurking in the background. When it attacks, the person is once again set a-running on the treadmill. At the 'normal' end of the anxiety scale, the person experiences butterflies in the stomach, restlessness and possibly sleep disturbance. In more severe anxiety and panic, the physical accompaniments increase with the severity of the psychological disturbance. Anxiety which produces crippling emotional and physical symptoms (that is, other than that which comes within the 'normal' range) is pathological. People who suffer from such anxiety need expert help.

Anxiety thus operates on three planes: emotional, cognitive and physiological. The more severe the anxiety, the more these three planes will become distorted. Very often it is what is happening within the body that brings the person to the notice of the physician. Such was the case of Andrew.

Andrew Fisher had been treated by his family doctor for about two weeks: he had complained of palpitations and was worried that he might be heading for a coronary attack. The doctor had prescribed suitable medication but the symptoms persisted. An electrogardiogram had revealed nothing abnormal. The night before Andrew was seen by a psychiatrist, his wife had called the family doctor in the middle of the night because Andrew had a panic attack in bed, with racing pulse and palpitations. This extract, taken from a case study, demonstrates the point that physical symptoms often become the first focus of psychiatric attention, and emphasises how necessary it is to consider the whole person and not just to treat the presenting symptoms.

One of the characteristics of anxiety is that the more severe it is, the more it erodes every aspect of the person's life; and the more this happens, the less able is the person to function effectively. His or her total psychic energy is taken up with the anxious feelings. Thinking becomes unclear and problem-solving ability is diminished. The inner struggle and the constant feeling of pressure, coupled with the feeling of not coping, leads to exhaustion and defeat. The prisoner collapses on the floor of the treadmill, while the gaoler laughs. Who is this gaoler?

I would like to suggest that the gaoler is whatever, or whoever, it is that seeks to drive the individual on to exhaustion. This may be a punitive conscience, guilt, ambition, fear of failure or any one of a multitude of fears. Less may be achieved by trying to fit the person into a theory than actually helping him or her identify what or who the gaoler is. It is possible that there are multiple gaolers, each one of whom may be at war with the others; the resultant conflict increases the tension felt by the victim. Pathological anxiety is the likely outcome.

The analogy of the gaoler, or gaolers, picks up the idea of sub-personalities. If one, or more, of a person's sub-personalities is victimising him, then that sub-personality needs to be brought under the liberating influence of the psyche. It might be opportune to remind ourselves that every person is made up of body, emotions and mind and that these three parts are influenced by energy, warmth and light emanating from the psyche. Not all sub-personalities are malevolent. Some exert a benign influence. But many work against the concept of wholeness; their influence is turned into disintegration, not integration. I would suggest that pathological anxiety is the person's response to the negative feelings produced by one, or more than one, sub-personalities. They are the gaolers; it is they who force the person onto the treadmill and keep up the pressure. They will resist all attempts by the psyche to modify their punitive influence. They, the sub-personalities, have much to lose by surrendering their power. The fear that drives the person on will be replaced by peace and wholeness from the psyche. That is what the sub-personalities fear. They survive on power based on fear. When that fear is replaced by peace, they lose their sting. The person stops running and may then step out onto the firm ground of manageable, rather than pathological anxiety.

Case Illustration – Susan

I have said how anxiety can be likened to being on a treadmill, where the person often feels pursued by some fear. Susan was such a person. A doctor in her late thirties, she had recently become very afraid of being alone in the house and could not sleep without a light on. She had lived alone since her divorce and had recently been receiving obscene telephone calls, sometimes in the middle of the night. As we talked, it gradually became clear that the telephone incident had triggered off a deeper, older fear.

When she was in a relaxed state, I asked her to let her imagination take her back to the last time she felt fear. That was related to when someone smashed her front door. A few other incidents took her back to the age of four.

SUSAN:　　　I'm standing at the front door of my Gran's house in Wales. I don't feel afraid, though. I feel quite happy. Why has that image come to me?

Still in her imagination she explored the house, starting at the 'parlour'.

There's a bowl of bulbs on the table. I haven't remembered that room in such detail before.

She moved up the creaking stairs to the bedrooms. When she got to her room and stepped inside, she physically shuddered, but could find no explanation. Then it was time for her to settle down to sleep.

Dear Lord, I lay me down to sleep,
I pray, Oh Lord, my soul to keep.
If I should die before I wake,
I pray, Oh Lord, my soul to take.

Good gracious, I haven't thought of that for years. What a horrid prayer to teach a child. 'If I should die before I wake'.

She then had a dialogue with her mother. Mother, leave the light on.

MOTHER:　　Now don't be silly, Susan.

SUSAN:　　　Mother, leave the light on, please (*becoming agitated*).

> *The light was left on. Into her imagination came a white, shiny object which terrified Susan. She took hold of my hand which gave her some reassurance.*

MYSELF: Describe this object.

SUSAN: It's just white and shiny. It doesn't seem to have any definite form to it.

MYSELF: Can you touch it?

SUSAN: I'm terrified, but I'll try. Now it's turned into something white – like a sheet hanging in the air.

MYSELF: What does the sheet want to do?

SUSAN: It's coming towards me; it wants to envelop me.

MYSELF: Let it.

SUSAN: I'm terrified. Don't let go of my hand. It's changed into a wooden chest, the chest that was in my bedroom.

MYSELF: What would you like to do with the chest?

SUSAN: I'll open the drawers. I've got it! *(her voice rising with excitement)*. It's a shroud. Gran kept all her burial clothes in there. I can remember being very puzzled when Grandfather disappeared. He had died and I knew that he had been wrapped in one of Gran's sheets.

> *As we talked this through, Susan linked the feeling of fear of the dark with the line of the prayer 'If I should die before I wake' and with the mystery of her Grandfather's disappearance.*

How could I know the difference between 'going to sleep' and Grandfather 'going to sleep' and being wrapped in a sheet?

This example used the power of imagery to release Susan from her tyrannical gaoler. It is interesting to note how the image changed from something vague 'white and shiny', to the enveloping sheet, then to something solid – the chest. If Susan had not, in her imagination, had the courage to reach out to touch the 'object' and to allow the sheet to envelop her, she might not have been able to identify what her gaoler was and so release herself from its power.

I have included this brief extract from a number of sessions with Susan because it demonstrates, in some detail this particular approach to dealing with anxiety. Not every counsellor would feel comfortable using such a technique. Nor may it be appropriate for every person or every situation. But it worked for Susan.

Case Illustration – Sheila

The second case is of Sheila, a student nurse, who was anxious about her mock finals. She had never done well at exams at school. Her parents were middle-aged before they had her, and the marriage was not a happy one. Her mother was the senior partner in a print shop. When Sheila was about six, she discovered her mother in bed with a lover. She was sworn to secrecy, but now the anxiety over the exam had brought it to head: 'I can't carry the burden any longer.' She went to boarding school and hated it until the last two years. She felt caught in a double bind: when she came home she felt unwanted; when she opted to go for holidays with friends, her mother criticised her. 'It's still the same,' she said through her tears.

My first strategy was to help relieve the immediate stress, by helping her to relax and give some guidance on exam technique. During relaxation I gave her instruction on how to substitute positive suggestions for negative ones. She had her morale boosted when she took and passed her ward-based assessment, in spite of acute anxiety that manifested itself in diarrhoea.

In the run-up to the exam we went through this procedure several times together, and Sheila practised this 'self-talk' on her own. She would sit quietly, relax then start the visualisation that she had written down from my dictation.

'I am getting up in the morning of the exam in good time, so as not to rush. I wash, make my bed, then have a good breakfast, and set off walking to the hospital. As I walk I control my breathing and I feel really calm. In fact, I think I'm going to enjoy this exam. I walk up the stairs to the exam hall, and I feel calm and confident. I tell myself that I've studied well, I'm well prepared, and I can't do any more now. I'm now going up to the desk, and I feel calm. I'm sitting down, putting my pen and pencils on the desk, taking off my watch and putting on the desk, and I feel calm. I've already worked out how much time to give to each question, so I'm well-prepared. The examiner says, "Turn your paper over, read through the questions, but don't start writing until I tell you." I'm reading through the questions, and I feel calm. The examiner says, "You may start now." I've decided which questions to answer and in which order, and I feel calm. I pick up my pen and I start on the first question.'

On the day after the exam, a very different Sheila came in. 'I took the exam and felt OK. I told myself that it didn't matter if I did fail. At one stage I actually put my pen down and said, "Sheila, my girl, you are great!"'

Although Sheila didn't pass the mock finals, neither did two other students, and this helped her morale. We agreed to continue working until the finals. Her anxiety had taken her to her GP who put her on medication which gave her headaches; she had one when she came to the following session. She imagined the pain to be a tangled ball of string. I asked permission to use touch and helped her to focus on the pain, which gradually eased. She said, 'I see myself held in a brown, rusty, mummy-like case. I can't break out completely. That would make me too vulnerable. I'm too afraid of being hurt again'.

I said, 'See if you can get a part of you out'. She managed to get her right foot out, but that was all. I said, 'Ask your foot what it feels like to be out'. 'It says it feels good.'

While she lay in this cage, an unidentified male figure came to help her. He held her hand and it felt warm and comforting. 'But I still can't break out.' I was struck by how close her account was to that of Sleeping Beauty being wakened by the prince. Was this her feminine principle that felt trapped, caged, vulnerable?

One of the characteristic features of counselling is how important information is often not disclosed until the counselling relationship is firmly established. This must be something to do with the level of trust. It was in Sheila's ninth session when she disclosed, 'English is my weakest subject, and I can't get my thoughts down clearly on paper'. She then went on, looking acutely embarrassed, 'I took English O level six times, and I'm thoroughly ashamed of my writing. I'll do anything I can to hide it. They made me write with my right hand; trying to make me like everybody else, I suppose. I know I write in a funny way, and the girls poke fun at me about it, even now'.

I asked her to write something for me, but she could only write a few words. We then used imagery to how she could cope with this fear, particularly at the exam. We agreed that criticism, ridicule and punishment were the three big fears. She worked out her own imagery techniques for coping with these, which involved much positive self-talk, praise and affirmation.

Sheila went into the exam feeling, if not 'high', certainly almost blasé. She thought she didn't do too well, but said she didn't feel crippled by anxiety. I met her in the college on the morning the results were posted. She was among those who rejoiced; she comforted two who did not.

Summary

In this journey we considered anxiety as a normal experience although when it is pathological the person usually requires psychiatric help. The treadmill analogy was used to describe anxiety, where the person experiencing it is often pushed to physical, intellectual and emotional exhaustion. The fact that most people would acknowledge that they have experienced some of the normal symptoms of anxiety provides a common base for an examination of a fairly universal phenomenon.

For those people whose experience of anxiety has moved from the 'normal' end of the dimension toward the 'pathological', the theory was put forward that they are the victims of antagonistic sub-personalities who are at war with one another. Identifying these sub-personalities may be enough to drain them of the destructive power they hold over the person.

People who suffer from crippling anxiety also suffer from a battered self-esteem. Counselling support may help to restore self-esteem, so essential to optimum recovery. Cognitive restructuring, information-seeking and threat minimisation, to help the person reduce the anxiety level, could be an appropriate counselling approach to use.

If we can help the client to identify the gaoler of the treadmill, we may have given the client a powerful weapon to control anxiety. As with all counselling, it is essential that we use a broad repertoire of skills; a limited repertoire may prove to be too restricting on the client. While one approach may suit one client, it may not suit all. One technique may suit the personality of one therapist but not of every one. One of the aims of counselling is self-awareness; this applies to both clients and those who counsel. We who counsel need to know why we do it and why we prefer to use the particular approaches we do. If our counselling is to be truly effective, it is our duty to extend our awareness of ourselves as well as the approaches to counselling which other people have developed.

Exploring Depression

The Limbo of Depression

As in the discussion of anxiety, depression will be considered mainly as a concomitant of illness or injury and not as a psychological disorder in its own right. But in order to do this, it is necessary, first of all, to examine the tenets of depression. Some of the ideas that will be introduced are fairly traditional; others do not fit easily into any one 'school' of psychopathology. I have deliberately taken a broad approach to this distressing condition because it needs to be tackled on as wide a front as possible. Our knowledge of depression is great; but our understanding of this condition can never be fully satisfied. In this section I attempt to plumb, still further, the depths of the bottomless pit of depression.

In exploring anxiety I suggested the analogy of the treadmill. There the person was constantly driven to exhausting activity. In many ways depression is the opposite: people are caught in a trap that cuts them off from their environment, so preventing them reacting appropriately to it and with the people in it.

It was this feeling of being cut off – of not being able to make emotional contact – led me to the analogy: the limbo of depression. Limbo (*limbus* in Latin) means 'border' or 'edge'. In Roman Catholic theology, limbo is the abode of the dead whose souls are excluded from heaven through no fault of their own; those who died before the birth of Christ, and who died without Salvation. The name arose from the ancient belief that the place was situated on the edge of hell.

Theologians distinguish two forms of limbo: the limbo of the fathers, where the souls of the just were detained until their redemption was accomplished by Christ; and the limbo of infants, where the souls of unbaptised infants, and others free of personal sin, enjoy a natural bliss but are denied the supernatural beatitude of heaven. It is also the place of unbaptised infants, and of people whose mental state does not permit them to distinguish right from wrong. Some theologians maintain that the infants in limbo are affected by some degree of sadness because of felt deprivation.

People who are depressed complain of: loss of enjoyment in life; sadness; guilt and worthlessness; paranoid feelings; loss of energy and interest; disturbance of sleep; disturbance of appetite and weight; disturbed time sense; suicidal tendencies; anxiety and obsession; disturbance of sexual function; slowing of bodily functions; and agitation. Only a few of these symptoms will be discussed.

Sadness

Sadness is unhappiness brought down a degree. Most people know the feeling of unhappiness. Many know the feelings of sadness. Not everyone understands the deep, lasting, incapacitating sadness of a person depressed to the point where he or she feels 'like a dried out husk', and where tears – therapeutic in normal sorrow – dry up in the eyes before they can be shed.

It has been suggested that the sadness of depression has its genesis in loss of some valued person, possession or status; in the way we attribute meaning to our ideas, feelings, ideals and circumstances, the sense of lack or loss of positive emotions, such as love, self-respect and feelings of satisfaction; in a sense of deprivation, pessimism and self-criticism.

While sadness is a normal and healthy response to any misfortune and is common, sorrow that does not lessen with the passage of time is pathological. People who experience normal sadness are usually able to talk about it, to know why they are sad, and still to feel hope that the sadness will lift. Depression sets in when normal exchanges are absent or greatly diminished. The words that would express how a depressed person feels are blocked in the well by the dried up tears. Sadness is also referred to as 'psychic pain' – pain that is not physical but mental. If sadness is psychic pain, is the psyche able to tolerate only so much pain? Is it possible that excess psychic pain is transformed into other feelings – anxiety, anger, rage and psychosomatic manifestations?

Sadness, particularly when it follows a specific event, such as a death is some sort of compensation, although renewal may take a long time. People who pass from normal sadness to depression are likely to be those in whom the reparative work of sorrowing has not taken place; they cannot do 'grief work'. It is possible that such people are psychologically ill-equipped (because life experience has not prepared them) to resolve their sorrow or sadness.

Sadness is characteristic of a depressed state and, whatever their culture, depressed people are fairly consistent in the way they use figurative language to describe their feelings: the heart may be 'heavy, 'dark', 'constricted, 'sunk'; the client may feel as if he has a 'stone in the heart': may feel a 'dark cloud is hovering overhead'. Sadness tops the list in many studies of depression.

Loss of joy

A close second to sadness is 'loss of joy', 'inability to enjoy', 'lack of pleasure'. This particular feeling is so closely related to sadness that it is helpful to consider them together. There is an increasing inability in depressed people to enjoy themselves. This affects relationships with their families; hobbies become boring; appreciation of art and music, which they previously enjoyed, lose their appeal; the world of nature and sound is dull and insipid. The fact that life is dull and cheerless causes them concern. They know the joy has gone but they cannot find where or how to recapture it. Not all depressed people are able to express this spontaneously, but when helped to do so, it is obvious that they do experience this loss.

The fact that the person finds no pleasure in things or people has the effect of cutting her or him off emotionally from activities and people who would normally stimulate them. That such a feeling of joylessness causes problems should come as no surprise. When any mood separates husband from wife; parent from children; working colleague from his mates; neighbour from neighbour; and when all of these relationships are affected *all at once*, our emotional world shrinks so much that even we, ourselves, are reduced to nothing. This is how some people express the depth of the feeling of isolation their depression has brought. Depressed people find themselves alone, separated from all human contact and in a world which has taken on a hostile appearance. Each person can describe his or her experience in an image, and all these images have one common feature – the depressed person sees himself as imprisoned in an inescapable isolation.

One of the characteristics of depression is that it is contagious. Counsellors may well find themselves 'picking up' the sadness, and reacting to it, by themselves becoming sad and losing some of their own joy. The effect which depressed people have on others is an important factor in their increasing isolation. On the one hand depressed people desperately need human contact yet, on the other there is very little that they can offer to establish or maintain friendly relationships. It is possible that in depression, the person's ability to love, and be loved, is impaired. A measure of this – which reinforces the feeling of isolation – is a decrease in libido. The decrease may range from 'little desire' to 'total inability' and 'impotence'. For couples who have hitherto enjoyed satisfying and fulfilling sex, loss of desire, or inability, may put their relationship under great strain.

Another part of an affectional relationship is communication. Yet the profound feeling of isolation usually makes communication difficult. Communicating becomes a burden. One of the difficulties expressed by depressed people is that the conversations of other people jar; their normal laughter seems totally out of place; their attempts to 'keep things going' become sources of irritation. The wavebands of communication have become distorted by depressed feelings. Communication – of any meaning – virtually ceases. This can make counselling difficult, particularly where the process is heavily dependent upon 'talking'.

Guilt and worthlessness

In a severe case of depression, the person becomes preoccupied with feelings of guilt and worthlessness: 'I am worthless'; 'the world is meaningless'; 'the future is hopeless'. Others take a relatively hopeful view of the future and believe that they will get well. This must obviously be influenced to some extent by their basic personality and by the support they receive. People who have always been negative and pessimistic may be more prone to take a pessimistic view of their depression. Someone who has the support of a loving and caring family may take a more positive view than someone who lives alone. People who 'think' they will get well may do better than those who 'feel' they might. This may be worth focusing on in counselling by using a cognitive approach of strong affirmation rather than always exploring feelings.

In the most severe cases of depression, these feelings of guilt and worthlessness assume full-blown delusional proportions. In such cases the belief cannot be reversed by evidence to the contrary despite the fact that this belief may be out of keeping with the person's social or educational background. Minor misdemeanours and omissions may be blown up into mountainous breaches of morals. Delusional responses may include the firm conviction that the person is the worst possible sinner; has committed 'the unforgivable sin'; is to blame for the state the world is in; and so on. It seems that when depressed, our normal feelings of doubt become so exaggerated as to 'take over' and crowd out rational thought and feeling.

Self-esteem

Self-esteem is the degree to which one feels valued, worthwhile or competent. Very low self-esteem equates to feeling worthless. Illness and disability alter one's self-esteem but may plunge a person possessed of a low self-esteem into a state of depression.

Lowered self-esteem is likely to be accompanied by feelings of unhappiness, anger, sense of threat, fatigue, withdrawal, tension, disorganisation, feelings of constraint, conflict and inhibition. High self-esteem equates to feelings of integration, freedom, positive emotion and availability of energy. The first list equates very directly to the list of symptoms of depression, and one cannot help but speculate as to the place of self-esteem in the onset and course of depression.

There is a close relationship between parental warmth, acceptance, respect and clearly defined limit-setting and positive self-esteem in children. Children who are expected to conform to ambiguous limit-setting standards tended to remain dependent or tended to withdraw. A child reared without boundaries will forever seek to escape from the wilderness of the wide world into which he or she has prematurely strayed.

It could be said that people with high self-esteem carry a loving parent within them, and that people with low self-esteem carry a non-loving parent within them. If this is so, such people are likely to become life's vulnerable personalities, prone to becoming caught in the quicksand of depression. It is also true that esteem for others is as necessary as esteem for one's self. People who have little self-esteem, or esteem for others, are already programmed for feeling helpless or hopeless in the face of loss. Self-esteem influences the way a person deals with loss; low self-esteem leads to generalised hopelessness.

Anxiety with depression

Symptoms of anxiety and those of depression are common companions. The outstanding features of anxious, depressed people is that they tend to be tense, jumpy, irritable and apprehensive, worrying about trivial matters and agonising over decisions. It would also seem that the majority of anxious people who become patients are also depressed.

To recapitulate, anxiety is the emotional reaction to the expectation of danger or damage. When the event has taken place – for example, death of a loved one or loss of job – and the damage has already been done, sadness results. But in many people the anxiety has become trapped in the feelings of sadness, thus preventing the completion of 'grief work'.

Finally, anxiety is linked with tension, and this tension may be reflected in a *feeling* of inner restlessness, particularly in the inability to relax. If anxiety and depression are twin sisters, and restlessness and tension contribute to an inability to relax, then it would seem logical that one way for clients to control how they feel is to be taught relaxation, *and to practise it regularly*.

Limbo revisited

The picture of the depressed person which I have painted may appear sombre and perhaps depressing. This is precisely the effect depression has. Very often we recognise with our intuition and feelings what we may not always be able to describe in words, for it is with radar-like intuition that we try to pierce the limbo-gloom that surrounds the depressed person. One of the points about limbo is that it is a prison: a prison from which the only escape rests in eternity. Nothing the condemned soul can do, no prayers, no oblations – neither by himself nor by others still in this world – may effect an escape. The soul is powerless to escape from the darkness. In limbo there is no light. Milton, in *Paradise Lost*, contrasts Hell (and with it, limbo) with Heaven. The one is dark and punishing. The other is perfect.

On page 116 the 'Emotional Awareness Wheel' was presented. The quarters represented the four seasons. The emotional content gets progressively more negative as one moves from 'pessimism' to 'optimism'. Many of the feelings that have been described in the preceding pages are to be found in the lower half of the wheel. In my theory I suggest that this is so because one is removed further from the light, and so becomes exposed to cold. I would suggest that they have been drawn (or pushed) into this state by the negativism of one or more sub-personalities.

Depression becomes a spectre who comes uninvited and whose presence mars every feast. Depression imprisons people within invisible, yet impenetrable, walls. The word-pictures painted by people are of dark prison cells; of being in a deep dark hole; of being wrapped in an impenetrable cloth; in a vast empty desert; of being enclosed by thick soundproof glass. The images vary, but the underlying concept is the same. The person is in solitary confinement. As the days pass, the torture grows worse, and the person becomes totally engulfed within the viciousness of negative thinking.

None of us is entirely free from negative thoughts about ourselves and others, but when most of our thinking and reacting is negative, we will spend increasingly more time (and emotional energy) in the dark halls of limbo, represented by the lower half of the emotional wheel. This becomes the prison of depression.

Cognitive theorists see depression, and other mood disorders, as being caused by irrational thinking. The person interprets events, his own self-worth, and the expected outcome of events, in a negative fashion. If this view is correct (and it would be wise to retain a healthy scepticism that any theory has 'the answer') then it does suggest that the person gains something from such a philosophy.

The 'learned helplessness' model of depression maintains that when we are faced with a situation, over the outcome of which we have no control, we learn that response is futile. One may infer that we then become a victim of circumstance, and as such we cannot be held responsible for whatever happens. We learn, therefore, to exploit our weakness and complaints, in order to force others to give us what we want. But this drives us still deeper into the darkness, and isolates us further from others. Every manipulation that results in increased isolation, reinforces the negative view we holds of ourselves.

Illustrative Case Study – Jenny

Jenny was referred to me by her GP for depression following her second miscarriage. Jenny had been married to Ben for two years; this was Ben's second marriage. Jenny was 21, Ben was 25. The first miscarriage happened at 12 weeks, one year before the second, which happened at 16 weeks. The GP said, 'Jenny has been on medication since the miscarriage eight weeks ago. The medication doesn't seem to be helping. I think she would benefit from more skilled counselling that we are able to offer at the clinic. I would appreciate your opinion and feedback'.

Miscarriage is a traumatic, depressing and despair-producing event. About 30 per cent of all pregnancies end in miscarriage. Although most miscarriages occur before 12 weeks, the longer the pregnancy continues, the more devastating it is when miscarriage happens.

The desolation is often overwhelming, because it is the loss of life within. It is as if a part of one's self has died with the unborn baby. When miscarriage is coupled with infertility, the loss is the bitterest of pills. The medical and nursing professions often find it difficult to help. Miscarriage, for many of them, is routine, and they do not always understand the full impact on the couple concerned.

Miscarriage is loss of life, of hopes and plans, and this means that grief would be a natural response. *Grief is the price we pay for loving.* When pregnancy is confirmed, the bonds of love have already been strongly formed, and the wrenching asunder of these early ties produces the pain of death before ever having given life. The situation is not eased by lack of understanding by many people who expect the woman to 'pick herself up', as if what happened was no more than a delayed period. Repeated miscarriages increase the burden of doubt and guilt felt by many women following miscarriage. Every miscarriage may resurrect the grief and guilt from previous unresolved losses.

When I met Jenny I was immediately struck by her total sadness, and there were many times when she seemed to drag the words out of the depth of some hole without a bottom.

I said this to her, and she acknowledged this to be so. Our dialogue proceeded as follows:

WILLIAM: Would you be able to describe this hole to me?'

JENNY: It's not a hole, it's a dungeon, like I've seen in a castle somewhere.

WILLIAM: And where are you?

JENNY: Sitting on the floor in a corner, huddled up, with my knees drawn up and my head on my knees. I used to do this when I was a child, when... (*She stopped.*)

WILLIAM: Take a good look round: where is the window, and where is the door?

JENNY: There is no window or door.

WILLIAM: Then all there is, is you, totally alone, in this stone dungeon, without light or any way to escape?

JENNY: That's right, and the ceiling is very high.

WILLIAM: And how do you feel shut up there?

JENNY: Cold, terrified, and so lonely.

WILLIAM: And what would you most want.

JENNY: To get out of here. To get back to the outside world again.

WILLIAM: But there's no window or door, so how could you get out?

JENNY: I don't know. Maybe I never will. Who cares anyway?

WILLIAM: Your story reminds me of the Count of Monte Cristo. Do you know that story? (*She shook her head.*) A French nobleman was falsely imprisoned on an island for many years in solitary confinement in a dark cell. Eventually another prisoner made contact with him by tapping on the wall. He makes his escape, found an island with treasure on it, and spent the rest of his life pursuing revenge on his enemies.

JENNY: Yes, that's me.

Although Jenny felt that picture fitted, there was little enthusiasm.

WILLIAM: How did you get in there?

JENNY: I did it. I built the walls, to keep me safe, but couldn't stop, then it all closed over and I was trapped.

WILLIAM: So you felt you had to protect yourself from somebody or something, and now to come out would put you back in danger?

JENNY: Yes. It's too dangerous.

At this stage I heard a very frightened little girl speaking. Experience has taught me that when a person imagines themselves in a trap, a cage, or now, in a dungeon, it is wiser to concentrate on effecting a release, an escape. Exploration of all the other points can be left until later.

WILLIAM: It seems that, like the Count, you've been in this dungeon for a long time?

JENNY: Years.

WILLIAM: Jenny, when you were a little girl, did you like fairy stories.

JENNY: I did, and spent hours with books; they were safe.

I heard the word 'safe', and wondered if there was a possible link with her earlier, 'I used to do this as a child,' and stored it away for possible future use.

WILLIAM: What was your favourite story?

JENNY: Cinderella.

WILLIAM: Why was that?

I hoped that by tapping into the past, she would draw energy from some happy memory.

JENNY: I liked it when the Fairy Godmother came and changed the pumpkin into the coach, and the mice into horses.

This was the first time there was any sparkle in her voice.

WILLIAM: So you would like her to wave her magic wand and take all this away, or something like that?

JENNY: (*Sigh*) That would be nice, if only...

WILLIAM: Why not ask your fairy godmother to come, and see what happens.

JENNY: She's come, all bright and glistening. What do I do now?

WILLIAM: Tell her your story, and ask her if there's anything she can do to help you.

She repeated much of what she had told me, ending with, 'How can you get me out of this mess?'

WILLIAM: And what does she say?

JENNY: Damn! She says she can't get me out just like that. I've got to do something for myself. I'm cross with her. I thought she'd use her magic.

I found this interesting, for this was Jenny's psyche taking control. Although magic is often useful, it should not be relied upon all the time. What Jenny's psyche was telling her was that the fairy godmother could help, but her release depended on a partnership.

WILLIAM: If your fairy godmother could help you, how could she help you get out?

JENNY: If there was a window, she could get me a ladder.

WILLIAM: Is it within her power to make a window for you, and then provide a ladder?

JENNY: I'll ask her. She says it is. Now there is a window, but it's so high; that means I have to climb.

WILLIAM: So now you have a choice. To stay here where it's secure but dark and dismal and sad, or to break out where there is still some danger. What could you take with you as a talisman? What could your fairy godmother give you?

JENNY: I ask her for something to protect me when I get out. She gives me one of her rings. I put it on and feel really strong.

Jenny did climb the ladder, though she didn't find this easy. When she reached the top, the window opened by itself. She stepped out into a garden she had known as a child. This evoked tears, as she related how, at the age of six, she had been raped by her uncle. She had tried to tell her mother at the time, but she was not believed. Her uncle was still alive, and she finished the session with, 'The second baby was due to be born on his birthday'.

Discussion of Jenny

Jenny had made the connection between the abuse and the miscarriages herself; it was the first time she had done so. She looked relieved, and said she would have to confront her mother again. I was, quite frankly, disappointed when Jenny decided she wished not to continue with counselling, saying, 'I can't go into all that again. It's too painful'. I acknowledged her pain and her difficulty, and said that I felt she was brave to have tackled it the way she had, and added that at some time in the future she might feel she would have to take up where she left off.

What to me seemed important, was that although she had built her 'solid defences' around her from a young age, and would have liked a fairy tale ending to all her troubles, she had to work at it. I hope that although she decided not to continue, she had gained just enough insight to see her through.

Summary

This has not been a treatise on depressive neurosis and its treatment. There has been no discussion of the classification of depression with its 'endogenous' and 'exogenous', its 'unipolar' and 'bipolar' typologies. I have attempted to paint a picture of depression, not present a psychiatric illness.

Suicide has not been discussed; one reason why it is not included, is that it is too vast and complex a topic for me to do justice to in this book. Another reason it has not been included is that it would have taken the whole discussion too far into depression as a psychiatric illness.

The one theme that repeats itself is the isolation felt by depressed people, cut off, as they are, from emotional contact. In a sense, depressed people pre-empt and pre-experience their own death – the final isolation. The relationship between counsellor and client is crucial in maintaining contact, and thereby reducing the risk of isolation. Human contact has a calming effect on the cardiovascular system of a person under stress. Thus it is quite feasible that our very presence achieves as much, or more, than our words of counsel, however profound.

What we do when we counsel is to offer ourselves in a relationship that makes no demands for itself. When we reach out to make emotional contact with depressed people, we break through the invisible barrier that keeps them isolated. This emotional contact builds a bridge. Across this bridge they may walk away from their limbo.

The Client Within Society
Separation or Reconciliation

Introduction

> A body is not a single organ, but many. Suppose the foot should say, 'Because
> I am not a hand, I do not belong to the body', it does belong to the body
> none the less. Suppose the ear were to say, 'Because I am not an eye, I do not
> belong to the body', it does still belong to the body. If the body were all ear,
> how could it smell? But, in fact, God appointed each limb and organ to its
> own place in the body, as he chose. If the whole were one single organ, there
> would not be a body at all; in fact, however, there are many different organs,
> but one body. The eye cannot say to the hand, 'I do not need you', nor the
> hand to the feet 'I do not need you'... If one organ suffers, they all suffer
> together. If one flourishes, they all rejoice together. (The New English Bible.
> I Corinthians 12:14–26)

This journey is by way of an epilogue to the first part of the book, but it also puts
forward a philosophy in which we do not regard clients as inferior and blemished,
weak or less than adequate, and think of counsellors as being superior, strong or
perfect and unblemished. I know that if someone suggested this we would hotly
deny it, yet some people may regard counselling as an ego-boosting exercise, rather
than the humbling process which I often think it is.

I say this because although I have my problems and difficulties, I often reflect
that if I had the problems and difficulties of some of the people I work with, what
would I be like? Would I still be able to smile and joke, and would I still find within
me the courage and strength to struggle through the pain of, for example, sexual or
physical abuse? May I never become so complacent and self-satisfied that I miss
what *that* means to *this* client.

Many people have to overcome great resistance to become 'clients'. Ken said, 'I
knew for months that I should do it, but somehow part of me wanted to manage it
by myself'. Ken expressed the fear that by coming for counselling, he would be
stigmatised, and that he would stigmatise himself, as being less than perfect. He
took a significant step forward when he was able to disclose to his parents that he
was in counselling. In many ways he regarded himself as 'disabled.'

For the purposes of this 'journey', I will refer to 'disability' in its broadest sense. What I say applies to many people who have 'visible' disabilities. However, for the client whose disability is 'invisible' – such as stress and anxiety, or pain and depression, the effects of, for example, stigma, are just as real.

There is a dramatic change of role from 'healthy' to 'disabled' and the problems that disablement often brings, as the person and the significant people in his life struggle to make sense of what has happened. They have to establish new identities for themselves. Part of those new identities involve the remainder of society. For every person who becomes disabled society is forced to establish a new identity for itself.

Many people with disabilities find this struggle too great, and give up. If society is to function effectively, and that means the disabled too, there needs to be far greater understanding and acceptance of every single person as someone without whom the rest of us cannot function to our full potential.

The 'Body' Concept

The analogy of society as a human body is apt when one thinks of 'all parts working together'. The human body is complex in its composition, construction and function. But the perfect functioning of the body depends upon all parts working together in balance and harmony. Any disturbance or disharmony in one part of the body will affect the whole body; the body will feel 'out of sorts' and will misfunction.

When we consider the body we think of its various systems; every single one functionally perfect, yet unable to exist independently of any of the others. If every system of the body was a personality in its own right would they each claim pre-eminence? Would each battle for supremacy and seek to adopt a dominant position over the others? No one system could isolate itself from the others by adopting a 'superior' attitude. Nor could one system, or a number of them, 'gang' up on another and isolate it. No one system may, because it feels 'more important' or 'more needed', demand more attention than any other. When every system is interdependent, no one is less, nor more, important than any other. For it to be otherwise would impose intolerable stress on the body and chaos would result. This is what happens in illness.

Illness is not caused by one part of the body 'deciding' that it will assume dominance; neither is illness caused by one system being isolated by all other parts. Yet in a sense, at that time, the affected part *is* demanding more attention from every other part; the other parts respond in sympathy. Their own needs become subservient to the needs of the affected part. Witness the reaction of the hand when the leg is injured; the natural response is to hold, or rub, the affected part and so to soothe away the pain. When disease strikes the body, defending white blood cells rush to devour the intruders. All parts work together.

This analogy, taken from the Biblical quotation that heads this journey, was used by St Paul to demonstrate the interdependence of every member of the Christian church, where each may have a different function. These functions were generally thought of as gifts or talents which, if not used, caused the rest of the Christian fellowship to function imperfectly. Paul was exhorting his readers to work together in the same way as the elements of the body do, for the good of the whole.

Body-Image and Society

Society's view of itself is similar to the view we have of our own body. This is the body-image, which in turn is part of the self-concept. I propose that society has a 'collective body-image'. The inner picture that society has of itself is as complex as the picture we have of ourselves. We have an 'ideal self' and a 'personal self'. A significant point is that the body-image is constantly changing – at least for the majority of people who realistically accept changes. A dramatic change in body-image results from chronic illness and disability.

The self-image that society has internalised corresponds to the idealised image which people hold of themselves. The discrepancy between the ideal which society has and the realistic image is great. This is because there are many individuals and groups of people who 'spoil' that image. People with chronic illness and disability form such a group. Individuals who retain a 'healthy' and realistic body-image are those who have accommodated changes. Societies who reject disabled people – striving desperately to retain an unchanged body-image – are not 'healthy', but 'sick'. A pathological example of such 'disassociation' was Nazi Germany's attempt to exterminate the Jews. The 'healthiest' societies are those who accommodate people who are 'different', and disability makes people different.

Most people would regard as pathological the man who, not liking the shape of it, cuts off his nose. In much the same way, parents who 'disown' their son because he does not match up to their ideals, are regarded with suspicion by other people. Yet on a larger scale, society does this to those who are disabled. It cuts them off and disowns them because they do not match up to an ideal; they spoil the image.

The man who cuts off his nose mutilates himself, yes, but he also does irreparable harm to his body-image. Although his intention was to improve his looks, he has disfigured himself, thereby creating a massive scar in his body-image. His ideal self is pushed further away. The parents who disown their son have carved a hole in their family body-image, a hole that no other person can fill and which, if it is not filled by the son, will never shrink.

When society cuts disabled people off and disowns them, it mutilates and creates holes that cannot be filled. The result is a spoiled body-image. Society has achieved by its actions what it hoped to avoid – a spoiled identity, a spoiled self-concept. A society which acts like this toward disabled people is not whole, and never will be until it incorporates those whom it has cut off and isolated – those whom it regards as not 'normal'. Individuals, if they are to remain emotionally healthy, have to accept themselves as they are, warts and all. Society must do likewise.

The concept applied

The man who, as the result of a stroke, is left with the legacy of a weakened arm, may do one of two things. He may totally ignore the arm – 'It is no longer mine' –

and end up emotionally crippled; or he can tenderly love it back to a degree of usefulness. The one approach is 'separation', the other is 'reconciliation'. Separation implies incompleteness; reconciliation, wholeness.

The man needs to discover what his arm can do and what it cannot. He may regret that it can no longer function alone, that it has to be aided by his good arm, but he adjusts to its limitations. He – and the rest of his body – adjusts to his arm's limited function. But they, all the body members, become reconciled to what is, in effect, a 'new body'. Similarly, society is given two choices to deal with those who are disabled – separation or reconciliation.

Society, at its peril, says, 'We don't need you. Go away, we cannot stand the sight of you. Look! we have provided you with this beautiful place, where you can be happy with people who are like yourself. You can be sheltered there, protected, fed, watered and groomed. We are a caring society'. But this is separation, not reconciliation. Is this not the hand saying to the foot, 'I have no need of you?' This is not all parts working together for the good of the whole.

The weakened arm could say 'I am weak, no good and useless. I want to be looked after. It is my right'. The other members of the body could then rightly say, 'We will help you, but we cannot do everything for you. There are certain things that you, and only you, can do. If you do not do them, either they will not be done at all, or they will be done badly because we were not designed like you. Without you we are incomplete'.

Some people become so immersed in their disability and self-pity that they expect – as their right – that other people will function for them. But these are a minority. Many more desperately want not to be separated from society, but to be reconciled to it, to be restored to active partnership, to function once more as a hand, foot, eye or tongue. Reconciliation accepts that the function may not be quite as vigorous as before but even reduced function has a definite place.

Separation may be easier for society to bear than reconciliation. The one approach is governed by legislation and money; the other is hard work, and emotionally demanding. In the process of reconciliation, many of the feelings within society are thrown into sharp relief against the back cloth of chronic illness and disability. For it is as the person with disability struggles back to a degree of independence that society's attitudes toward disability are questioned.

If we are to be reconciled with people who have disabilities, we need, like the body, to establish a new identity in which the reconciled person has a definite place and is able to function as an integrated 'member' *in spite of their limitations.*

The foregoing discussion does not imply that society should do all the giving: reconciliation is a relationship of give and take. We all have rights, privileges, needs and wants. But hand in hand with these go responsibilities, obligations and duties. None of us, and this includes the person with a disability, may expect to exercise rights, privileges, needs and wants, without accepting responsibilities, obligations and duties.

Not to do so is like the hand saying to the foot, 'I am more important than you'. The more people with disabilities are reconciled to society – truly reconciled, accepted and helped to function as valuable, wanted and needed members – the less they will need to regard themselves as 'special' and expect (and sometimes demand) what may be denied to other members of society who are not disabled.

Much has been accomplished in the past thirty years to make known the feelings of many people who are disadvantaged, not only by illness and disability, but by bad housing, poverty and hunger.

Perhaps at no other time in the world's history has the impact of suffering of whole communities engendered such response in the way of aid. The impact which suffering millions have made on many people has been made possible by rapid spread of information by radio and newspapers but more startlingly, by television.

In much the same way illness of all kinds has been brought into people's sitting rooms, *whether they want to know about it or not*. This may produce favourable results, and people respond by wanting to know more, thereby increasing their understanding of other people. Sometimes, however, people react in much the same way as when confronted with the sight of starving, dying people in Africa, or the dying wounded in Bosnia or Northern Ireland – they switch their emotional receiver off even though the television set is still receiving. Some people are so overwhelmed by suffering *over which they have no control* that their only safeguard is to 'switch off'.

Publicity which aims to raise awareness may be constructive, but it can also be so stunning in the way it is presented as to be counterproductive. People who respond to the suffering of others by turning away cannot be protected from chance encounters with people who are disabled, any more than people who are disabled can, or should, be shielded from possible contact with people who would shun them because of their disability.

But if provision for people with chronic illness and disability is to be improved, more people – of the sort who are prepared to do something to change the system – need to be better informed.

Illustrative Case Study – Dave

Dave was 55 years of age when his job, as a senior nurse teacher, was made redundant. Dave was unmarried, and had been in the health service for thirty years. 'I lived for my work, now I feel lost.' Now follows a short extract of our time together.

WILLIAM: It sounds as if your world has stopped spinning.

DAVE: Yeah, that's how it feels. I feel cut off.

WILLIAM: Something feels severed. If you were to put that into a picture, what would it look like?

Dave was a keen experienced gardener.

DAVE: A tree that's been cut off near the ground.

WILLIAM: So you are lying there helpless on the ground, cut off from your roots?

DAVE: That's what it felt like, but not what I see. No, it's more like a branch that's been damaged, hanging.

WILLIAM: So part of you has been vandalised and left. Something like an
           arm?

DAVE: Yes, like my right arm.

WILLIAM: And its hanging there, useless, maybe blowing in the wind. Not
           much good. As a gardener, what would you do?

DAVE: I could get a saw and make a clean cut.

WILLIAM: Painless, neat and tidy. And then what?

DAVE: I'd paint it over with preservative, to stop disease getting in. Like a
           surgical operation.

WILLIAM: And then the branch?

DAVE: Well, it would be thrown away, burnt, or something.

WILLIAM: Now take a look at that tree, say, an apple tree, what does it look
           like now?

DAVE: (*His lip quivering.*) I don't like it. It's spoiled, unbalanced.

WILLIAM: So? What else could you do?

DAVE: I could bind up the branch, hope it would heal.

WILLIAM: Why would you want to do that?

DAVE: So that it would fruit again.

WILLIAM: If that tree is you, and if your job is the branch, what then?

DAVE: OK! You say I have a choice. Cut off those thirty years, or heal the
           wound and be fruitful. Yes, I've got experience, training and
           skills. I'm not ready for the scrap heap.

WILLIAM: Before we end, imagine it's one year from now. What does the tree
           look like?

DAVE: It's one of my Cox's trees and that branch is covered in blossom.
           I can see the scar, but the branch has healed.

Discussion

The relationship between the branch of a tree and the limb of a person is obvious,
and there is little doubt that Dave felt cut off, isolated, separated from a vital part
of himself. He felt he had been vandalised. Working with a client's image is
important, for unconsciously he had made the connection between the fruitfulness
of the tree and his lack of fruitfulness. Cutting off the damaged branch could have
been a solution, but he chose the way of healing. This fits in with the principle of
reconciliation in the Second Journey. At the start of this imagery Dave presents a
discrepancy between what he feels and what he imagines; this is important to clarify
and test it out, for what I interpreted did not match with his image. The apple
blossom points the way to promise.

Summary

A quote from a speech made by Alfred Morris, during the second reading of his 'Chronically Sick and Disabled Persons Bill' in the House of Commons, 1970, is a salutary exhortation to us all.

> If we could bequeath one precious gift to posterity, I would choose a society in which there is a genuine compassion for the very sick and the disabled, where understanding is unostentatious and sincere, where, if years cannot be added to the lives of the chronically sick, at least life can be added to their years; where the mobility of disabled people is restricted only by the bounds of technical progress and discovery; where the handicapped have the fundamental right to participate in industry and society according to their ability; where socially preventable disease is unknown and where no man has cause to be ill at ease because of his disability.

When society becomes better informed, and when the majority of people accept illness and disability as a part of a 'healthy' and 'whole' society, then, and only then, will reconciliation and not separation operate. Then and only then will the hopes of reformers like Alfred Morris, which hitherto have been little more than images drifting in the wind, take on solid form and become reality. That reality is a society where quality has been added to years and disabled people are truly members of, and working together as, one body.

Journeying with Fifteen Clients

Introduction

The 15 clients,[1] around whom Part Two is built are drawn from my case book, and illustrate different aspects of the use of imagery. The extracts are recounted more in the spirit of 'this is how it was done', rather than 'this is how to do it'. These accounts have been written up from my notes and from notes kept by clients, in some cases. I speak as if with their voice. They deal mainly with the use of imagery: naturally there were many occasions when imagery was not used.

I feel very privileged to have been given the opportunity of working with these clients, and learning from them. The various journeys they took became my journeys also, and have added to my own awareness. Several of my 'clients' are counsellors, either seeking a mentor, or needing to work through some particular difficulty in their own life. Many of them have acknowledged that their understanding has been enhanced by how they have been encouraged to use imagery in their sessions with me. I believe this applies also to clients who have been quoted in the whole of this book and not just in this part.

Counselling is not about 'curing'; it is rather about 'enabling'. Some of the clients quoted wanted no more than to be able to get through a particular crisis; for others, counselling was an introduction to counselling training. I hope that for all of them the experience of the counselling relationship was as rewarding as it was for me. If the images that they created, and that we shared, have lived as long with them as they have with me, then I am quite certain that when they recall those images, they will again experience something of the magic, as well as the hard work, of that relationship.

Finally, I would urge you, as you read through these cases, to try yourself to enter into the imagery, for in this way the clients' journeys will become yours.

---

1   Again, names and situations have been changed.

Bill
Crossroads

My name is Bill. I'm 23, and a student nurse. When I came to William, on the advice of my girlfriend, I felt under stress. William helped me to work out the reasons for this:

1. My parents were both unwell.

2. My sister had married because of pregnancy.

3. My career; I'm a pupil nurse and desperately want to became a registered general nurse (RGN).

4. I no longer love my girlfriend. I want to end the relationship, but she doesn't want to.

I'm not doing too well at my studies. I don't feel able to concentrate; there are many pressures. There's mother who expects me to be the father, and she says she can't manage without me. I have to go up to Manchester on days off, and that's a strain.

WILLIAM: I see you attached to a long length of elastic.

BILL: (*Smiling*) That's true, and I hate it.

WILLIAM: How do you feel about trying to put those feelings into some sort of picture?

BILL: I'm trapped in a corner. Dark and cold, sitting with a half-emptied booze bottle. I'm scared, lonely unloved and rejected.

WILLIAM: So you feel cornered right now, and pretty desolate. Imagine that somehow that image could be changed.

BILL: Somebody's come, a man in a white staff nurse's uniform.

WILLIAM: And how does that feel?

BILL: Warmer. He tells me to get up and do something. I get up and follow my friend into the light.

There was an awful struggle before I could take the step into the future. Sweat was pouring from me, and I wanted to cry, but didn't want to leave with red eyes. I felt

I'd done what I came for, and although we only had two sessions, it was enough to see me through.

Comment

Bill felt trapped between a girlfriend and freedom, between responsibility towards his parents and his career. The position of being in the corner, in the dark, speaks of depression. His father has a drink problem, and this probably accounted for the image of the half-consumed bottle.

The staff nurse in the white coat probably represented his ultimate goal, so he was really telling himself to get up and go. The 'friend' possibly meant that he had to learn to befriend himself; possibly this was his psyche, whom he had to learn to trust.

At one stage Bill saw a crossroads and someone, leaning on a wall, cigarette in hand, and he knew he had to make a choice to go on or to go back. I encouraged him to look back, and he saw the corner of the room with some faceless person sitting there. He was tempted to go back, but he took a step forward into the light and felt better, towards his goal which is to become a RGN. He knows how easy it would be to go back. He spoke about alcohol and the image he saw of someone whom he didn't want to become. 'That really frightened me.'

Getting the client to look back is often useful, particularly when there is a crossroads. Crossroads represent choice, as Bill found out, and by looking back he could see what he had left behind.

Alan
Sexual Identity

I am Alan, an older-than-average psychiatric student nurse, with a degree in Modern Art. I'd come into nursing because I couldn't find a steady job in Sunderland. I was about seven months into training when I felt the need to talk with William. It was incredibly difficult for me; I was quite scared and ill-at-ease. Since starting the course I'd been forced to take a good look at myself, and thought that some of the confusion I felt would have to be sorted out if I was to continue training.

I wasn't sure what to expect from counselling, and asked William to fill me in. He explained quite simply that we would set up a contract for so many sessions, and that his style was to leave the direction of the session to me, and that he would try to stay with me. He also said that he would try to understand what things meant to me, and that if ever I thought he wasn't with me, I should tell him. I felt comfortable with most of that, except that I didn't want to commit myself to any fixed number of sessions. So we agreed on that.

I started off by telling William that none of my relationships ever worked out for me. And gradually I disclosed that I was more comfortable with women than with men. I don't know what it was, but I felt safe in that room, safe to say what I wanted, what I needed to say. I blurted out that my older brother thinks I'm gay. Just saying that took all the courage I could draw on. Many of my acquaintances think the same, I'm sure. This is probably because I'm not macho, and because where I come from unless you're constantly boasting about all the women you've screwed, you're not a man. That was never my scene. Plus my 'puffy' subjects at university, as they called them. It wasn't just people around; my father and brother too were scathing about me.

What I was trying to say to William was that I wasn't sure if I was gay or not. I know many people regard me as effeminate. I wasn't sure where I would stand on a masculinity–femininity scale. That's what I wanted to explore with William. I left that first session feeling I'd taken a gigantic step forward.

WILLIAM: It seems that what we're speaking about is your self-esteem. How about writing on the board all the positive things about yourself?

ALAN: Goodness! That's not easy. 'Reliable', 'tolerant' and 'easy-going'.

WILLIAM: That's a good start. We can look at those again later, and see if you can add to them. Now what about negatives?

ALAN: There are so many negative things about myself, I don't even want to write them down. What I will write is, 'Don't present a good image to other people.'

WILLIAM: That's fine, but a bit vague. How could you make it more specific?

ALAN: I'll expand it to not liking my appearance, or my qualities, particularly my appearance.

WILLIAM: That's good progress. Now use your imagination to create an inner picture of yourself, what you feel like inside.

ALAN: That's really scary. I see myself as a twelve-year old, round-faced, curly-haired boy.

Alan sat looking at this inner picture for several minutes, and seemed very near to tears.

WILLIAM: A boy not yet mature?

ALAN: That's exactly it, the real part of me is still a boy.

After a long, reflective silence.

I'd like to tell you about what happened at the weekend. I met Charles who took me back to his flat. I felt loved and cared for. I don't want to go into details, and I know you well enough to know you won't pry. All I know is, that brief encounter boosted my self-esteem.

For many years I felt that other people controlled what happened to me. Now it was time to take charge, to be responsible for my own life. All the time I allowed others to decide and they could take the blame when things went wrong. In a strange way, that revelation came out of the counselling relationship. William, all the time, was refusing to take control, and by his doing this, I had to, and I was starting to enjoy it.

I remember William and me spending a long time discussing the counselling relationship. I suppose it was some sort of model for me to work to in my training. I expressed some concern that it could become a dependency, that I would come to rely on it. At the same time, I knew that if I was to get the most out of it I would have to trust how the counselling relationship would develop. From the discussion about trust, power and dependence, William and I moved on to what I wanted from other relationships. For me those things would be interest, affection and intimacy, although I wasn't at all certain if this was to be with men or with women.

I spoke about one disastrous relationship with a woman. That didn't last, possibly because she criticised me out of my mind. There wasn't any respect or trust there. William wondered how I would react if he criticised me. I thought about this, then decided that it would depend on the criticism. He then related criticism to trust. I realised that although I'd come to trust William, it was something that needed to develop.

ALAN: Something else I've realised, William, is that I need criticism, almost to confirm my low self-image.

WILLIAM: That sounds quite a revelation, and brave of you to disclose it.

ALAN: I also realised that I often mistrusted people when they said anything in my favour.

WILLIAM: I wonder if your low self-esteem was linked to insecurity.

ALAN: I think probably you're right, and it feels lousy just admitting that.

WILLIAM: Can you use your imagination to picture what that insecurity looks like?

ALAN: A plain, cardboard box, with absolutely nothing on it to distinguish it from any other box. That was me, ordinary Alan.

WILLIAM: How you feel about looking inside?

ALAN: No! I'd rather not know, at least for now.

I wanted to cancel the final session, but went anyway. After session three I began to feel OK about myself. William and I looked again at our relationship and at this session that was to be the final one. It must have been the contrast that made me think of the relationship between my brother and father. They were always at each other, hammer and tongs, with me in the middle, siphoning off their bad feelings. William wondered if I'd taken these bad feelings into myself. I probably had, though I'd never thought about it. All I know is that the four sessions with William started me on a road of discovery and of learning to be comfortable with myself as I am.

Comment

Throughout the four sessions with Alan, I was acutely conscious of the need to tread delicately. There were several occasions when he hinted at homosexuality, yet there was something in the way he gave the information that caused me to hold back from actively pursuing that line. My intuition led me to believe that he almost wanted me to confirm his sexuality for him. I did not feel this was right for me to do so. How could I? How could anyone? When he talked about his brother's opinion of him, thinking he was gay, Alan looked very directly at me, and I could sense an unasked question; what did I think? I thought it more appropriate to ask Alan what he thought about himself. This led on to his talking about self-esteem. He felt his self-esteem bucket to be very low.

When one takes into consideration the family climate, and all the things Alan talked about – his degree course and the caustic comments associated with that, and the fact that certain of his mannerisms could give the impression of his being effeminate – it is little wonder his self-esteem was low.

Alan was a man who liked order; he would often arrive with a list of topics he'd been thinking about, and wanted to cover in the session. And he always made sure that anything that was written on the board was rubbed off before he left. We talked about this, and he linked this with still not fully trusting me. Alan came for only four sessions, so it is quite understandable that he should still be wary. Trust cannot be established quickly. His comment about holding back on trust led to an interesting discussion about his being able to accept criticism from someone rather than praise or trust. In my notes for that session I heavily underlined, *I must not criticise.*

When he was describing that ordinary-looking box, with nothing to distinguish it from any other, I felt a deep sadness within me for this man who was putting himself down. I told him so, but he had difficulty accepting my feelings for him. Although he agreed to examine the inside of the box the following week, when he arrived, it was obvious he didn't want to; he wasn't ready.

Although we only spent four sessions together, we were able to work through an ending of the relationship, and he left knowing that he could return if he wished. He never did. He did complete the course and moved to a job outside of the area.

For Alan this was something of a crisis, although that is not how he presented it. On looking back on it now, after a lapse of several years, the one thing that really strikes me is the image he had of himself; as a boy, not yet mature. If the sessions we had helped him through what is often called 'an identity crisis' then he will have experienced something positive that will be of benefit wherever he is. What Alan and I saw in that image was the psyche of a man trapped within a boy sixteen years younger than the man's age. Is it any wonder Alan had been confused?

Arran
The Depths of the Lake

I'm Arran, a Hindu from Mauritius. I have been in England 18 years, since I was 20. My wife Aysha is Tamil, and we have two daughters, aged ten and eight. I work as a nurse teacher in Southampton, and am currently studying for a Master's degree in psychology and counselling. As part of that I have to be in therapy myself.

My early life wasn't happy; my father was a lazy man who was always drunk, and left everything to my mother, who owned the property. He had little time for me or my siblings. For instance, I can't ever remember being hugged by him. When I was 14, I took on a lot of what he should have been doing. It was then that I made a conscious decision to be the opposite of him in every way possible.

Mother died and I was cut out of her will. I'd told her I didn't want any of the estate – my siblings needed it more than I did – but I wasn't even mentioned, and that hurt a great deal. I feel rejected by my father, because I've invited him over to see us, but he refuses to come. I think it's because I married Aysha, who is of a different faith.

One of my characteristics is that I just can't say 'No' to people. If somebody wants four hours of my time, I have to give it. If somebody wants my money, I have to give it. This leads me into all sorts of stress. I know it's something to do with wanting to be perfect, but it's also to do with feeling responsible for people. If my students don't pass their exams, then I'm to blame, I haven't worked hard enough. I have to work so hard not to fail. I must not fail, so I take on more and more work to prove how responsible a man I am.

I know I have high standards, and this creates friction with Aysha. I insist on buying expensive clothes for her and the girls, because I want them to look their best. I know I probably do this to compensate for what I never had. I blame my father for the fact that I didn't achieve more; my parents had seven children. I wasn't going to repeat that, so I had a vasectomy. Ideally I would have liked one child, but Aysha wanted two. I would die if my children ever said an unkind thing about me.

When I started with William I had to get rid of a lot of bitterness about two sets of relatives who had treated my wife and me very unkindly. They had visited us for long periods, had borrowed money from us, had never repaid us and and we had got into debt because of them.

WILLIAM: Last week when you were talking about your relatives, you used these words: doormat, rejected, bled dry. These are fairly powerful words.

ARRAN: I know, and it applies particularly to one brother who has stabbed me in the back, yet I love him so much, I'd lay down my life for him, and he does this to me. Why?

This was a very tearful session, although Arran struggled hard not to cry.

Session Four

WILLIAM: We've spent a lot of the time in the last three sessions talking about your relationship with your parents and siblings. You feel totally rejected by them, feel you can't trust them any more, that they have let you down. I wonder how you view our relationship. Could you imagine how it might be if you were creating a picture?

ARRAN: I have difficulty with that. I don't think imagination is my strong point. I'm learning to trust you, and I certainly think you care.

WILLIAM: Let me give you a start. I imagine you having climbed over a very high wall, and on the other side there is a lake.

ARRAN: That's funny, for I saw a lake, but couldn't work out how that could be what you meant.

WILLIAM: It sounds as if you want me to lead you and tell you what to do.

ARRAN: I suppose I do. You know me, I like to have things black or white.

WILLIAM: That seems to relate your high score on judgment. How does that judgment attitude show in you?

ARRAN: I want people to do what I want them to do, because I feel I'm right.

WILLIAM: One of the things about high judgment is a strict sense of time. How does that apply to you?

ARRAN: Yes, definitely. If people are late, I get angry, and I think they are not responsible people.

WILLIAM: I expect we'll pick that up again, but for now, let's return to the lake. How would you feel about exploring it?

ARRAN: Oh, I don't know, it looks deep.

WILLIAM: Tell you what, get yourself a scuba outfit. How does that sound?

ARRAN: OK, but could I have a rope and you hold on to it?

WILLIAM: Sure, that sounds really good. What about a weapon, or a powerful torch?

ARRAN: No, the rope is all I need. I'm going a long way down, it seems like miles, the water is very murky. I don't want to go any further. I feel there is some predator near, though I can't see it. If I don't draw attention to myself, it won't notice me.

WILLIAM: So you feel really stuck. You can't go on, and if you move, you feel it might attack you.

ARRAN: Yes, that's right. I'm starting to panic.

WILLIAM: I've still got the rope. Give it a tug to reassure yourself. How do you feel about trying to befriend this thing?

ARRAN: Oh, I couldn't do that.

WILLIAM: Could you get close enough to see it?

ARRAN: I can just see it. It's black and ugly.

WILLIAM: Does it remind you of anything.

ARRAN: It reminds me of my sister.

WILLIAM: Now you've identified what it is, how about trying to befriend it?

ARRAN: I don't want to. I'd like to stop there, please.

WILLIAM: Fine, just take time to surface. You don't want to get the bends. Then, in your own time, return to this room.

ARRAN: That is incredible, where did I get to? I know it was my unconscious, but it was dark. My goodness, I need to get some light in there. When I started, I thought I'd go straight to the bottom, and there I would find bright light, with clear sand and flowers. So all that was a disappointment.

WILLIAM: And your sister?

ARRAN: I'll have to work on that. It sounded as if I hate her, didn't it?

WILLIAM: It sounded as if you were afraid of her in some way.

ARRAN: So that black thing was my fear?

Session Six

WILLIAM: How does the creature look now?

ARRAN: Still black, still ugly, but not so threatening. Somehow I feel more empowered.

WILLIAM: Empowered enough to befriend it?

ARRAN: No! I want to put it far away from me.

WILLIAM: Tell it to go.

ARRAN: It won't go.

WILLIAM: How do you feel towards it?

ARRAN: I feel pity. I'll ignore it.

WILLIAM: The last time you visited the lake you were disappointed. How is it today? Can you describe the lake.

ARRAN: Shaped like a bowl. Still dark, but if I go further down I can see some light. So, I'll go towards that. Now the light is getting brighter. If I squeeze through this narrow bit... No, I can't do that. I want to but something seems to be stopping me.

WILLIAM: Arran, I wonder if the water is muddy because the creature has stirred something up, and maybe you can't get to where you want to because there's unfinished business in the dark bit?

ARRAN: Something to do with my sister, yes?

WILLIAM: Possibly, or maybe it's the dark side of yourself, your shadow?

ARRAN: I don't like what I'm hearing. I'd rather be in the light, for the creature can't live in the light. I'll be safe there.

Comment

I asked Arran to try to qualify the counselling relationship for a specific purpose. As a trainee counsellor I thought it would help him to try to put his feelings into words. This clarifying of feelings helps to look at negatives and positives. A second point is that he had been talking so much about negative relationships, rejection and loss, that I wanted to give him the opportunity to examine our relationship.

Arran had come through an educational system that had emphasised authority and didactic learning rather than experiential learning. In Jungian terms they had concentrated on sensing and thinking, rather than on intuition and feeling, so it was no surprise that at first he found imagery difficult, although he had said he wanted to work in this way.

Arran admitted that he is very judgmental, of himself and of others. Judgmentalism often shows itself in black or white terms, and in an inability to suspend judgment.

The journey into the lake took a lot of courage, even though Arran is an experienced swimmer. The fact that he did not want a weapon is significant. He is a very gentle man who, although he gets angry, would be hard pushed to become aggressive. The lack of a weapon seemed to indicate that he could cope with whatever lay in the depths. The rope attached to me speaks of a lifeline, security, and that said a great deal about trust.

If water represents the unconscious, then the journey through the murky waters would suggest that Arran's unconscious was pretty dark, that there wasn't much light around. It also suggests that he was travelling through unknown territory, getting the feel of it. He took a very long time to 'surface' from that imagery.

Whenever the client feels blocked in some way, then is the time to go back a stage and look at any unfinished business. Arran still had to deal with the 'creature', and he could only move into the light when that had been dealt with. The light he saw at the 'bottom' drew him like a magnet, and this suggests that even in the depths of the unconscious there is hope for him. Although the unconscious is often presented as it was here as something one goes in to, with the conscious 'up there', it might be more profitable to think of it as circular, like a ball, with the conscious all round, gradually moving deeper into the unconscious as one moves from the periphery towards the centre.

Using this analogy it is easier to see how Arran imagined light at the bottom, not really the bottom but a coming back 'out of' and drawing nearer the perimeter, the outside.

We spent parts of many sessions exploring Arran's drive to succeed, spurred on by his obsessive perfectionism and fear of failure. He traced this to his conscious decision not to be like his father, whom he regarded as a total failure. There were many times, therefore, during his time with me, when we explored his frustration about what was happening between us, and how difficult it is to measure success and failure in counselling.

This particular characteristic, if not understood and modified (modified, not eradicated, for it has its positive side), could create tension between him and his clients. Certainly in the image of the lake, and not being able to 'break through' to the light, proved very frustrating. He was learning that his mind was no longer in control. This was difficult, for there was a strong rigid streak in him, and any unbending was, in his eyes, a lowering of (impossibly high) standards.

Arran's circumstances changed and he was promoted away from the area, making it difficult for us to continue. We were able to work through to a satisfactory closure of the relationship. We both felt that Arran had a lot of work to do on modifying the parts of his personality that created stress for him.

Andy
The Neglected Cornfield

I'm Andy, I'm a third year student nurse. I came for counselling because of pressure of exams and personal pressures. I'm the youngest of five children and really I don't think my parents ever trained me to take responsibility. That's one of the pressures of the job, too much responsibility at times. Another thing is that whatever people want me to do, I do it. I give in far too easily. I want to change all that, and hope that counselling will start me on that road.

WILLIAM: You seem to put yourself down quite a lot. See how many good points about yourself you can write on the board.

ANDY: I know I'm not unintelligent, and I want to put 'intelligent', but I can't.

WILLIAM: Whose voice do you hear telling you that you're not intelligent?

ANDY: I know it's my own voice.

WILLIAM: So you see yourself as unintelligent, what else?

ANDY: Oh, I'm the clown, the fool, always making people laugh. My eldest brother, Martin, he's an artist, and he's OK. June is the eldest, and she and the next two brothers, Jim and Tom, they ruled my life.

WILLIAM: How?

ANDY: Always making decisions for me, always putting me down. Never felt I had any independence.

WILLIAM: Andy, as you're talking, I feel a lot of pain here in my gut. My hunch is that I'm picking it up from you.

ANDY: (*Close to tears*) You're right. I want to scream at them, 'Leave me alone. I hate the lot of you'.

WILLIAM: Even now you don't feel independent of them? It seems as if you're blaming them for that?

ANDY: I am, but that's not right, is it?

WILLIAM: Let's look at this way: all the time we blame other people for how
            we are, we're refusing to take responsibility for how we are. How
            do you feel about that?

ANDY: That hurts, but you're right. What can I do about it, William?
            (*Tears of helplessness in his voice*).

WILLIAM: Andy, this is a major step forward for you, and I think you're brave
            to have taken such a step. It takes courage to accept some
            responsibility. The way ahead might not be easy; in fact it is often
            difficult. How do you think you'll handle that?

ANDY: I don't really know, but I'll have a go.

In session three William and I spent a lot of the time speaking about childhood and
adolescence and how I felt. I remember saying something like, 'the child needs to
be loved.' William picked this up and asked if I felt in need of love. That was too
direct for me, so I sidestepped it and talked about women. I'd never had much success
with them. 'What have I to give?' I really was putting myself down.

WILLIAM: In transactional analysis terms and of parent, adult, child, which
            mode do you think you operate mostly in?

            We had already discussed the PAC model.

ANDY: It has to be my child, probably a sulky, spoiled child.

WILLIAM: And how do you view our relationship?

ANDY: Adult, definitely. That's one of the good things about it. I thought
            you'd ask a lot of questions, you know, strip away all the layers of
            the onion, and get at the cause, why I'm like I am.

WILLIAM: And as that's not happening, how do you feel?

ANDY: OK. I like the adult bit, but I don't have to get rid of all my child
            do I? I wouldn't like that.

WILLIAM: No, certainly not, especially the free, spontaneous child. I often
            think that my child was stifled too much by responsibility too
            young, quite the opposite to you, from what you say.

Session Four

            We had agreed to make more use of imagery starting this session.

WILLIAM: Now you feel relaxed. Imagine a meadow on a warm, sunny
            afternoon. As you look around you will see a wood, and a hill, a
            stream and a house. Tell me what you imagine.

ANDY: It's a field of corn, sort of square, and the wood is in one corner
            behind me. The field stretches away to my right and up a hill. I
            can't imagine a house anywhere.

WILLIAM: How do you feel right now?

ANDY: I don't think I've any right to be here. I keep expecting to hear somebody tell me to get up and do something useful.

WILLIAM: I now want you to imagine you are lying down, looking up at the blue sky. Feel the corn rise above you, and then feel the full ears. Now imagine roots going down from you into the ground and merging with the roots from the corn. Stay with this for as long as you wish, and just take in what the image is telling you.

             He started to cry very softly, then spoke.

ANDY: I know this field is me, and I know it's been neglected. I got down a little way into the roots, then it got sort of scary. Part of me wanted to go right down, but there was another part that kept saying, 'watch out.'

WILLIAM: Tell that to the field, to the corn, to anything else that's there.

ANDY: (*Speaking aloud*) I'm sorry you've been neglected, I mean, I'm sorry I've neglected you.

             Towards the end of the session.

WILLIAM: Now we've talked that through, I see time is almost up, so I suggest you go back into the meadow, and see if it's changed in any way.

ANDY: Yes, it has changed. I'm now facing uphill, where the sun is shining. I'm telling the meadow I'll cultivate it and look after it. I won't allow other people to build concrete roads all over you, not all over my meadow.

WILLIAM: That's lovely. What does the meadow say?

ANDY: It's telling me that other people could not destroy it. It says that I and the meadow are bound together and only I can destroy it. But if I do, I will be destroying myself.

             Andy got up and looked out of the window, obviously struggling with some deep emotion. This was a powerful session for us both.

Session Five

ANDY: I'd like to talk about last week, if that's OK. I left with very mixed feelings; part of me kept wanting to cry, another part felt on a high, and another part kept saying, 'a lot of stupid rubbish'.

WILLIAM: That sounds pretty confusing. Which part won?

ANDY: The tears. When I got into my room, out they came. I'd wanted to cry here, you know, when I went to the window, but couldn't. Sorry.

WILLIAM: I guess that crying might seem as if you would be giving in, and that's something you're trying hard to deal with.

ANDY: You know that's right. I used to cry very easily, and my two brothers were always calling me names because of it.

WILLIAM: Such as?

ANDY: Oh, you don't want to hear them.

WILLIAM: Sometimes articulating the dreaded words often helps to remove their sting. Try it?

ANDY: 'Cry-baby', 'mummy's boy', 'girlie', 'softie'. That used to make me cry all the more.

WILLIAM: It sounds as if those arrows have left their barbs still in you. Could you just look at that. Close your eyes, and imagine being shot at.

ANDY: I see one arrow stuck right here, on my forehead. It's not a barbed arrow, it's one of the suction arrows we used to play with.

WILLIAM: So it's been there a long time?

ANDY: Years. How can I get rid of it?

WILLIAM: Imagine someone coming to your aid. This person is carrying a bottle of oil, and gently smears the place with oil, and slowly the suction starts to lessen. You feel the suction pad slipping, as the oil gets underneath. The person takes hold of the wood and gently pulls, and now it's gone. He hands you the arrow, and gently rubs the spot until all the soreness goes.

By the end of this directed imagery, Andy was crying. Crying often accompanies healing.

ANDY: You know, I really felt that. It was wonderful. You won't laugh? That man, it was our priest. I'm Catholic, not practising very much, but I was in church, in front of the altar. He took the holy oil, that's what it was.

WILLIAM: And now, let me guess, you feel that part is healed; the pain has gone?

ANDY: Not gone, but much better. I've been thinking about this imagery. I like it, and I've enrolled for a course of meditation, I think it will help me to get into this 'inner world' you talk about. I'm really determined to start taking control and not to blame others for what and who I am.

WILLIAM: That sounds fine. Now to your meadow. Feel like looking at it again?

ANDY: Sure. I'm looking at the hill, now I see there's a tree on top of it,
           but I'll leave the hill. Looking over to my right I see a great open
           space.

WILLIAM: What does it remind you of?

ANDY: Funny, it reminds me of years ago, when I was lost on the moors.
           I'd be about ten. Did I get a telling off when they found me.

WILLIAM: So this open space could be something to do with that, that
           feeling of excitement mixed with fear.

ANDY: That's very accurate, but I think I'll go on, just the same. I go a
           little way, but what strikes me is the loneliness, and I feel
           disappointed somehow, yet it looked so attractive.

WILLIAM: Could you link what you said about being lost with this new
           feeling of the open space. Imagine you are a child again, just
           setting off to explore.

ANDY: I'm scared. I want my three brothers to come with me, but they've
           run off in front, leaving me trying to catch up.

WILLIAM: How do you feel about that?

ANDY: Like a hanger-on, a nuisance.

WILLIAM: Like a pain in the bum to them? Why not you take control now,
           take the lead, and discover something.

ANDY: Right! I find a lorry, half buried in the ground. It's robust and
           durable, and won't be easily knocked down.

WILLIAM: And how about your brothers?

ANDY: Martin's OK about it. Funny, he says, I always knew you'd find it.
           The other two, they're jealous, because it's mine and they haven't
           got what I've got.

WILLIAM: That sounds pretty important. Perhaps we can both think about
           that before we next meet, but for now, it's time to leave the
           meadow and return to this room. In your own time...

Comment

When Andy was in the cornfield, and telling it how he had neglected it, this was a
representation of his inner world, possibly his imagination, possibly the feminine
principle. Corn represents the promise of fruitfulness, and is linked with Demeter
(Ceres), the goddess of the harvest.

What I did discuss with Andy was the possibility that what he had neglected
was his right brain function. I offered a short explanation of right/left brain
function, and how many of us do a good job of developing the left brain and neglect
the right brain functions. I suggested that his left brain was the part that was warning

him to be cautious of going too far into the root system, in fear of becoming lost. The left brain wants to be in control.

I also spoke of the psyche, striving for integration and wholeness, and told him that although his journey may, at times, be uncomfortable, and even painful, the psyche would always work for the ultimate good. This reassured him that he could learn to trust that part of himself.

It is helpful to end the session back in the meadow, particularly where discussion has taken the client out of it. While no great harm would result from closing the session there and then, it is a bit like leaving a book open; all sorts of things could happen. I also think that going back into the meadow does allow the client an opportunity to compare before and after.

Andy's experience with the 'holy oil' was one of those rare, hair-tingling moments of tapping into the client's unconscious. I had no idea that Andy was a Roman Catholic, but when he saw the arrow stuck on his forehead, I had a flash of a priest anointing the head with oil. Not wishing to 'direct' the imagery by suggesting a priest, I left it open for him to choose 'the man'. The choice of 'oil' has obvious links with healing. Sometimes I will get the client to imagine warm oil being poured gently on to a place that hurts.

On re-entering the meadow in the fifth session, and deciding to explore the vast open space, I interrupted him with a question, 'What does it remind you of?' I did this to inject a cautionary note, without actually saying, 'Watch out.' Wide open spaces can prove frightening, when landmarks disappear. This proved fruitful, for he made a link with a 'forgotten' memory. Not all open spaces are frightening; they can symbolise an enlarging of the horizons, and that is exciting and full of possibilities.

I asked him to discover something. I did this because I think it asserts his position, gives him some sort of kudos, a reward for taking the initiative. His discovery of the truck is worthy of interpretation. A vehicle represents movement (the wheels) and power (the engine). A lorry also represents something practical, something of use. Half buried represents not totally hidden, waiting to be discovered. Andy and I discussed this at his final session, and thought that he had discovered something precious about himself, half hidden in the subconscious.

As things were, the truck wasn't going anywhere, it needed digging out, and when it was dug out, it was found to be robust. Andy discovered that he had a lot more about him than his two brothers gave him credit for. He possessed something they did not have, and this gave him something to be proud of.

Andy never felt the need to come back for any more counselling, and he did well in his final exams, and took up a post in the Paediatric Unit.

Tracy
Integration and Rebirth

My name is Tracy and at the time I started in counselling I worked in a private psychiatric hospital in Hampshire. William and I had met when I attended one of his counselling workshops about three years before. I had been a 'client' for William who was demonstrating counselling to the group. The problem I presented was a real one, and that experience made such an impression on me that I knew whom to approach when my life started to turn upside down.

I had been feeling under tremendous pressure for some time, cried a lot, was experiencing nausea, had spots on my face and work had lost its appeal. William and I identified the major pressures as:

1. Doing a degree course.
2. Doing a demanding job.
3. Listening to other people.
4. My husband, Hamish, who is a self-employed builder.

Hamish supports me fully in my work and in my study, although he made it quite clear that he refused to have his life changed by it. This left me feeling burdened and stressed. Hamish wanted to start a family. I'd put off making that decision for as long as possible; there was something about the thought of having a child which I couldn't cope with. Anyway, I eventually agreed to start 'next year' (which was 1988).

A recurring theme throughout the early stages of counselling was my previous hospital and the feelings of inadequacy connected to it. I'd worked with imagery during the counselling demonstration, and found it helpful.

WILLIAM: Can you imagine what that inadequacy looks like?

TRACY: A picture is slowly emerging of a canyon.

WILLIAM: It might be scary, but can you look into the canyon?

TRACY: I'm looking into it, and you're right, it is scary, and it's something I don't want to do. Away to my right is the canyon with absolutely no way over, and it's too terrifyingly deep, rugged and steep to get into.

WILLIAM: So right at this moment you feel stuck, with no way to go, and nothing to help you?

TRACY: It's just total confusion, mixed with tremendous fear.

WILLIAM: Are you able to look at the confusion?

TRACY: A very small person, has appeared, ugly and misshapen. She repels me, and she won't go away.

WILLIAM: How do you feel about trying to make friends with her?

TRACY: She's starting to grow, now she's getting smaller. It's really weird.

WILLIAM: What do you want to do with her?

TRACY: All I want to do was make her look pretty and nice looking, and to be acceptable.

Through my tears I said to William, 'I can't do it all at once. I will do it, though'. By about session eleven, the child was not so ugly, and I liked her better. It was the first time I'd recognised just how low my self-esteem was, and certainly the first time I'd ever put it into a picture. I left that particular session feeling fragile, yet, in a strange way, stronger. We continued the imagery in the following session.

That canyon represented the experience of my last job. Only when we looked at it in this way did the full impact of those four years hit me. By this time I had come to accept that my self-esteem was at rock-bottom, the rocks at the bottom of the canyon. I couldn't take anything good about myself without qualifying it, or minimising it. Over the years I had grown up with the awful feeling and belief that I wasn't worth very much. That's why I had allowed people to walk all over me. I hit back at them, in anger, with aggression. Now I was beginning to face up the fact that I had a right to be me, a right to be alive.

Eight sessions was the time William and I had agreed on, so we spent some time reviewing where we had come from. Over the two months I had reached a decision. Ever since the counselling workshop I attended, the germ of an idea had been developing. I would train as a psychotherapist when my degree was finished. William encouraged me and asked me what I wanted to do about our relationship. Although psychotherapy was my long-term aim, I just knew that there was a lot of healing to be done before I could even think about pursuing that course. So William and I agreed a new, open-ended, personal therapy contract, which was to continue, including the introductory eight session, into a three-year relationship. If I'd known then what lay ahead, I wonder if I would have chickened out!

William and I started another phase of therapy when Hamish and I returned from a a month's holiday in the Bahamas. I didn't want to come back to all the problems. The Bahamas called me back, for I'd fallen in love with a handsome, fairly well-off Bahamian called John, a little younger than me. If there had been an opportunity, I'd have given myself to him. Having been confronted with my feelings so dramatically, it was painful for me to admit to William that now I wasn't sure if I loved Hamish. My feelings were in turmoil about whether I wanted our marriage to continue. Hamish didn't know, but suspected that something had gone on. What

I did tell him was that I wanted to go back to Bahamas and work there. I agreed with William not to make any decision for a month, although my heart was shrieking at me to get on the next plane. Although I had talked with William about Hamish, this was the first time I'd faced up to the fact that our marriage had a problem. More than that, I was having to make a choice.

In session thirteen I stated, 'Hamish and I have been together for fifteen years, and he's just the same as he was at the beginning. He often puts me down, never give me attention, and I don't love him any more'. As we talked, I accepted that the incident with John had only been the trigger to a lot of frustration, resentment and loss. Hamish hadn't done a lot for my confidence and self-esteem. He had remained dependent on me, and I no longer wanted that. I was no longer sure that I wanted the hard work of trying to put everything right again.

William asked if I thought I could tell Hamish that our marriage was on the rocks; I didn't think I could do that either. I'd never been a totally rational person, but now anything rational and logical had deserted me, and I felt bewildered, confused and uncertain. I had no idea which way to go. If only William could have given me some direction, told me what to do!

Part of me wanted to tell Hamish my feelings, that was probably my heart; another part, my head, looked at all the possibilities if I did. Another, more selfish reason, was that I didn't want any upsets just before my exam, but I wasn't sure if I could contain the uncertainty. William helped to put my feelings into focus: 'You can't face a future without him, yet you can't face a future with him'. In imagery I saw myself up very high, much higher than in a plane, and could see the horizon, perfect, although far off. This gave me hope that Hamish and I were entering a new phase in our relationship.

I did try talking to Hamish about our relationship, but he couldn't see that there was anything wrong with it. 'I'm still the same. You're the one whose changed.' This was true. I had changed and was still changing. I knew that if he didn't, or couldn't, change this would eventually cause a split. Yet I knew that just as William was enabling me to change, so, in some way, that's what I had to do for Hamish. William pulled me up with a very strong challenge: 'If he was like this when you lived together, why did you marry?' That was a question I didn't want to answer. 'It was convenient. We got a cheaper Council mortgage.' Saying it made me cringe. Was that really all it meant to me?

About a month after coming back from Bahamas, when I was still talking about John, William said, 'It sounds as if you are already emotionally divorced from Hamish.' To accept that would have been too threatening, and although it was near the mark, to have admitted it would have been too final. I changed it to 'separated'. Just admitting that helped in some strange way. For the very first time I began to feel anger, directed at John as well as myself. Slowly I was beginning to accept a degree of responsibility for what happened, or didn't happen. I'd tried to convince myself that I was innocent. I worked through to a grudging acceptance of the truth.

At one stage I asked William, 'Will I ever reach self-awareness?' I wanted him to say, 'Of course you will.' He simply said, 'Self-awareness is like going on a journey with many staging posts. Look back and see the various posts at which you've stopped on the way, the discoveries that have pulled you onward, then decide if you want to continue.'

I'd been in counselling for about six months before I felt free enough to talk about sex. William knew I didn't want children. That was the statement, but underlying that was a tremendous fear, not of the birth but of becoming pregnant. This was something that even just talking about it filled me with fear, although I'd no idea why, and it was something I'd never talked over with Hamish. That probably is an indication of the barriers we'd created. Added to that fear was the feeling that I already had one child – Hamish. So much of the time I was mother to his child. I wasn't sure that I could cope with a real-live baby, too.

It seemed that whenever Hamish and I were at loggerheads, I regressed into my ugly little girl, and I thought of myself as being horrible. My mother-in-law's sarcasm was a factor in this. It was painful for me to accept that I had taken on board so much of mother-in-law's low opinion of me, reinforced by Hamish. Why did I do this? Another painful admission: to gain favour with Hamish. No wonder my little girl felt so ugly and insignificant, and why I so often allowed Hamish to put me down in front of other people. I was able to talk this over with Hamish, calmly and rationally, and although it was difficult for him to accept, he really tried to see it from my point of view.

My relationship with my parents was, for most of the time, not easy. My mother was a very judgmental and critical person, qualities I was now striving so hard to overcome in myself. Just as Hamish and I had been brought closer through a crisis, so it was with my mother and me. Father had a suspicious growth removed from his gut. Mother needed my support then, and for probably the first time ever, spoke to me as a woman, not as her child.

A significant milestone was reached about nine months into counselling. I wanted to go on holiday to Italy with a girlfriend from college. Hamish and I had always gone away together, and I ran over with William how to put it to Hamish. William said, 'It sounds as if you need permission from Hamish?' It was that word 'permission' that stung me. 'Of course I don't need permission,' I jumped at him, but then knew that was exactly it. So that was something I had to work through before I even mentioned it to Hamish. By the time I did, it was said, not apologetically, not aggressively, but with conviction, that I was taking his feelings into account, but that this was something I wanted for me. Much to my surprise, he thought it was a good idea, and even offered to buy my ticket as a present, which I accepted. That holiday was wonderful; however, I was quite unprepared for the depth of feeling at missing Hamish. There was no question about it, Hamish and I were reaching a new level of understanding.

I had been complaining to William about Hamish, who had accused me of nagging. What William did say, which struck home, was that perhaps my nagging was my way of exercising control over Hamish, just as his way of putting things off was his way of trying to control me. At one stage I'd invited Hamish to join me in counselling, but he'd refused. Again, that was probably my wish to see him changed. Writing this now only emphasises just how *I* have changed and grown. Such perspectives would have been totally alien to me before I started counselling.

William challenged me once about making mother out to be the 'baddie', and said, 'What about your father?' I then had to face the truth that they had both rejected Hamish and me when they found out we were living together.

Mother didn't seem to understand children, and this was all tied up with rejection. Father was more understanding of me when I was small, but he couldn't cope with me as a young woman. In fact, on one occasion, he hit me so hard I had a black eye, and that was embarrassing. It was all the more embarrassing because it was linked with early menstruation, and not wanting to explain what I was doing by going into the bathroom when he was working on the stairs. So, I suppose I was now admitting to William that there were things about both my parents I needed to work through. Once I had begun to explore rejection, it seemed that I couldn't get rid of it, even in my dreams. One dream in particular was the start of a whole new adventure.

I was in an empty room, aware of a cupboard high up on a wall. There was a deep sense of foreboding, and I knew there was a ghost in that cupboard. When I re-entered the dream with William, it took a lot of courage to open the cupboard. When I did, water swept over me in several waves. When the cupboard was empty, it looked frightening, black and horrible. It looked like a coffin. When William asked who I could get to help me, Auntie Joan appeared. She said, 'It's my coffin'. William asked me if I could touch the coffin. When I said I couldn't, he asked if I could look into it, but that was too much for me and tears took over. Although I did not work directly with any of the elements of the dream, I was able to continue with the imagery and light gradually came in *through the ceiling* and the whole room was less frightening. The cupboard slowly changed into a flattened cardboard box.

At the time I wasn't at all clear how that dream fitted into the theme of rejection. All I know, is that I left that particular session feeling extremely fragile and that I'd been emptied of something, although I didn't know what. I realised that the collapsing of the box meant that its work was accomplished. I also wondered if the water that enveloped me was to do with birth. In a later session I re-entered that dream. This time I was able to crawl into the cupboard. Because of the water, I felt safe.

Over the weeks since the first encounter with the room, I'd come to the conclusion that the room represented my mother's rejection, and this became clearer the second time, as I came under my mother's powerful 'critical parent', which overwhelmed her 'caring parent'. As a result the child (me) was totally confused and browbeaten. Mother couldn't cope with my developing sexuality, and this, for me, was the ultimate rejection. I also came to the conclusion that because my mother was essentially critical and uncaring, I had not had much of a role model of caring.

At one stage, when I was talking of lack of caring, and crying at the same time, William cuddled me. It was a strange feeling. I felt secure and at the same time uncomfortable. We talked about these conflicting feelings, and came to the conclusion that somewhere within me I equated rejection with lack of physical contact. I could not remember the last time either of my parents had cuddled me. I think I must have been very young. That session was the anniversary of my coming to William, and he drew attention to the significance of that by asking, 'Is this low state an annual feeling?' I can honestly say, for the first time ever, I knew, without a shadow of doubt, that it was. But why did I always feel low around December? I also realised that this low feeling started, in fact, about mid-November. Had I suffered any bereavement about this time? That was it! Auntie Joan died toward the end of November. That was something new for me to work on.

As it happened, it was six weeks before I felt strong enough to explore it again. What that dream also did was to bring to the surface some of the fears I had about enclosed spaces; school assemblies, trains and crowds. I was always afraid of people being ill or sick. That sounds really weird, coming from a nurse! William took me back to the first time I consciously remembered feeling like that. My brother Trevor is two years younger than me, and I remembered watching him feeding from the breast and asking for a suck, to be told by mother, 'Don't be silly! Grow up'. I wondered if that was something to do with my jealousy. It was many months before I could speak to Trevor about my jealousy of him. When I did, it was a pleasant surprise to find how understanding he was. That moved us on to a more adult relationship.

Whether or not I suffered more rejection than anyone else, William said, was not relevant. It's what it meant to me that was important. William introduced me to the concept of the 'self-esteem bucket', and that some people seemed to have large buckets, others, small ones. Mine was a child's seaside bucket, and even that had holes in it. The holes had been punched in it by the rejection of my parents, but also by me. My sexual experiences with men had started quite young, and by the time I went to live with Hamish I was worried about how many men I'd been with.

Now, many years later, I realise that I felt shitty about myself, the same sort of feelings I had when mother said I was tainted. Now, with a lot of insight, I wonder just how much self-hurt I'd inflicted. This question directed at myself showed just how much growth had taken place; the question could never have been formed, and if it had been, I doubt if I would have had the courage to voice it. At the same time, I had no idea that emotional growth could create so much discomfort. I was helped to understand it when William used the analogy of the daffodil, which lies dormant for many months, yet in the end, if it is to bloom, must break through the hardness of the soil to seek the light.

That winter I had to take some time off sick, and when I returned, although still fragile, I felt more able to cope. For the first time I'd admitted to my boss that I wasn't the superstrong person who could cope with everything. My return coincided with the dramatic changes taking place within the NHS related to grading, which I felt as another rejection.

WILLIAM: What does that rejection look like?

TRACY: I see myself as a pile of rubble, at the foot of a broken-down wall, with no whole bricks visible.

WILLIAM: And what do you want to do with that rubble?

TRACY: Nothing. There's no strong desire to try to clear it up, or to try to make anything of it. There's no responsibility there, no hassle.

That surprises me – normally I would be consumed by the need to be up and doing. I just needed to feel OK at being part of a pile of rubble.

WILLIAM: I wonder what will be rebuilt?

TRACY: A wall, I suppose, that's what the rubble was.

WILLIAM: It might be something different.

TRACY: Might, but can't imagine what.

In another session, soon after starting her second year of counselling.

TRACY: I'm looking again at the heap of rubble, and surprise, surprise, I see a seed, lying dormant. I know it will grow into a tree, although I'm not sure what. I would like it to be evergreen, but in the end, I decide it will be a silver birch, beautiful in leaf, and also presenting a beautiful, leafless tracery against the winter sky.

WILLIAM: That image seems to something to do with birth?

TRACY: Probably, and does that relate to this dream that I often have, of being trapped in a giant pipe?

WILLIAM: It could be connected with your own birth.

TRACY: Maybe, but right now this isn't something I could cope with.

I looked at the seed from time to time, and it lay dormant for a long time. What was interesting was the relationship of the seed to the wall. The wall was an enigma. It served no purpose, other than to protect the pile of rubble, and therefore, the seed. William asked me to try to project myself forward in time, to see what the seed was doing. It was now a tree, and the wall had disappeared. So, whatever purpose it once served, it was now redundant. We wondered if it was some sort of façade. William suggested that at some stage I might need to transform the heap of rubble into a medium suitable for the seed to grow. I accepted this, but wasn't yet ready.

About half-way through my time with William I realised that my seed had grown into a sapling, about a foot high, still on the rubble, but looking healthy. This growth, I felt, was linked to my growing self-esteem, and to the fact that I'd forgiven my parents for the pain they caused me. All this meant that I was quite content to leave my sapling where it was. It would grow in its own good time. Having reached the stage of forgiveness, William and I were then able to explore again my own part in the pain, for example, my conquests of boys while at college. I no longer felt proud of that period.

A nightmare I had led me into a fruitful imaginary journey of discovery. Hamish and I were walking down some steps, but it was too frightening to go any further. I chalked an X on the wall, for I knew I would return. When we started to climb back up, the stairs kept moving, as if I was trying to climb a downward moving escalator. That was scary, so I asked Hamish to stop the movement and let me off.

WILLIAM: How do you feel about going back into the dream?

TRACY: I don't know why, but I felt I can't take Hamish with me.

WILLIAM: Look for something to take with you as a guide.

TRACY: I'll take a lantern to guide me through the dark and frightening tunnel ahead. My mind keeps leaping ahead, but my body doesn't want to follow.

WILLIAM: Something feels really scary. Just take deep breaths, and tell yourself you can do it.

TRACY: I'm moving slowly along the tunnel. Just around a bend I see a fierce cat, but there's no time to explore that image, for the tunnel keeps closing behind me. I'm really terrified now, William. I need Hamish.

WILLIAM: Visualise Hamish holding the other end of the length of stout string, which you've held on to all the way through.

TRACY: Thank you, that's better. I think the tunnel closing around me are the constraints put upon me by my parents.

WILLIAM: Try loving the tunnel.

TRACY: I'm gently stroking the walls. Now they're revolving rapidly, yet giving me much more space and freedom to breathe. I'm turning back, and I confront the cat. It's snarling and spitting, quite ferocious.

WILLIAM: Try befriending it.

TRACY: I began to fuss it up, now it doesn't want to leave me.

WILLIAM: This might be too soon, but how do you feel about integrating the cat into yourself?

I didn't want to integrate it, so we left that for another occasion. I didn't like admitting that this angry spitfire was me. We wondered if it was this I was afraid of meeting in my dreams of tunnels. We did, in fact, explore other tunnels, which all seemed to be minor ones; it was as if I was delaying something, not being able to explore the major one. In one of them I discovered a little mouse wearing a red jacket. I liked that. He became my mascot of confidence. It was around the end of my second year in counselling, and it was winter. Somehow I knew I was going to get through what had become a dreaded date on the calendar.

Fresh insight had come, related to Christmas and my low feelings around that time. I'd associated it with Auntie Joan's death, and that was partly it, but there had to be more. Through discussing a dream, the details of which are not important, I just knew that it was the pain, bitterness and resentment surrounding the Christmases when Hamish and I lived together and were not permitted to visit my parents together. They would have allowed me to visit, but not Hamish. I couldn't stand that, so I didn't go, either. Some of these insights I felt free to discuss with Hamish, for he was part of them. Others I kept to myself.

I know perfectly well that I'd kept putting off coming back to my first tunnel, but as I was going to have a break from counselling, to go away on a course, I needed to reenter it. The steps were the same, although I no longer needed to be tied to Hamish. There was now a rock almost blocking the entrance to the tunnel, with only enough room for me to squeeze through. My cat was there, but no longer unfriendly.

Previously he had looked like a tiger, now he was a lion, which I called Leo. Together we went through the tunnel and came to a bright, blinding light. I was afraid. 'I don't know if there is anything to step out on.' William suggested a ladder. I went across an abyss of great depth. The other side went on indefinitely. I didn't want to go any further. I came back and Leo was waiting for me. I didn't want to leave him. I absorbed him into my body through my legs. I know he represented strength and courage. 'I can pull him out at any time. Only I know he's there.' I knew that I didn't have to explore the tunnel any more. I hadn't recognised my own strength and courage, which had been proven by what I had achieved in my journey.

In early January, my old cat, Thomasina, became very ill. She had been with us ever since we started living together. As a nurse I'd coped with death, of course, but this was the first time, since Auntie Joan, that I was having to face letting go a part of me. William didn't think it at all bizarre to be talking with me about a dying pet. Although I had William to talk to, Hamish only had me, and I was aware of trying to *give* him insights that were for me. That was a valuable lesson; that we can never give anyone our own insights. However, it was painful for me to watch Hamish struggling.

Her death was more than the death of a pet; she was a symbol of our relationship. I felt, in many ways, that she'd kept us together; the one thing we'd shared all those years. William helped me understand, by putting into words what I felt but hadn't verbalised. Thomasina was like the child we'd never had.

It was a red-letter day when I told William that mother had apologised for the way she treated Hamish and me all those years ago. There were tears between us, as I told her that I had been able to forgive her. William and I talked about unfinished business, and how it had been essential for me to forgive myself before I could find it in my heart to forgive my mother.

One of the bits of 'unfinished business' was Auntie Joan's death. I hadn't had the chance to say 'goodbye' properly. I know she thought of me, for she left me some of her jewellry, which I often wear. It had taken me almost three years of work to admit my anger that she had left me. Tears, yes, but I was also angry at the way she died. I also realised that I hadn't let go of her. I had always said I was agnostic, until William asked, 'Are you angry at God?' Had he asked that even a year before, I would have denied the very existence of God. Now I found myself questioning the reality of God, rather than his existence.

The realisation about not letting go was brought sharply into focus when our training group was viewing a video on the subject. William was the facilitator. The film touched us all very deeply, and I related this to my journey. I told the group about Auntie Joan, and as I did so, I saw her quite clearly, standing in front of my parents, and much larger. This broke me. She was not even a relative, yet I had invested so much emotion into her memory. She had assumed far greater significance to me than my parents who were still alive.

When William and I next met, I knew this was something I had to work on. I imagined myself in a room with several other people. I was writing a letter, which said 'Dear Auntie Joan, I have to say goodbye'. As I wrote, I saw myself tied to Auntie Joan's apron strings, and was unable to separate from her. I took her along a candle-lit passage to Chris (the man in the video). There was a tremendous struggle as I tried to separate myself. Eventually, after what seemed ages of tears, I managed this and passed through a door, not into the light-filled room of the video, but into a sun-lit field, where there was an eagle and a lion. The eagle represented freedom. Although I had separated, I knew there was still the slenderest of threads still attaching us, and it felt OK.

With a little more work I was able to attach the thread to a harness, which meant that I could choose to take it off and when. Suddenly, and totally outside of my control, I was being taken up by the harness into a helicopter, and with lightning speed was being transported, no longer in the helicopter, down a tunnel. I could see light at the end. The tunnel was pulsating and contracting. I had the impression of being in a tube-train, with the walls flashing past. Then I was sitting facing away from the light.

Then out of the blue I realised what was happening. This was the birthing process. It was ages before I was 'born'. In a curious 'double take', I was both a baby and the watching mother. I felt myself being held upside down, and felt the pain when the cord was cut. I saw father running to tell Auntie Joan. Felt really good, but exhausted, when it was all over. I can't describe my tears, or the healing which that incredible, profound experience brought. I knew, then, that Auntie Joan and I were finally separated, and that mother and I were very much closer, indeed, bonded. At that stage, and through many tears, I said to William. 'Now I'm ready to try for a baby'.

Comment

Tracy is a sensitive, caring woman who finds it difficult not to take on other people's burdens. She initially presented in a slightly disjointed way; she expressed a lot of negative feelings, and felt she was not getting anywhere. Session three was essentially a practical one, as I helped her work out a structure for her first clutch of essays. We both agreed that this was necessary to relieve some of the immediate anxiety. Some counsellors would not see this as part of the role; my belief is that if that is how the client wishes to use the time, then it is client's choice, particularly if it does have a direct bearing on the process.

The essay results were excellent, and were a tremendous boost to her morale and self-esteem. Throughout her academic work she was pushed by a powerful drive to achieve. Not only did she have to achieve good grades; they had to be the best, and she was dissatisfied with anything less than an A grade. This drive to achieve added greatly to her stress levels.

When Tracy was talking about her other self, we followed on with a discussion about her child. It seemed obvious that Tracy had invested in this little girl all her own unacceptable characteristics. Healing would only be achieved to the degree by which she felt able to own that child as part of herself.

The relationship between Tracy and Hamish was often disturbed by rows, quite aggressive ones, with objects being thrown by both of them. Tracy's behaviour pattern was to sulk, or to withdraw. The way she was speaking conjured up a picture of a child. I suggested to her that this was her child reacting to the critical parent in Hamish. She had done some work with transactional analysis previously, so this gave her a real life situation to work on. Tracy said that she is often in the critical parent mode. She thought that her nurturing parent was seldom around with Hamish.

By session 11, things were happier between Tracy and Hamish; she'd taken him some flowers, and he'd helped her with an essay. He's a very clear thinker and helps her cut through some of her woolly thinking. In many ways they complement each other.

Session 13 seems to have been a turning point. For the first time Tracy had been prepared to look at the possible failure of their marriage. The fact that she couldn't decide to live with Hamish or without him was an indication that the line had not yet been crossed.

The relationship between Tracy and Hamish was very strained after their return from the Bahamas. Tempers were short, Hamish was puzzled and hurt by her refusal to make love. At one stage she said to me, 'Whenever he starts, I see John, not Hamish. I can't make love to a mirage'. If John was a 'mirage', he occupied a great deal of many sessions, as Tracy slowly worked him out of her system. Only as she did so was she able to let Hamish assume his rightful place.

Many times in my relationship with Tracy I was conscious of holding a delicate creature in my hand, a creature that needed nurturing and careful attention, if she was to survive. The most accurate analogy would be a chrysalis, with all the promise of a beautiful butterfly.

The journey toward self-awareness, of course, will never be completed all the time we are clothed with the garments of mortality, but when we step into that river, as we think of it, we shall never be totally satisfied if we step out and refuse to get our feet wet again. The journey along the river often brings pain and discomfort, as we are faced with painful decisions of letting go. When we do reach a particular staging post of decision, it is as if unless we let go, we are unable to proceed, and we become stuck.

About six months into counselling, I introduced Tracy to Jung's theory about the shadow, and how we often invest into our shadow all the things about ourselves that we do not like and wish to hide away. She recognised this in her ugly little girl. Yet, for integration to take place, we have to accept our shadow. As she reflected on this she admitted that for much of the time she tries to present a glittering, coping persona, which is frequently a denial of her true self.

Quite often during our relationship, Tracy would arrive and announce, 'I don't seem to have anything particular to talk about today'. This is a curious phenomenon in counselling. It is possible that there really is nothing pressing on the client's mind; it could mean that things are improving and the client is experiencing a sense of wellbeing. It could also mean that there is something which is not yet ready to be brought into consciousness. Whatever the reason, I generally find it useful to encourage the client to sit quietly and wait, certainly not to engage in small talk. In Greek mythology Psyche is referred to as a butterfly. If we approach a person's psyche in that way, delicately, softly, cautiously, we shall be rewarded with watching it open up like the wings of a peacock butterfly. Rush in, and the beautiful creature will be scared off.

One of the most precious things about counselling is watching the growth of the client. Growth is seldom visible from day to day. One does not measure a growing child every day. Parents very often do not see the growth that has taken place, until, for example, the child needs a new pair of shoes, or a new school uniform. So with clients; they very often are unaware of the growth taking place within them. That is why I think it is important, from time to time, and particularly in long-term work, to take a look at where we have come from.

When counselling has taken place over a long period, the original reason(s) may have faded into insignificance. Counselling is like taking a journey; we know from where we have come, and roughly the route taken, but on looking back, the starting point has become obscured, partly through distance, but also through time. Unlike a journey, it is necessary for both counsellor and client to look back in order to firmly establish the final position. Looking back to where and why the journey began may prove difficult; feelings, as well as memories, fade with time. Looking back is not always comfortable. It may reveal obstacles not previously recognised.

One of the things I've discovered is that when listening to clients I often experience something happening within me, such as physical pain, or the need to cry, or just that 'ouch' in the pit of my stomach. At first I used to try to control what was happening, so that it didn't intrude. I thought that if I did disclose what was happening within me, it would get in the way. Through my own therapy I have been able to use this in a positive way, by offering it to the client as something that may also be happening within her or him. In Tracy's case, usually whenever I this happened, it led to new exploration.

In session 35, Tracy, who had been struggling for several weeks with the subject of rejection, recounted the dream about the cupboard. Confronting a person with aspects of a dream takes a lot of courage on both sides. I had to be fairly sure that Tracy had the psychological strength to try, and that I would have the sensitivity not to push her beyond her ability to cope.

I am always very careful about interpreting dreams, preferring to ask the client, 'What does that mean to you?' It is also dangerously easy now, with several years of hindsight, to work through it with some degree of certainty. So, bearing this in mind, this is how I might have interpreted it.

The cupboard represents something that contains. This may mean the unconscious, or closed mind, or the past. It may also mean the womb. The possibility of the womb seems to be confirmed by the water – the waters breaking. Tracy did not want children, and it is possible that there was a deep fear underlying that. The fact that Auntie Joan appeared when Tracy was working on rejection suggests a link between her and Tracy's parents. She is the one who brought about a reconciliation, but she died before Tracy and Hamish could be married. So she was not alive to see the fruits of that reconciliation.

I also wonder if Tracy, by not wanting children, was rejecting her parents and punishing them for their rejection. Subsequent events do seem to support this hypothesis. A coffin represents death and decay, the past. Whatever that meant to Tracy, it was too difficult for her to handle, even to touch the coffin. In any case, the cupboard (and the symbolic coffin) changed their character. This is a useful point to pause and explore.

In all psychotherapeutic work, therapist and client must learn to trust the psyche. The psyche is constantly searching for, and working towards, wholeness and integration, and if we are patient, it will lead us gently on. By waiting, Tracy and I were able to experience a gradual change from darkness to light, *through the ceiling*. The direction by which light came seems to suggest 'from above'. 'Above' suggests the sun, warmth and life. In the end, the cupboard changed into a flattened cardboard box, something quite ordinary and useful, and not at all frightening. Tracy re-entered that room several times more during the course of counselling, and each time there was something new to explore. This brings out an important principle: if I had taken charge of the direction, I might well have assumed that one, or at least two, visits to the room would have emptied it. But no, that was not the case, and it seldom is. Let the client always be in control, and trust the client's psyche to travel in the direction and at the pace most appropriate to the client.

In one session Tracy related a dream, in which she was counselling, and I was sitting behind her. I interrupted the client to seek clarification. Tracy was indignant and, when the client had gone, I told her how useless she was, and that I didn't want to see her again. We discussed this, and her interpretation was that she feared rejection from someone whom she respected.

This could be an indication of transference. In a way, Tracy is saying she has put me on some sort of pedestal, this is often an indication of transference, where the therapist can do no wrong. At the end of the session, after the break of five weeks, I wrote, 'I feel she has achieved a lot of growth since we last met, and done a lot of thinking'. Perhaps that time out was necessary for her to consolidate the gains she'd made over the first year.

In session forty-four, Tracy again spoke about the seed, which was still lying dormant, but did not cause her concern. She spoke about death and rebirth. I now want to spend some time on the details of that session, for it marks a significant stage in the therapeutic process.

She had gone back to her quarrel with Hamish, and how she felt so much pain as she lay crying on the bed. This is the dialogue.

WILLIAM: Where is the pain?

TRACY: In my head.

WILLIAM: A bright light will come and reveal things to you.

TRACY: Helplessness. Can't cope.

WILLIAM: What does this helplessness look like?

TRACY: A little girl. She doesn't want to be touched, and certainly not cuddled.

Tracy wasn't at all sure if she wanted this little girl to come out. I felt somewhat helpless. I felt that integration was essential, but how? Whenever I experience this helplessness, and don't know what to do, I just wait, and stay with the image as I see it.

WILLIAM: Take the little girl by the hand and go outside where it is bright.

TRACY: Where?

WILLIAM: Take her into your meadow.

TRACY: Now what?

WILLIAM: Look around. A house will appear, take the little girl towards it, and when you get there, go inside.

TRACY: I can't, it's not mine.

WILLIAM: You have the owner's permission. Now explore the rooms, and introduce the little girl to the house.

TRACY: I don't want to go upstairs. (*This was said with great resistance.*)

WILLIAM: Somewhere downstairs you will find a bedroom that is to be the little girl's.

TRACY: She doesn't want to stay here. She wants to come with me.

This was a positive sign of the move towards integration.

WILLIAM: Is there anything you want to do with the little girl?

TRACY: Give her a hug.

WILLIAM: How can you integrate her?

TRACY: By her hugging me. She keeps coming in and out of me, and there are still two of us. (*This was said through many tears.*)

WILLIAM: Keep me in touch with what's happening.

TRACY: I'm carrying her now in front of me, but I can't close the door. She's in the way.

WILLIAM: How can you work on that?

TRACY: She's now inside of me.

WILLIAM: How does it feel?

TRACY: Fairly comfortable.

WILLIAM: Close the door and go back into the meadow. Then in your own time, return to this room.

We had agreed the previous week to increase the length of time so that we could work on imagery. As so often, I didn't interpret what took place, and Tracy didn't seem to want to discuss it. She needed time to integrate what, in my opinion, was something significant. She had started the session with a great deal of resistance to integrating the little girl, probably the same one we'd met very early on in the relationship.

It is always difficult to portray the depth of feeling in a session such as this. It was intense and powerful, and I was conscious of something like the birthing process. Yet in another way, I wondered if this was an image of conception and pregnancy. This style of working requires, for me, an ability to enter fully into the struggle taking place, yet to have the ability to remain the counsellor. It is as if I am attached to the outside world with a very strong elastic cord that pulls me back in order to help move the client on.

Tracy's seed lay dormant for a very long time, waiting for the correct season. At the end of one particular session, when we'd looked again at the rubble and the seed, I wrote 'Will Tracy's journey be complete when she reconstructs the heap and the tree is grown?' Tracy had become much more confident, and I wondered if the new-found strength came from her seed that was about to burst.

Tracy's imagery of the tunnel took place over several sessions. It is difficult to always find words to express some experiences. The inner struggle that Tracy engaged in during that imagery was rewarding in its outcome. She was afraid of tunnels and confined spaces anyway, and to choose to enter imagery that focused on a tunnel was very brave of her.

The first part of the imagery – stairs – represent a connection between the conscious and the unconscious, just as stairs are a connection between the upper and lower worlds. My study of mythology and symbols immediately conjured up the picture of Ariadne and her magic ball of thread and the labyrinth of the Minotaur. A person does not need to know the story to be able to relate to the image. String (or cord) also represents birth and rebirth, the umbilicus, and in this instance, an image of safety and return. Tracy herself gave an interpretation of the tunnel closing in around and behind her as the constraints of her parents. To my mind there seemed a very strong feeling of this representing birthing, which Tracy could see as a possibility.

When animals, particularly ferocious ones, appear in imagery, they often indicate some part of the person, usually kept well-hidden, suppressed. Tracy's cat, appearing as it did underground, probably represented part of her dark side. After she had made friends with it, I said to her, 'Ask its name'. She said quite sharply, 'You know perfectly well who it is; it's Tracy'. When Tracy didn't want to integrate the cat, I said to her 'Tell it you will be back soon'. This was important, for it told both Tracy and the cat that there was still work to do. It was almost five months before we re-entered the main tunnel.

In my work with imagery, I am constantly amazed how clients often tap into timeless, archetypal images. It is doubtful that Tracy could have known the full meaning of the transformation of her tiger into a lion. Firstly, the blazing stripes of the tiger give it its name. The tiger is linked with Dionysus, the Greek God of ecstasy and wine (the Roman god, Bacchus), and Dionysus married Ariadne. Thus, another link was made between the string image and the tiger. The tiger is associated with wrath, cruelty, darkness and the unbridled expression of the base instincts. It represents the wild beast. The lion corresponds principally to god and to the sun, hence it is often found as a symbol for sun-gods, such as Mithras. It also represents the masculine principle.

So, for Tracy, this transformation from tiger to lion, with its strength and courage, was highly significant, the more so as she wanted to integrate him, *through her legs*. At first this puzzled me. On reflection, legs symbolise strength, stability, support, mobility, independence, standing alone. Tracy, unconsciously, was integrating part of her that she had recognised previously (the tiger), but had been unwilling to integrate; over the intervening weeks, however, it had been transformed into something positive. And certainly her journey up to that time had taken a great deal of courage.

The final session before her planned three-month break was taken up dealing with her anticipated grief over the approaching death of Thomasina. To me, grief is grief, no matter what the person is grieving for. This event, and the period that followed, helped Tracy to get in touch with previously untapped feelings. Grief over a pet very often taps into previous unresolved or partially unresolved grief and affords the person a further opportunity to work through it. I wondered if Tracy was ready to do imagery work to see where Thomasina was, but she wasn't.

When Tracy finished her course, she seemed to be in something of a backwater; all this was tied up with her feelings about one of the tutors on the course. We talked about how much energy it takes, for example, a bit of wood, to escape from a backwater, instead of going round and round and not getting into the flow of the stream. Sometimes the only way for it to escape is for a greater flow of water to change the pressure, and so effect a release.

Tracy's work with letting go of Auntie Joan was beautiful. She was approaching three years in counselling, and it had been obvious from the start that something like this would have to happen before she could integrate the reality of Auntie Joan's death. Jung speaks of synchronicity, the coming together of two events which have psychological significance. My showing of the video at that precise time coincided with Tracy's stage of growth. Of all the people in that group, and we were all touched by it in some way, it seemed to mean the most to Tracy. There is no telling, of course, what impact it has had subsequently on the others. Watching other people in the video go through the agonies of letting go helped her. Not only was she able to let go of Auntie Joan, but she began to view her parents with a different perspective, which holds hope for improved relationships there.

Tracy's final major work, her rebirthing, was probably one of the most profound experiences I have been privileged to share as a therapist; hers and Phil's in the Fourth Journey. There were several times during our hundred sessions when it looked as things were heading that way. When it came it took us both by surprise, because it was neither planned nor engineered.

The separation from Auntie Joan was but one of the elements that made this possible, and this event must be viewed from the perspective of three years' work.

There had been the building up of Tracy's self-esteem, which involved her husband and her family. She had achieved a great deal of integration of the dark side of herself, and had worked through a great deal of pain and guilt. The relationship between herself and her immediate family had improved. She had been able to let go of Auntie Joan and to replace her with her parents. All these were antecedents in the final adventure. Tracy and Hamish now have a delightful daughter.

Hazel
The Brass Candlestick

My name is Hazel, and at the time I came for counselling I was a general student nurse, doing my stint in psychiatry. It was one of the staff who recommended I spoke to William. Although the work was stressful, I think I could have coped if my life had been happier. My parents had split up two years before and their recent divorce was still fresh in my emotions. Father is a solicitor, a very introverted man, who has never found it easy to communicate with people, other than on a professional basis and this made it hard for me when I was so upset. He now has another partner; Mother doesn't have anyone else. I feel torn apart, for they both make different and difficult demands on me, as well as dealing with my younger brother and sister who both live with mother. The stress shows itself by my being swamped by feelings of low self-worth and hopelessness, being very irritable and very often reduced to tears.

WILLIAM: You used the word 'hopelessness': can you imagine what it looks like?

HAZEL: What a strange thing to ask me, but I'll try. Now that's really weird, I image quite clearly a brass candlestick. There's no candle in it and it looks as if it hasn't been cleaned in an age.

On the face of it, there seemed no logical connection between hopelessness and a brass candlestick. It might be stretching a point, but possibly the association is with light, being the opposite of darkness, and the empty candlestick was saying, 'There is no light, therefore there is no hope. But there could be'.

WILLIAM: Perhaps the candlestick is you, and that something within you has been neglected.

HAZEL: I can go along with that.

By the end of the first session, William had given me a lot to think about and a couple of strategies to use to help with the stress. I felt that at last that someone had heard my unspoken feelings about myself.

Session two was a surprise. William had brought a brass candlestick, that had been stored in a cupboard for years, and was badly in need of polishing. It wasn't of much value as it was; I asked if I could take it away and clean it.

WILLIAM: Let's use this as an object lesson. Last week you said it represented your feelings of hopelessness. I've been thinking about that, and wonder how you feel it relates to your self-esteem, and your feelings of being useless and helpless.

She sat looking into the distance for several seconds.

HAZEL: I have a memory one of my teachers who always used to put me down, and told me not to set my sights too high, or I would come a cropper. I feel bloody angry, at her, but also against my parents. I'm not comfortable expressing that. I'd rather talk about a strange dream. I had lost a male patient on a desert island, and it was my fault.

WILLIAM: Male patient? Lost? What do you associate with those words?

HAZEL: My father, and perhaps I feel I've lost him. Perhaps, somehow, I did think it was my fault, or that I should have been able to prevent the split up.

WILLIAM: And this feeling of responsibility weighs quite heavily on you?

HAZEL: Yes, silly isn't it? Why should I? They're old enough. That's the logical part, but I do feel it.

She looked as if she was about to cry, but bit her lip.

WILLIAM: It looks as if you're head is struggling with your heart, right now.

HAZEL: (*Smiled, then said*) Let me tell you another dream, a few nights ago. I was admiring a vast lake and wondering what lay in the depths. There was an island in the middle, but it was too far away for me to see what was on it.

WILLIAM: I wonder if that lake is something to do with your untapped resources, things that lie beneath the surface.

HAZEL: Thank you, that's very encouraging. What resources lie beneath my surface?

I left that session with two more ideas to help me cope. I often caught myself thinking, 'I'm no good'. William suggested I replace this with 'I'm effective', to write it down and put it somewhere prominent so that I'd read it often. The second idea was a roundabout. I could imagine things quite well, so I was to imagine myself on a roundabout, which carried a huge label 'negative thinking'. I was to imagine going round very fast, and then to slowly stop it and step off and go through a door marked 'positive thinking'. I found this worked really well.

Third and Final Session

HAZEL: I've done the best I could with your candlestick, William, but there are still some marks I can't get off, sorry.

WILLIAM: It looks really good, thank you. Let's leave on the table. You sounded really disappointed that you couldn't do a better job.

HAZEL: I am. It took me ages, and really enjoyed doing it, you know, bringing it back to look bright again.

WILLIAM: So getting things perfect is important to you?

HAZEL: That's spot on. I don't like failure, coming secondbest. I feel I have to listen to my father's grumbling, and my mother's grumbling, and if I don't listen, then I'm a failure.

WILLIAM: It sounds as if you really are blaming yourself for their failed marriage.

HAZEL: I knew it sounded silly when I said it. I would like to be more assertive, but find it incredibly difficult. This is something I must work on.

WILLIAM: Hazel, several times you've referred to what you've said or felt as being silly. It sounds as if you might feel I'm judging you, a bit like a parent who always says 'Oh stop being silly'.

HAZEL: Right again. I was always being told I was silly, mainly by my father. He was so logical and I wanted to read fairy stories and fantasy things. So yes, I think I was afraid of you judging me, like he did.

WILLIAM: Mm.

HAZEL: I seem to be dreaming a lot these last few weeks. Is it all right to tell you another? I was on top of a partly broken down wall. Behind it lay the 'secret garden'. Outside was all bright and green; inside was cold and grey. I needed to be helped down from the wall.

WILLIAM: That sounds like a contradiction. The secret garden, yet it's dark and grey. Not a very nice garden. If that garden was you, how would you feel?

HAZEL: I think that's it. Inside I'm pretty miserable, outwardly I'm OK, put up a good front.

WILLIAM: And the wall?

After discussion I thought the walled garden was really me, and the wall was the defences I'd built around myself, although now they were partly broken, and that I must accept that I needed help. As I looked again at the dismal scene behind the wall I felt very sad. Perhaps one of these days I may re-enter counselling, and try to discover more what lies behind the wall.

Comment

Hazel came for only three sessions, but whenever we met in the college after that, she was coping well. She felt caught in a tug-of-war between her parents, and this added to the stress she felt. Many people cope very well with stress at work, provided they are relatively stress-free in their personal lives. She was an introverted person (this was her own assessment) and as such she would prefer to solve problems by herself, so it was fortuitous that her charge nurse had her confidence enough to suggest she contact me.

The first session, because her need was urgent, was carried out in the side ward of a large psychiatric hospital, with patients milling around outside in the corridor. As the college counsellor I made myself freely available and very often went to the students if they were unable to come to me.

Hazel's image of a tarnished brass candlestick is full of symbolism. Brass is a durable yet workable alloy. A candlestick is both functional and decorative. Hazel's candlestick had no candle in it, so it was not functional; its beauty was marred by it being tarnished. So, all in all, it was of not much value, although it had potential. The light given by a candle is functional; it illuminates and shows the way. A candle also has a spiritual significance. For Hazel, the candlestick probably represented herself, although she originally imaged this as her hopelessness. Her feeling of hopelessness made her feel useless, like a tarnished, unused candlestick, badly in need of being cared for. This was a powerful image, and although Hazel didn't cry (probably because the environment was not supportive), she was deeply moved.

One of the two strategies I offered her was *Thought-stop*, which is used to bring negative thoughts under control. Every time a negative thought enters the mind, it is ruthlessly pushed out by a conscious effort of the will, by saying, either mentally or aloud, STOP! This brings thinking under the person's control, rather than the person being controlled by the thoughts. The second strategy was learning to relax. Very often I would teach clients progressive, deep relaxation; sometimes, however, circumstances or the environment are not conducive to that, so a shorter form is useful. By concentrating on one part of the body, such as the right arm, for example, and inducing deep relaxation there, one finds that the whole body becomes relaxed. Of equal importance, is that the mind also becomes relaxed.

Self-esteem is like a delicate, fragile flower, so easily mutilated by thoughtless words. The wounds we carry from such thoughtlessness often remain unhealed and cause much pain. People in authority, parents and school teachers particularly, because of their positions of power, can so easily wound sensitive children. Hazel found this out, as she recalled the put-down by her teacher. Hazel's first dream (of the lost patient) evoked emotion, and the conclusion reached did seem to point to the feeling that she had lost her father. A desert island is also a lonely place, from which escape is difficult. At the same time, land in the middle of sea indicates a solid base, however small, but it is also vulnerable to being swamped by rough seas.

Hazel's inability and frustration at not being able to remove all the stains from the candlestick provided an excellent opportunity for looking at an aspect of her personality, not being satisfied with anything less then perfection. Linked with this was the feeling of failure, which led into an exploration of how her family expected her to be able to cope with anything, and her feeling of failure when she didn't cope, when she wasn't the perfect person she felt they expected her to be. Although I didn't suggest to her the image of tug-of-war, it is often a useful analogy to offer people, with its emphasis on one side winning. A related image is to get the person to imagine being the rope, and to feel the strain.

In three sessions Hazel achieved a great deal of insight. In addition she found out how to use a few techniques that will stand her in good stead wherever she is.

Janice
The Picture Gallery

I am Janice, a 27-year-old art teacher who came into counselling because my relationships with men were always going wrong. I would find myself sexually attracted to certain men, but after a time the relationship fizzled out, and I was left feeling depressed. When this happened several times, my self-esteem and self-worth took a severe bashing, and I thought it was time to do something about it. I met William through a mutual friend, so I thought I'd give counselling a try.

My parents split up when I was 13; being an only child I found that devastating. Father remarried, and has children; mother didn't remarry, although she has a regular man friend. I decided to move away from Birmingham for various reasons, but mainly because of the relationship with my mother. During my 12 sessions with William I took a long, hard look at the way I related to both my parents, and to my male partners. I discovered that I was harbouring a great deal of anger toward my father, because he had left me. It wasn't just anger, it was the feeling of loss, something I hadn't recognised. This was released through the use of imagery. As an artist, this was a medium I could enter into without difficulty, although at times it was so painful I couldn't carry on with it.

WILLIAM   Just now when we were talking about feeling lonely, you used the word 'aloneness'. Can you imagine what that aloneness looks like?

JANICE   I feel it here, in my chest; now I'm immediately in a large, empty cave.

Janice was so overwhelmed by emotion of this great emptiness, that her tears rolled out like two waterfalls.

WILLIAM   There's obviously something very powerful about this cave, some powerful feelings.

JANICE   The cave isn't dark, but I feel tremendous fear.

WILLIAM   Do you feel able to explore the cave?

JANICE   I think so. I see what looks like a picture gallery, though they don't look like pictures, more like wallpaper.

WILLIAM   What is the feeling as you look at them?

JANICE   I want to destroy them.

WILLIAM   Hang on a minute, Janice. These seem to be too important to
           destroy.

JANICE   I agree, somehow it wouldn't be right to do so, although I really
           don't know why.

WILLIAM   Imagine a spotlight directed at the pictures, and see what happens.

JANICE   Yes, I can imagine the light shining on the pictures. Now that's
           strange, two childhood memories have surfaced. One is of me, at
           around the age of three, sitting on my father's knee, watching a
           regular TV programme. Somehow, and I'm not sure how, I just
           knew that my mother wanted to be with father, to have her for
           herself.

WILLIAM   And how do you feel now, remembering that scene?

JANICE   I feel intensely jealous, just as I felt then. I remember thinking,
           'This is my time', and I stuck it out.

WILLIAM   So you were a determined little girl then? And the second
           memory?

JANICE   I am outside a shop in Birmingham, in a car, crying because my
           father hasn't bought me a birthday present. I did get one, but I
           think it must have been late, or something.

These two memories awakened all sorts of feelings, particularly when I realised that
from that young age I had been jealous of mother and her relationship with father.
I then began to think about his leaving, and in a flash I knew that he had begun to
leave me long before I was thirteen. That was simply a date I could put on the event.
Emotionally he'd gone years before. I knew then that there was a lot of work to do
about that anger.

Part of it I was able to deal with when, quite soon afterwards, I went to my
father's retirement party. It took a lot of courage to tell him of my feelings, but to
my surprise he seemed to understand how angry I felt at being abandoned. More
of a surprise, however, was that mother and I became closer after I told her of the
loneliness I felt. I didn't tell her of my jealousy, and still haven't. We had never had
any sort of physical contact, mother and me, but when I left, on that occasion, we
hugged each other, and it felt good.

I felt I'd really made progress in self-awareness. I told everyone in the family that
I was having counselling, and it felt good, too, that I could be open about it. I was
only sorry that mother couldn't afford it. In some strange way, I still felt responsible
for her.

I said earlier that imagery was useful but that at times it was very difficult. I
wanted to explore this loneliness still further with William. We started one of the
sessions with me trying to find a quiet place. Nothing came. Perhaps I wasn't quiet
inside. William put me into a beautifully relaxed state of body and mind, then
suggested I imagine myself in a meadow somewhere. The meadow that came to me
was nothing like I'd ever seen in real life, but it was beautiful, calm, peaceful and

oh, so green, with birds chirping in the trees, and insects flying around, and tall grass waving in the slight breeze, on a warm sunny afternoon. William suggested that somewhere in the picture there was a stream, then a mountain, then a wood, and finally a house. I saw them all in vivid colours. He asked me which I would like to explore first.

The stream looked inviting. He asked me to look at the stream carefully and decide which way I wanted to explore. Downstream didn't look inviting, so I decided to go upstream. The stream led through the wood, although I don't think I deliberately arranged it that way. Then it began to widen out and suddenly I experienced fear, and told William, who suggested I imagine someone to keep me company. Again, I didn't 'think' about it. Andy, a man I fancied, just appeared. We walked a little way along the stream and then it was time to return to the meadow. I didn't know what to do with Andy. I decided to leave him there. By this time I was in tears (I did a lot of crying with William). But somehow I felt that Andy and I would come together sometime. The parting from him by the stream was incredibly painful; it seemed to hold all the pain of every parting I'd ever experienced.

Starting imagery the following session wasn't easy at all. I wasn't at all sure I wanted to go through the pain. The meadow was the same, but the stream looked more menacing than before. Andy wasn't around. Part of me wanted to get into the river, but I was too afraid that I would sink and not be able to get out. That was silly because I'm a very good swimmer. I scooped up a handful of the water and immediately sensed mother's presence. As I looked at the river I felt that under the water there were people creating a babble, although I couldn't identify them or their words. My secondary school appeared in the second handful. For some reason I saw myself being bullied and knew that I needed to develop defences against that. There was no way I could trust myself to the water, not in a boat, not attached to a rope, unless it was held by a man. I couldn't think of a man whom I would trust enough. What that session told me was just how much I mistrusted people. I'm not sure that I would have trusted Andy either, if he'd appeared, although it was him I most wanted.

Part of what was happening is also tied up with a gradual coming to terms with the reality about my parents. Unconsciously I'd taken mother's side against father; it was all his fault, and so forth. As I spoke these words to William, I could hear mother very clearly. I was at an impressionable age when he left us, and no doubt had to put up with a lot of nasty things being said about him, without hearing his side. So, my relationship with mother needed re-evaluating. My flat mate, Sharon, confronted me with, 'You're in a mess because you're tied to your mother's apron strings'. It was as if she had slapped me. We had a blazing row, but I knew she was right, in a way. Mother was tied to me, and I couldn't break free. Mother applied a great deal of moral pressure, almost blackmail 'You've all I've got now', 'I hardly ever see you', 'It's such a long way to Southampton:', 'Why can't we be like other mothers and daughters.' Somehow I needed to find the strength and the courage to confront mother.

In the session with William following that row with Sharon, I drew a picture of myself, looking very corpse-like, with three faces looking down at me and saying

'Blame', 'Blame', 'Blame'. I linked this with the voices of confusion I'd heard in the stream. I couldn't understand why I was just lying there passively taking it all, instead of fighting. I realised I felt helpless.

Something that did emerge, about half-way through counselling, was that I was just as possessive of the men in my life as mother is of me. I had been complaining to William about my mother's possessiveness, then later on I was telling him about one of my earlier relationships. All he said was, 'That sounds quite possessive'. He didn't need to make the connection. It hit me square between the eyes. I was possessive and jealous, just as mother was, and still is. That was a large chunk to swallow, but swallow it I had to. I then had a flashing image of me shooting out grappling irons into the poor fellow, to make sure I had him and would keep him. I think I'm one of these women who love too much.

My sessions with William were very much up and down; tears and laughter, with long periods of silence when I was allowed to think things through for myself. William had warned me that the journey could be painful, and that at times I would probably want to give up. It was like that, exactly. At one stage I felt I'd reached a crossroads. I'd accepted certain things about myself that I didn't like very much, but I also felt that I needed to confront mother, and tell her how I felt about being tied to her, and that I was trying hard not to play her game any more. William and I talked this through and I was under no illusion; this would not be easy. She and I were hooked into each other.

WILLIAM   Janice, how do you feel about dealing with that confrontation with your mother now?

JANICE   I've been putting if off, haven't I?

WILLIAM   As you say, challenging is not your strong point, but do you feel strong enough?

JANICE   I think so. But you know, we seem to be talking about separation again.

WILLIAM   Janice, there was something in the way you were looking just now, I don't know, a sort of wistful look, that prompts me to ask if you're grieving for something.

JANICE   Ouch! That hit me just here, in the abdomen, I'll have to think about a minute. Yes, although until this minute I hadn't put words to it. It's my youth. Part of me rebels against the staidness of a constant relationship, yet part of me is attracted to it. Something else, though. If I am able to successfully confront mother, and we are able to separate, it will mean that I can no longer hold on to that part of my life. I really will be separate, and that scares me quite a lot, if I'm honest. I'll no longer be the little girl.

WILLIAM   That sounds like a gigantic revelation, a real flash of light.

JANICE That's exactly what it feels like. I feel quite scared. Can I make it on my own? Help me, William. Tell me I can make it. Don't just smile enigmatically.

WILLIAM Sometimes the pain of discovering who we are is so great that we feel we want to give up, yet there is something that kicks us in the bottom and says 'Get up and go on, you're worth it'.

I remember ending that session, prompted, no doubt by William's use of 'worth', by telling him of one of my colleagues who only the previous day had said what a nice person I was, and that made me feel of some worth.

I would like to say that after having talked with mother everything was fine, but that's not how I felt. In fact, I felt awful, it's as if I was blaming her for who I was, and I knew that I had to take responsibility for myself. There was still a barrier between us. William suggested I draw this. I drew two figures in red, where I was turning away from mother; that one I labelled 'then'. Alongside I drew another picture, 'now', not so violently red, where we were facing each other. Both showed anger and grief, but the second was less angry. I couldn't get a picture for the barrier, however. All I felt was the lack of warmth.

William suggested an iceberg. This didn't quite fit, but it gave me a clue; it was a frozen stream, with me under the ice, looking up at mother. The awful pain of the separating ice broke me and melted some of the ice. I remember saying, 'What can I do, William, what can I do?' as the tears poured down. I'd cried with William before, many times, but this was different. It was as if years of frozen feelings were suddenly starting to melt. Between us we thought I could spend time composing a letter to mother. This I did and over several months we came closer, as two women, not only as mother and daughter.

A theme that kept recurring was my low self-esteem. Early on in counselling, William drew a bucket on the board and asked me to estimate my percentage of positive esteem. I put it at around one quarter. We then identified all the things that were negative, things that drained me of self-esteem. Some of those things were my looks. I didn't think I was attractive, so I didn't do much about making myself look attractive. My hair and clothes were ordinary, and baggy, and dull. That's pretty well how I thought of myself, a frumpy, ageing woman who, if she wasn't careful, would be left on some inaccessible shelf that no man would want to reach up to. Gradually I came to the conclusion that I had put myself there, to keep men out of reach. By the time counselling was over my self-esteem was up about half-way up the bucket.

I still have a long way to go, but I'm climbing. One of the things we identified was that I was determined not to be like mother and drive men away, as she had driven father away. Yet that was exactly what I did, by trying too hard. And every time it happened, ouch!, another hole in the self-esteem bucket. I can remember saying to William, 'I'm not going to be a doormat for anyone'. Just the vehemence of that statement jolted me into realising that is exactly what I'd become. Being a human doormat is downright degrading, humiliating and as low as I could get. I was determined to change that. When I started taking more notice of myself, other people did too. One of my best boosts was when a female student, around fifteen, said 'You're lovely, Janice, and I love you'.

Comment

These twelve sessions with Janice have so much in them and they demonstrate how complex counselling can be, and how cautiously we have to tread. Insight can never be given by one person to another. I could only stay with Janice as she struggled to open a particular door that led to fresh understanding.

One of the difficult things for me, and no doubt for many other counsellors, is to suspend judgment. It would be relatively easy to pass judgment on Janice's parents, for example, but if I had done this, and therefore taken sides with Janice against them, it is highly probable that Janice could have become alienated from them, instead of working toward healing and understanding. Something we all need to remember, constantly, is that people do not become parents after a stringent selection process that measures their suitability. Neither are there any blueprints for the task for which they receive no training. It is probably the only important job that is done totally by example and intuition.

As many people do, Janice wanted me to take control, to give direction. At the end of the first session, when we were discussing what she wanted to do, she expected me to tell her whether counselling would be worth it. I told her that that was something I was unable to answer, but that in my experience I had learned to trust the client. My expressing trust in her ability to make a decision added a substantial layer of cement to our embryonic relationship.

Janice cried a great deal during our time together. Tissues were always to hand, yet very often she would allow the tears to flow unchecked, great big tears that seemed to come from deep within her. Tears often embarrass the person who is crying, rather than the observer. Yet somehow I felt that her tears, free-flowing as they were, were not only expressing feelings, they were cleansing very deep wounds. I think, too, that the uncontrolled weeping I observed (and it was out of the ordinary) was reminiscent of a very distressed child. As I write this, I am, in fact, reminded of my own uncontrolled weeping over some childhood loss, probably a beloved kitten.

In all the time with Janice, in spite of the tears, I never felt it would have been right to have touched her, except to hold her hand on a few occasions. Toward the end of counselling I asked her about this, to find that my intuition had been accurate. She would have felt threatened by anything more than I offered. I long ago came to the conclusion that when I want to hug someone it's more for my comfort than for theirs. And very often too quick a reaching out in physical contact can cause the other person, if there are tears, to dry up.

Janice herself used the phrase, 'A woman who loves too much'. This is a concept applied to women who enter into a series of relationships in which they are constantly hurt, because of some deep need to be loved, even though all they receive is pain and abuse. It is thought that such women are reared in dysfunctional families where there is abuse of some kind, physical, sexual, alcohol or drugs.

The empty cave Janice imagined in session three generated a great release of emotion. I rarely interpret symbols to clients, but whatever they might have meant for Janice, this image was a powerful one. She was afraid of what she might find there, possibly the unconscious. The pictures, looking like wallpaper, could mean that whatever she finds are as harmless as paper cutouts.

It is rarely positive to allow the person to destroy objects that appear in imagery, for, in some way, they represent parts of the person. Transformation is more positive. Light is the opposite of dark, light is revealing; that is why I suggested a spotlight. What was revealed were two memories. In psychoanalytic terms, the first memory possibly points to the Oedipus complex, the jealousy the child feels toward the parent of the same sex who is taking the love of the parent of the opposite sex. The second memory, of the toy, is again linked with her father, and has a hint of the possessiveness that accompanies the Oedipal stage.

Janice appeared for session four with a complete change of hairstyle. Normally it had been frizzy and (to me, not very *au fait* with modern hairstyles) lacking in style. Now her hair was tied back with a blue ribbon, and the whole appearance was of a much younger person. Almost her first words seemed to confirm this impression, when she said that she realised during the week that her loneliness had its origins further back than she had first thought. I wondered if relaxation and imagery could help her get in touch with those early feelings.

Janice didn't care for the look of the 'down' stream, that travelled from left to right, which indicated that she was reluctant to journey deliberately into her unconscious and her masculine aspect. It is very important, in imagery, that one does not force the client. It is also interesting that although Janice chose not to travel downward, she found that the stream very quickly led her into a dense wood, her unconscious. When clients experience fear in imagery, it is often because they are intuitively aware of something that is waiting to confront them, then I suggest a travelling companion. In Janice's case, and she was hesitant about admitting him to her journey, Andy appeared; so in her mind, Andy is someone who would protect her. Her anger at Andy's treatment of her was replaced by overwhelming grief as she left him behind. This encounter with Andy, I think, reinforced her attachment to him, and, in the light of events, may well have been a prophetic encounter. She later entered into a relationship with him.

Imagery is an incredibly powerful medium, for it bypasses the intellect, something Janice discovered as she re-entered the meadow at the next session. I would not normally suggest immediately that the person get into the water, for that requires a great deal of courage and feeling secure. It was she who said she didn't want to get in, that she would sink and not be able to get back up. Water speaks of the psyche and also of being in the womb. What she did next was interesting: the handful of water she scooped up seemed to represent what she might have experienced in total immersion. Her mother's presence became very real to her, so in some way, the water was bringing her into closer contact with her mother.

The water also awakened memories of school and bullying. The experience she had of the babble of voices, of confusion, could relate to the conflicting voices within her; it could also be the confusion of memories as yet not brought into consciousness. Another point about the stream (although by now, in Janice's imagination, it was a river) was her total mistrust of getting into or onto it, and that the only way was for a rope to be held for her by a man. It was interesting that she couldn't bring any one man into her picture, not her father, Andy, nor me. This was a strong indication that she was not yet ready to trust herself to her unconscious, or, possibly to her masculine part.

At one stage, in session six, Janice asked me how she was doing as a client, on a scale of one to ten. She thought she was about five. My reply was that it seemed important for her to be able to compare herself with other people, perhaps to make her feel better, and added. 'If they were better does this lessen your worth?' She then went on to say that she really did need other people to give her a lift, she needed their approval so much, their opinions counted a great deal. She also realised, in saying this, that her mood often depended on how much praise she got from people. It was in this session that she drew a picture of herself with three faces looking down at her and saying 'Blame', 'Blame', 'Blame'. Janice didn't know what it was she was being blamed for, but something seemed to be hinting that it was the breakup of her parents' marriage. The repeating of the single word 'Blame' is very powerful and emphatic, so I encouraged her to say it aloud, with increasing force. This provoked an outburst of tears mixed with anger, in which she vented her anger harmlessly by punching a cushion.

One of the features that emerged in Janice as we worked was her developing assertiveness, particularly toward her parents, and in the way she initiated action, instead of passively waiting for other people to act. This is often characteristic of what happens in counselling, as if the relationship with the counsellor provides a more solid base for the client to relate more effectively to other people.

An observation I have made during my time as a counsellor is that many clients have a very low opinion of themselves, low self-esteem. When clients are in a relationship in which they experience empathy, unconditional positive regard, non-possessive warmth and genuineness, their self-esteem 'bucket' slowly starts to fill, as they realise they have worth.

The self-esteem 'bucket' starts to be filled from the moment we are born. Even before conception, the relationship between the parents creates a climate that starts the process of self-worth. In the journey through life, particularly the early years, holes are made in the self-esteem bucket that cause leakage. Many people receive more negative than positive strokes as children, hence the low level of opinion they have of themselves. The counselling relationship, in a way, neutralises these negative strokes, and (continuing the analogy) the person is then able to close some of the leakage holes.

Janice vividly conveyed her feelings about her self-esteem when she accepted my comment about being a doormat. Another point about Janice's self-esteem was that at the end of counselling she was much more able to be in control in the relationship with Andy. She also made an important distinction between 'being in love with', a sort of dreamy, romanticised idea, and 'loving' Andy. The one is often fantasy, and has a strongly physical side to it; the other is based on reality, and is personalised. Their holiday to New York (paid for by Andy), a long journey, seemed to symbolise the long, painful journey Janice, herself had travelled.

Lily
From Sexual Abuse to Sunbeam

I'm Lily, aged 32, divorced and a manager in a large hospital. I came for counselling because of two reasons, which are linked. I was sexually abused as a child, by my father, and I want to do something about my disastrous relationships with men. It was all brought to a head when, three months before I started counselling, I had my third miscarriage. I have no children.

Both my parents are still alive, and still together, although I have very little contact with them, and I know if mum died, that would be it as regards my father. With all that's happened I find it difficult to trust people, other than on a professional basis.

I cried a lot in my first session, and described my mind to William as a filing cabinet which has been turned over, and all the contents are scattered around on the floor. I want to get some sort of order into my thoughts and feelings. My major fear was that I would become an abuser, like my father.

We spent the next session talking about my relationship with one of the young doctors. I would like to think I am in love, but that would be kidding myself. I think it's more like desperation. In lots of ways Stan is the opposite of me, and saying that helped me to look at the opposites within me, the 'shadow', as William put it. It was only after talking through my feelings, that I realised just how low I'd been, and had even thought about suicide. However, after three sessions I told myself I was worth something. William suggested imagery; I wasn't too sure, as I'd done some of it before, and found it difficult to cope with. William's explanation of the way he worked reassured me, for it would leave me in control.

Session Four

LILY: I'm in this meadow on a hilltop, but I'm not seeing it properly: it's as if I'm looking at a reflection of it in my sunglasses.

WILLIAM: So that if you took them off, you might not be able to cope with what you see?

LILY: Something like that, as if I can't risk it just yet.

WILLIAM: That's OK, anyway you like. We'll work with what's there.

LILY: The wood is right in front of me. Do I feel anything? No, nothing. It's just a wood. The house is a long, white cottage with a stone wall. It looks interesting, and I'd like to explore it one day. I can see the stream, but it quickly turns into the sea. The mountain's about three miles away. A funny looking thing, with lots of shale on it, and a top like a volcano. I'm bringing the mountain closer, as if my eyes are telephoto lens. No, I don't want to climb it.

WILLIAM: It sounds as if with all that shale on it could be unsafe?

LILY: I'm doing as you suggested, lying on the ground, and my roots are growing downwards. They look like blood vessels, but white, and they're lightened by some powerful light, although I can't see where it's coming from.

WILLIAM: It sounds as if you feel quite comfortable down there?

LILY: Yes, I am. It feels, how shall I put it, as if I've come home?

WILLIAM: A bit womb-like?

LILY: That's it, exactly. I'm being drawn forward and find myself in a lake of bubbling liquid.

WILLIAM: Can you identify it? Is it a cave or something like that?

LILY: Not a cave, there's no roof.

WILLIAM: Any ideas about it?

LILY: I know! It's me. I'm looking at me inside. All bubbling and steaming.

WILLIAM: Ready to explode?

LILY: I suppose that's what it is, all churned up.

WILLIAM: I'm going to suggest that you will imagine something that will bring peace and calmness to you.

LILY: Yes, I see a beautiful white water lily bud, just on the edge of the lake. Oh, this is just wonderful. I'm watching it open so slowly.

WILLIAM: As if warmed by the sun?

LILY: Yes, yes. Now it's fully open, and in the middle is it's crown of yellow petals.

WILLIAM: Beauty from the mud. And that is you. Can you accept that? (*Tears*)

LILY: Now the flower is fading, and turns into a puff-ball and it has blown away. The stamens have landed on the lake, which is now quite still.

WILLIAM: I suggest you put your hand in the water, and see what happens.

LILY: The lake has changed: it's now the sea, with waves breaking on a
            rocky shore. I feel the wind in my hair.

WILLIAM: I suggest that it is now evening, and the sun is sinking low, and
            you imagine its beams touching the water, which is so calm you
            can see right to the bottom of the seabed.

LILY: Yes, I see that clearly.

WILLIAM: I now suggest that you go into the water and walk right into the
            sunbeam, so that you and the sunbeam become one.

LILY: I've gone so far, up to my waist, and I start to feel the warmth of
            the sun all around me. Now it's as if my lower half has dissolved
            into the water, yet I feel wonderfully whole and peaceful. Now
            the lower part is revolving in a different direction to my upper
            half. I know it sounds strange, but it's not uncomfortable, and I
            don't feel afraid, not even a tiny bit.

WILLIAM: Where do you think this is taking you?

LILY: Back to this room. It's over for today.

WILLIAM: Just sit quietly and let the journey sink in, and come back slowly.

Comment

Lily was looking at her meadow as if it were a reflection. She was seeing it, but not
clearly. Sunglasses are used to shield the eyes. This could be interpreted as meaning
that she wasn't ready to look at what was emerging in the real light of day, that
there was something she couldn't yet face.

The opening of the lily, from bud to full bloom, is symbolic of something
happening within her. The lily (a psychic pun?) speaking of purity, with its roots in
the mud, also speaks of beauty rising from the most unlikely places. The fact that
the image of the water lily brings peace is not surprising: the very image is peaceful,
and by this time we had already been in session for about twenty minutes, and the
whole process was having a calming effect.

Putting the hand in the water is making contact with the element. It is symbolic
of entering, of exploration. It is saying, 'I trust you'. This putting the hand into the
water, although I didn't know it, was a preparation for the scene with the sea. There
had been a steady progression throughout the session. Not everybody can imagine
themselves travelling down their roots, so her capacity to do this indicated that Lily
was not afraid of what was happening. The merging with the sun's rays is a truly
wonderful experience of integration, merging with creation.

In discussion afterwards, Lily said that she was totally aware of all that was
happening, and that she was aware that she didn't want to go beyond a certain point.
Where she stopped, the final image took her as far as she felt able to 'surrender'
herself. This was reassuring to her, that she was not being taken beyond what she
was capable of dealing with.

Meg
The French Connection

I am Meg, and I came to William for counselling when I was 27 years of age, and in my second year as a graduate student nurse. Life had been difficult for some time, and I felt that if I was ever to be happy, I would have to start taking control of my life; not letting things happen to me, as had been the pattern so far. My degree was in French and French literature; partly because my father is French, and many of my early years were spent in France on holiday with my grandparents. Our home was bilingual, so French was a natural choice – a far cry from nursing. My work as a translator lost its appeal after a time, and I wanted to do something with people; the usual corny comment one hears from many nurses, but it was the only way I could express it. When I was into it about a year, I started having serious doubts. I hated the routine and the insistence upon procedures, even though they were essential. So I started with my doubts with William to see if he would understand me.

I have decided that the only way I can cope with writing this is to approach it logically, and deal with the various strands separately, rather than in any chrono-logical order, even though many of the strands, are, understandably, connected.

I have two brothers, André, two years older than I, and Charles, four years younger, and a sister Katrina who is two years younger. We weren't very close, any of us, and this was something I very much regretted. I knew I was harbouring a lot of resentment against my mother. She is a very dominant, self-centred and possessive woman, towards us all, but particularly towards me, for some reason. At the same time, I was afraid to confront her; I wasn't at all sure I could cope with the aggravation. I was also afraid that if I let the lid off, things would be said that I'd afterwards regret. I was particularly angry with my mother because she wouldn't allow me to see my English grandmother (Mother runs a nursing home) when she was dying. I didn't get the chance to say 'goodbye' and I wasn't allowed to show my grief. Mother would have hated that. William and I tossed around the idea of my writing Mother a letter, but not posting it, which I thought was a really good idea, although I wanted to explore my feelings a lot more before I could even commit my thoughts to paper.

On talking things through with William I realised that Mother made very heavy demands on me. She would use words like, 'If you really loved me...' or 'Other daughters don't treat their mothers like you do.' I felt stifled by her. So strong were my feelings, that I was often troubled by bad dreams, in which, for example, I would be going upstairs with a knife in my hand, to kill her. In fact, I was afraid that someday I might actually do this. The thought terrified me. I didn't know how to deal with her. William talked through with me a way of responding called the 'computer mode'. I tried this and found I could handle my feelings better. I think mother is jealous of me, although I can't think why she should be.

William and I talked about dreams that troubled me. One such recurring dream started way back in childhood. I used to dream that I could make my mother burst into flames. This really shows the depths of my feelings, and the length of time I'd felt this way.

William suggested that I put these feelings about my parents into an imaginary picture. I didn't have to 'think'; right in front of my eyes, as it were, was a high, ugly brick wall, higher than myself and wide. I felt very sad looking at it, and wondered how the situation could be changed. I wanted to break the wall down, but was not sure if I would have the strength. William advised against violence as the wall would probably change in time.

As the sessions went on I was able to talk more about my father. He is a very cold man, absent a great deal through his work as a consultant engineer on the continent. Neither he nor my mother was outwardly affectionate to us children. It's funny how things 'pop up' when I'm talking with William. I had been talking about my jealous streak (just like Mother, I suppose), when an incident sprang into my mind. I would be about nine; I overheard my parents talking, and heard Mother say, 'Charles is my favourite'. This left me feeling very left out and unwanted. I took my jealousy out on Charles for a long time after that. It may sound silly, but I yearned for my father to cuddle me.

I never got any 'answers' about my parents from counselling, but just being able to express my feelings seemed, somehow, to give me more strength and under-standing. I found myself not reacting so violently to my mother, and I learned that I could make some approaches to my father, without him rejecting them.

I realised that if I was to get anywhere, I would have to be honest and open in counselling. My tangled feelings needed teasing out. It wasn't too long (it was in the second session, I think) before I disclosed that I'd recently had an abortion. I know I said this coldly and with detachment. I didn't mind talking about the facts, but I wasn't yet ready to 'feel'. I come from a family where 'feelings' are never, ever, talked about. To do so would be a sign of weakness. So, I couldn't tell my parents about the abortion, nor could I tell them I'd taken up again with Jim. There would be a dreadful scene with my mother if I did tell. I can't explain the relief it was just to talk, without feeling the need to justify, or explain. I hated the deceit, and wondered how long it would be before I had to 'confess'. That's another thing; I had not been to Confession since the abortion.

At first I thought that talking about the abortion would be easy; but it wasn't. I hadn't realised how much pain there was attached to that event which happened about four months before I came into counselling. I can't really talk about the abortion unless I also talk about Jim. We had had a fairly tempestuous relationship for about ten years. It seemed that when we were apart, we couldn't live without each other; yet when we were together we fought like two cats. I didn't tell Jim of the pregnancy; neither did I tell him I intended to have an abortion. When I did, he was very upset and tearful. He felt I had deprived him. He didn't show much concern for me and my feelings, however.

I said that my relationship with Jim was stormy; it was also quite violent at times. Until I started seeing William, I'd always blamed Jim. Now I realise that there was a lot about me that must have sparked Jim off. In my times with William I was able to discuss what was important to me. One such discussion was triggered by a dream. Jim and I were with a married couple on a river-bank. Jim was trying to persuade me to get into a brightly coloured houseboat. Everything became dark and foreboding. I ran off, chased by Jim, who was brandishing a knife. I felt that the dream expressed my feelings about my relationship with Jim, and also that something within the relationship was making me afraid. What that dream triggered was an incident that I thought I'd dismissed. While I was still pregnant, Jim and I had been arguing. Jim put his hands around my throat, quite firmly, as if he was going to strangle me. I was afraid then, for I felt in touch with a violent part of him I'd only been dimly aware of.

I've said how impossible it is for me to tell Mother about the abortion; this is partly because she doesn't like Jim, and that would create just too much hassle. So I keep quiet and deceive her. At one stage I asked William if he could see Jim and me together, but Jim wouldn't agree. 'It's your problem' he said. I got quite angry and hurt at that; I felt it was *our* problem. William challenged me by asking me what I wanted from the relationship with Jim. Without thinking, I said, 'Lover, friend, father, psychotherapist'. The last one surprised me, totally. In reality, Jim wasn't at all like that. I could see Jim as like my father, in that I was looking for caution and responsibility.

William challenged me on the 'responsibility', by referring to something I'd said several sessions before, when I'd attributed blame to Jim. I knew my thoughts were mixed up, and that challenge helped me to sort them out. I felt I couldn't really blame Jim; I thought sex was safe, and it wasn't, therefore I should shoulder part of the responsibility.

I found William quite challenging; at times I didn't like it! I'd been recounting the weekend spent with Jim, when William said, 'You sound as if you did a lot of nagging'. Although I didn't like hearing it, he was spot on. Not only do I nag (just like my mother), I know I wallow in self-pity.

While I was seeing William, I broke with Jim, and felt calmer and more able to be myself, but just before I did, William and I were talking about my dependence on Jim; I am dependent on him, yet at the same time, I know he pulls me down. For some time I'd been worried by the amount Jim was drinking, and his moods were really unpredictable. I found it quite easy to work with images, and for this feeling of his having a hold over me, I pictured a black, steady river that threatened to suck me down in a whirlpool. One of my male friends threw me a rope and pulled me out. As I stood on the bank, I felt a great weight drop from me. At the time I wasn't sure if my resolve finally to break with Jim would be strong enough to carry me through. Perhaps our need of each other was too great. Although I broke with him,

I still felt uneasy about going out and meeting other men. I suppose I didn't know what I did want.

A few weeks after the break, I accidentally met Jim, and was overcome with jealousy to find that he was seeing another woman. I could have killed her, and myself. If William hadn't been there for me, what would I have done? It was then I realised that I couldn't let Jim go. So I broke the promise to myself and entered again into an intimate relationship with him. Then I thought I was pregnant. It was what I wanted, but could I take the responsibility? William helped me to sort out my feelings about being pregnant, and this opened up some of the unresolved stuff about the abortion; stuff I thought had gone. One of the issues we talked about was my need to rebel (I was quite a rebel) and the responsibility of having a child. From this discussion emerged the half-hidden fact that I'd had far too much responsibility thrust on me as a child, by my mother, who was out at work. I was the 'little mother' and desperately sought approval from my father; but of course he could only see me as his daughter, and even then there wasn't much acknowledgment. In some ways, I'm afraid of taking responsibility. That was one of the early themes related to my nursing.

I wasn't pregnant. Part of me was relieved; part disappointed. I was able to admit to William that the main reason for my disappointment was that I would lose my hold over Jim. That was an awful admission, and I felt very bad saying it, but it helped just admitting it. What made all this worse was the fact that André's girlfriend was pregnant. They'd told my parents, who took it very well. Was I jealous! I felt usurped. It was my place to produce the first grandchild, or so I thought. How I wish I could get my feelings about Jim sorted out. He's an addiction. William must have wondered if he and I were making any progress, the number of times I kept returning to the same old theme. My thought was that when I qualified, I would go and nurse in Australia. William remarked that the place seemed significant. Yes: it couldn't be any further way from Jim.

It was ages before I could tell William of another strand of my problem. When I was twenty-four, I met a man who took me out for car ride, that turned into the most dreadful nightmare. It all started off quite innocently, a drive in the country, then through some woods, for several hours. It was then I began to get anxious. He became very quiet, sullen in fact. We stopped somewhere, miles away from any other track. 'Give me a goodnight kiss, darling' he said. I really didn't want to kiss him, but thought I'd try to placate him. When he started mauling me, my fear began to choke me. I could smell the drink that was turning this man whom I thought I liked into a beast. He was small, but very powerful, and he raped me repeatedly, so hard that my anus and vagina were tender for weeks. I was screaming obscenities at him through my pain and fear. It seemed to go on for ages. And I did nothing about it. I certainly could never tell my mother. I'd never had a positive body-image. I didn't like myself from the neck down. The rape and the abortion added to that dislike of myself.

WILLIAM: How would you imagine those feelings about the rape?

MEG: I see them as an iron fence, with thick bars, throwing shadows
             and I'm caught up in them. I'm not sure if I'm enclosed by this
             'fence'.

WILLIAM: Fence and defence: similar words, aren't they?

MEG: You mean an unconscious pun? Defence, yes that would be right.

WILLIAM: Strange how the unconscious works. What are you doing with the
             fence?

MEG: I'm putting my hand on it and walking round. That's funny, it's
             not a complete circle.

WILLIAM: How could the fence be transformed, and into what?

MEG: It's changed into a castle in the distance. It looks slightly
             forbidding.

WILLIAM: What do you want to do with the castle?

MEG: I want to explore it, although I feel a bit apprehensive. I'm now
             going over the drawbridge and am exploring the rooms. They're
             all empty. From the top, I can see trees; it feels cool up here.

WILLIAM: I think it would be exciting to find a treasure.

MEG: I've found a small warm, well-lighted room, lonely, as if it had
             been created just for me. I leave the castle feeling happier.

Some time after the rape I decided to have psychotherapy for agoraphobia. I
mentioned the rape on the personal details form but it was never explored. So, I
thought it wasn't important. That was one reason, I think, why it took me so long
to disclose it to William. The relief I felt when he took it seriously was incredible.
I could see how hurt he felt at my story. Together we explored the incident and my
feelings then and afterwards. I hesitantly put forward the idea that somehow I had
been responsible; that I'd led him on. William didn't agree. His view was that he
had to take total responsibility for what he did. Hearing him say that so adamantly
was a tremendous relief, and encouraged me to explore my feelings of worthlessness
and uncleanness. The rape had affected my lovemaking; there were times with Jim,
when I just couldn't relax enough to be free. Jim couldn't understand my feelings,
so I gave up trying to explain them.

One of the links William and I made was that the feeling of being dirty and
worthless after the rape were the same as I felt after the abortion. When I'd related
the rape to William, and I saw and heard his reaction, a great feeling of sadness
overwhelmed me, and I began to sob. I'd cried before with William, but not like
this. I knew I was reaching down into the very depths of my pain, not just about
the rape, but so many things. I remember William reaching out his arms, and I found

myself being surrounded by such undemanding love as I'd never before experienced.[1]

When some of my pain had passed, we talked. William encouraged me to use the imagery I'd become used to.

WILLIAM: Let your imagination take you to a beach, in late summer, where the tide had gone out where there was a lovely stretch of virgin sand.

MEG: The cool sand is comforting. I could stay here for ever.

WILLIAM: In the distance a man is approaching. He is not a man you know, yet you feel you have known him all your life. Tell me about him.

MEG: There is something that draws me to him, some expression, something about the way he walks. He comes close, and his eyes seem to see right through me, but I'm not afraid.

WILLIAM: I want you to imagine that he is putting his hands on your head, and as he does so, you will feel all the dirt in you drain away into a pile at your feet, and in its place, in every part of your body, there will be a beautiful peace, and all the hurt and pain will have gone.

MEG: For the first time in years I feel whole.

The last strand of my problem was my fear of going out; my panic attacks. In my mind I'd linked this to the rape, but in reality it had been there for longer than that. William encouraged me to go back into my childhood, at about the age of seven, in France. My parents had gone out, leaving me with friends. I remember the panic when I couldn't find my parents. This connected to the feelings I used to have when my father went away on trips. He never prepared me; I would get up in the morning to find him gone, and I would panic, wondering if he was dead, or something.

My panic attacks won't allow me to travel on the underground, for example, and I hate going in lifts and on buses. In my mind I thought all this sounded silly, but the way William listened, and developed various themes, made me feel that it was OK to talk about them. Something I'd only been dimly aware of, but which was made clear, through exploration, was that I was afraid of being taken ill in the underground or on a bus, because then I'd be out of control; and being in control was something important to me.

One of the things that did emerge was that I was more prone to these panic attacks when I was tired. William had introduced me to relaxation and I had one of his tapes, which I'd started using regularly, so that helped me not to get too stressed.

---

1   Some counsellors would strongly avoid physical contact to the exent of holding clients, while others, particularly those who work holistically, accept this as being part of the healing process. But it must be appropriate and for the needs of the client, not for the needs of the counsellor. Physical contact is not something to be undertaken lightly or without the client's permission. Touch of any kind should be as carefully considered as the words we use. Some clients accept touch, others refuse it, and that is their choice.

We looked at what it was that could be causing the panic attacks; several different things emerged.

One was of a memory when I was about the age of two, being lost in a fish market in France. That was quite scary, even to recall. Another thing was that I often felt as if something behind me was holding me back from doing things, like travelling in the underground. In my imagination I pictured this as something black and shapeless, with a great amount of fear attached to it. Although I didn't get any real insight on that particular occasion, when the third thing emerged, I did.

Together, William and I worked out a number of situations in which I knew I would feel panic. Some I knew would take a long time; some I thought I could cope with. I wanted to visit a friend in Chalk Farm, which meant I'd have to choose between the underground or the bus. I thought the bus would be less dreadful than the underground. So, in imagery, helped by William, I started the journey. Even before I got on the bus my hands were sweating and my heart was pounding.

I stood in the street and controlled my breathing, and relaxed enough to get on the bus. Then I was conscious of a black, shapeless something behind, waiting to engulf me. My terror almost made me jump up and leave the room, but William encouraged me to 'stay with it', and suggested I think of someone who could be with me, to give me support and strength. I wanted my granny, and she held my left hand. Somehow I found the strength to turn round and face whatever it was. Could I reach out and touch it? It was so horrible, I felt powerless to reach out, although I knew I could, if I really wanted to. Was it male or female? Again, instinctively, I knew it was male. It had a space somewhere in the middle, which I was able to touch. Could I make friends with him? I could, but didn't want to. Neither could I get a name for him. Why was he there? The answer that came sounds silly and spooky: to teach me to be strong and how to die. Could I lie in the space? This took all my courage and determination. William suggested I hold on to granny. I knew this would help, but I felt it was something I had to do on my own. I allowed myself to relax into the shape, and gradually it changed to become two hands, large, strong, rough, stroking my hair. I felt fear, and wondered aloud if there was something dreadful I couldn't remember. The man was a mixture of father and someone else who I didn't know. Then he began to change, to become the memory of a man giving me red balloons in a French market. Then I was in a room (at about the age of five) with a man whose name was, I thought, Philippe. I had never 'remembered' this incident, so wasn't certain if was real or not, but if felt significant. That was a longer journey than going to Chalk Farm, but somehow much of the fear of confined spaces went, although I still have to work hard at it from time to time. I now have some techniques and strategies to help me through the difficult times.

Comment

Meg had twenty-three sessions spread over almost one year and I feel we did some very useful work together. One of Meg's strengths was her flair for imagery, something she learned to use very well to get in touch with her feelings. As a thinker, she was more comfortable pushing her feelings up into her head and talking about them, rather than actually 'feeling' or exploring them. When we imagine something long enough and strongly enough, it starts to take shape in our behaviour, and this applies equally to either positive or negative images.

When Meg was first relating her story about the abortion, she did so with a marked degree of detachment, which was, of course, her way of coping. I felt it would have been unwise to try to push her too rapidly into her feelings. When she found herself accepted, she then felt more safe to explore her feelings. Another factor to Meg's story was the lack of feeling – she described it as 'coldness' – of her parents, and their inability to express affection openly. Bearing all this in mind, and working with my own intuition, I decided to approach things cautiously.

Her presenting problem (dissatisfaction with nursing) was real enough; it wasn't a lie, and needed to be dealt with sympathetically. However, one should always bear in mind that rarely is the opening problem the only one as, of course, Meg clearly demonstrates. The relationship with her parents, particularly her mother, caused her great concern, and she shows the dilemma many of us find ourselves in: the need for affection from our parents (or significant others) coupled with the resentment that so often accompanies such relationships. Meg's mother was dominant and possessive: Meg desperately wanted independence (remember she said she was a rebel), and yet that independence could cut her off from ever receiving the affection she craved. Reality told her, as she often said to me, that it was very unlikely that her parents would change now, yet there was another part that held on to that hope.

People who are dominated by possessive parents generally lack assertiveness skills. This is understandable; the development of such skills would be actively discouraged, for they would threaten the power base. To help her cope with her mother's 'blamer' mode, I introduced the work of Virginia Satir's 'computer' mode. The blamer is the person who makes statements like, 'Why don't you ever think what *I* might want?' This seemed to be Meg's mother's mode, which usually put Meg into the 'placater' mode – anything for peace, even at the expense of feelings. One way to cope with the blamer is to adopt the computer mode.

A computer has no feelings, does not react from an emotional base – *Star Trek*'s Mr Spock, is a classic computer. Everything directed at the computer is filtered through the impersonal screen that deflects the other person's feelings. Computers work very hard to avoid saying 'I', for that would be too personal. A typical computer response would be something like, 'That's an interesting idea, how does it fit into your general philosophy of life?' The computer response is aimed at taking the heat off. It helps the target person by putting the question back to the sender. Meg was able to achieve some success, and a little success paves the way for other successes.

Meg was obviously carrying a great deal of 'hate' toward her mother, as evidenced by her various dreams of going to kill her, of making her burst into flames. When Meg was relating these dreams, she was getting in touch with some very real feelings. Her image of the brick wall, related to her mother is significant. A brick wall in imagery represents a barrier of substantial proportions, and in Meg's image it was high and wide. A word she associated with this wall was 'unsurmountable'. The associated feelings were frustration and powerlessness. This, then, is how she viewed herself in relation to her mother. Meg wanted to break the wall down, but wasn't sure if she had the strength. It is also possible, although this wasn't explored, that she may have wondered if it was worth it. Something else to bear in mind about a brick wall: it has been carefully built, brick by brick. It has not occurred naturally, or by accident. Meg saw her wall as being 'ugly': this suggests something to be despised, unacceptable.

Several times Meg spoke about my challenges. I was generally careful to challenge her strengths, not her weaknesses. For example, thinking was a strength; feeling was less of a strength. When I challenged her thinking there was no problem. There was one occasion, however, that is worth mentioning.

In session seventeen, Meg had been saying how she wanted to end her relationship with Jim, and then added that she had telephoned him. I picked this up later in the session and asked 'Why did you phone Jim?' The session ended quite soon after that, and the next week I felt a constraint between us. Meg said something about not always finding it easy to say what she wanted to say. There was a certain quality in her statements, reinforced by her facial expression, that made me say, 'Like here and now?'

I continued, 'Last week I thought you looked disturbed as you left'. This encouraged her to challenge my statement of the previous week. She felt my comment about her phoning Jim had been judgmental, but she couldn't challenge me. I had now given her the opportunity she needed, and she took it. I had to agree with her; it was judgmental. I also realised that it was a challenge to her feelings, not to her intellect. I congratulated her on her courage at offering a challenge in that way. On thinking about it afterwards, perhaps this would have been more appropriate: 'It seems that you were torn into two; part wanted not to ring him, and the other part did. That was quite a conflict'. Such is the benefit of hindsight.

Her abortion and rape were very closely related. The feelings were similar. Unlike some therapists, I do give opinions and views, but make it clear that they are mine, and come from my values and standards. Yes, I was angry at her account of the rape, and in no way could I have permitted her to bear the burden of thinking she was responsible. Some therapists would no doubt argue with me as to the wisdom of this; many would simply reflect the client's statement and attempt to discover more of the client's feelings.

Coupled with this was the fact that this was one of the few times in our relationship when I offered her physical comfort; it was accepted, and was therapeutic. Some therapists would also argue with that. For me, at the time, and for the client, it was right. It also says a great deal for the relationship that Meg was able to trust me sufficiently to allow me to enter her world and experience some of the pain she felt.

The particular imagery she mentions, on the beach, is an image I have used more than once. Other imagery is specific to the client at that particular time. For example Meg's image of her relationship with Jim, where she picture him as a black river that threatened to suck her down in a whirlpool. That is a dramatic image, and portrays vividly the fear she feels, but may never have put into words.

My work with Meg emphasised the importance of going at the client's pace. In the first session Meg had mentioned, a little casually I now realise, in the light of events, about her agoraphobia. Somehow it was never discussed until almost a year had passed. I may have missed the importance of it within the whole. I may have missed it because Meg didn't give it emphasis. I may have missed it because she was obviously not now agoraphobic.

Later, however, she started talking about 'panic attacks' and gave specific examples. The whole idea took on a new urgency, and she was now ready to work on it. Whatever the roots of her panic were, it is probable that even if Meg gained a great deal of insight, she would need active help to overcome the attacks. Imagery would have been the first stage; getting her to cope comfortably with a bus journey (and this may have taken several sessions), then undertaking a journey on the underground, or travelling in a lift, would then follow.

As it happens, after the session in which we did that imaginary journey, and somehow got sidetracked into France, Meg only came back once more, and not to work on her panic attacks. She had taken her final exam and was coping better with life. I felt that her last real journey with me was charged with significance, which may only be revealed to her in the future.

Meg passed her finals, practised for a while in England and then did as she'd planned, and went to work in Australia. Counselling, or therapy, whatever one calls it, is seldom, if ever, complete; there are always loose ends somewhere. Perhaps someone, somewhere, will work with Meg and build on the work she has already done, in order to achieve a little more wholeness.

Moira
The Well

I'm Moira, I'm 25 years of age, and a teacher of English in a large comprehensive school. After a long hard debate with myself, I've decided to take a year out and tour the world. So why do I feel the need for counselling? Since my father remarried two months ago I've felt totally demotivated and lacking in energy. My parents divorced 18 months ago.

My family is a strange one. My mother originally had an affair with my grandfather, who used to beat her. His son, my father, often came between them. Eventually mother left and married my father. She is 18 years older than my father. Now father is remarried, to a woman only seven years older than I am. At the wedding I met a whole lot of relatives I never knew I had. Now I feel obliged to get to know them, whether I want to or not.

WILLIAM: You sound angry and hurt and you're struggling with your tears.

MOIRA: Correct, but I also feel betrayed by my parents, both of them. I don't want to sound as if I'm against men, but I know my father fancied me; he'd surprise me when I was undressing, and sort of leer. And my step-mother's father wants me, I can tell. Anyway, all this puts me under a great strain when I visit father and Jane, who then take me to visit her father. I can't think why I don't just keep away.

WILLIAM: I'd like to share an image with you. I see a river that is suddenly divided into many tributaries, all the energy is being drained.

MOIRA: Yes, that is something like it. I just wish it wasn't so painful.

Session Two

WILLIAM: Moira, while you were talking just now, I imagined you climbing down a deep well. How does that sound for you?

MOIRA: I'm looking down that well, but do I want to explore it? I don't know what's down there. Can I cope with it?

WILLIAM: You sound as if you want some sort of reassurance from me.

MOIRA: I suppose I do, but that's not the way of it, is it. All right, I'll give it a go.

WILLIAM: Do you want to prepare yourself in any way?

MOIRA: No, I'll be all right, thanks. (*After a few minutes.*) Gosh this is difficult. Just imagination, you say. There's no ladder, just bits of rock for handholds and footholds. I'm getting scared of falling.

WILLIAM: I suggest you find a platform and rest for a while.

MOIRA: That's better, but I know what's wrong. It's my clothes, they're not right for this.

WILLIAM: Change them for something more suitable.

MOIRA: I have, and it hasn't made any difference. That was just an excuse. It's not the external that has to be changed, it's something within me.

WILLIAM: Have you any idea what that could be?

MOIRA: Well, I'm pretty stubborn, pig-headed, you could call me, and so independent, I hate accepting help.

WILLIAM: How does it feel, then, coming here?

MOIRA: I find myself struggling against it. I wish I could change.

WILLIAM: I suggest that if you look around where you are, you will find something that will help you change.

           After a little while, with astonished expression.

MOIRA: I've found this small pearl.

WILLIAM: You look, and sound, delighted with the find. What does it have to say to you?

MOIRA: It says, I love you and you are precious.

WILLIAM: The 'pearl of great price'. How do you feel about that, Moira?

MOIRA: (*Starting to cry*) That's really lovely. That means that I'm precious. I'd forgotten that. Thank you.

WILLIAM: The pearl is formed out of pain, perhaps that's the meaning for you. Now it's about time to end. How do you want to end this; climb up, or just get out?

MOIRA: I'll put my old clothes back on and climb out.

Session Three

MOIRA: I was thinking about last week and the pearl, and I certainly feel brighter and more optimistic, it's as if the pearl has given me assurance and a vision. The minister used part of Psalm 119 as his sermon on Sunday, 'They word is a lamp unto my feet and a light to my path', and I felt that the pearl was that for me.

WILLIAM: That's a lovely image to start our journey today. How do you feel about exploring the well again?

MOIRA: Oh, I don't know, is there more? Yes, I suppose so, it's not finished. I'm wearing the same clothes, and I feel more comfortable with them. I'm quickly at the platform, and the footholds are more definite today, and there's more light in the well.

WILLIAM: Where's this light coming from?

MOIRA: It's been there all along, I just hadn't seen it.

WILLIAM: You've sort of had your eyes opened.

MOIRA: I'm at the bottom of the well now and there is nothing of significance, only some burned out matches.

WILLIAM: And what do those tell you?

MOIRA: That somebody has been here, and because there are no skeletons around, they've made it out again. Now don't laugh, but it seems familiar.

WILLIAM: As if *you've* been here before last week?

MOIRA: Something like that, but it feels comfortable, like a stronghold, a place of refuge.

WILLIAM: How about giving it a name?

MOIRA: How about 'Nocturne'? Calm and peaceful.

WILLIAM: Sounds very appropriate, for it's your secure place, a place that nobody can violate.

MOIRA: I'm going up now and this is strange. The bottom third was dry, but the top bit is quite damp, and it's not so comfortable.

WILLIAM: It could be that this is the bit that needs further exploration.

By the end of the third session I was feeling much calmer and more in control. I've been to see my father and step-mother and they gave me a super birthday party. I realised just how strong the tie was. In the fourth and final session William and I talked about the way I tend to relate to people, usually by remaining aloof; then I feel under great pressure and I make a dash for people who are not wholly desirable and the relationship doesn't develop. I now realise that this is not productive, and I feel that my newfound strength and awareness will help me slowly to change this. This last bit was a painful admission: that I'm very intolerant of people who only talk and don't converse. I'm off on my world tramp soon, but that's a different sort of journey to the one I've just completed. I'm not sure which will be the easier in the long run.

Comment

Imagery work is two-way. I certainly don't expect clients to take on my images if they don't agree with them. However, often they do, and if the images don't totally match, often they provide a departure point. The image of the divided river is a powerful one when one is thinking of energy, and in Moira's case, the dissipation of that energy.

Going down a well is, of course, a descent into the unconscious, and even in the natural would such a descent would be a daunting prospect for many of us. Moira's insistence that she didn't need any preparation, such as a rope, gives some clue as to her independent nature. Wells, certainly older wells, were hand dug, then normally lined with brick or stone, and they were deep. This symbolises a man-made structure, and that someone has gone that way before, and has provided a way out.

The well is similar to the dungeon, in that it is dark, and underground, and when a person imagines being in a dungeon, it is sometimes profitable to have them change the image to a well, and to find a ladder or steps to help them out. When the well is open one can see the light, and that acts as symbol of hope.

Providing a platform, or something similar, like a plateau when climbing a mountain, is essential when there is evidence that the client is finding the going to be tough, or there is fear. The pearl in the well is a most exquisite example of finding beauty in the most unexpected of places, symbolic of light in the darkness, and treasure within the unconscious. By putting her old clothes on, Moira was symbolising a degree of integration, saying that her old self was now more acceptable.

My comment the previous week about the 'pearl of great price', referring to one of Jesus' parables, seemed to have triggered off the connection between that and the sermon on the 'lamp'. This is not an infrequent happening, and is an illustration of Jung's concept of 'synchronicity'. It seems that Moira was already prepared to 'hear' the allusion. Being nearer the top of the well is symbolic of being near the conscious level: wherever the client feels discomfort it is probably a reliable indication that there is more work to be done near the conscious level.

Neil
The Lighthouse

I'm Neil, a first year medical student from Newcastle, studying at Southampton. The studies aren't a problem, it's more to do with confidence, so my tutor thought a course of counselling might help. I met William for an exploratory session, and felt we could work together. I was very anxious during that session, and had to keep wiping my hands, they were so sweaty. I don't much like living in the hall of residence, it's a bit like living in a cell. I know I'm drinking too much, and it's a drain on my finances. I think I drink because I'm lonely. We agreed on six sessions. William introduced me to relaxation, which I found very helpful, and I agreed to practice it during the week.

Session Two

WILLIAM: Last week we spoke about using imagery. This week I want to introduce you to the first stage, the meadow.

I went through the introduction, in which he imagined it very much as I described it, and the meadow was entirely imaginary. The house lay behind him, quite some distance off; he could hear the stream, but couldn't see it; the wood was away to his right, and the mountain was some distance ahead, covered in trees.

As you lie in the grass, and look at the daisies, I suggest you become microscopic and explore one of the daisies. Tell me what's happening.

NEIL: I'm looking at this massive something which I know is a petal, and I walk all over it. Then I wander into the middle of the flower, where I find a tunnel going all the way down, with steps that I know are tiny hairs. I'm not at all frightened, I'm just eager to explore. I'm now at the bottom of the tunnel and see the roots spreading out and going down into the earth. I decide to go down one of them. It starts to feel really warm and moist, with a lovely smell. The roots are a pale brown. I go right to the end, and find myself in the earth. I really feel a part of nature, it's great.

WILLIAM: That sounds quite an exploration. Now it's time to come back. In your own time, come back up, into the flower, into the meadow, in your normal size, then back into this room (*I gave the date and time*).

NEIL: Wow! that was just wonderful. I'd no idea my imagination could take over like that. What did it all mean?

WILLIAM: I wasn't sure how you'd get on with imagery, but obviously you can, but what do you think that journey represented?

NEIL: Going within myself? It certainly felt like that.

Session Four

WILLIAM: Take a good look round, and see if the meadow has changed. Which bit of it do you want to explore.

NEIL: I'm moving towards the house, and I come to the stream. It looks really inviting, I'll paddle a while, and enjoy it.

WILLIAM: How old are you?

NEIL: Oh, ten, I think. Now why? I don't know, but I'm a kid again, and I'm running and splashing in the water.

WILLIAM: It sounds as if you haven't a care in the world.

NEIL: I didn't then.

WILLIAM: How do you feel about exploring the stream?

NEIL: No, I think I'll move on to the house. I'm leaving the stream now, and that's strange, the wood has moved, now it's between the stream and the house.

WILLIAM: What does that seem to be telling you?

NEIL: I have to explore that first, I suppose. Gosh! it's really very big, a forest, I'd say, like one I've been in in Germany. It's dark.

WILLIAM: Just hold on a minute. Look for a path, and maybe there's somebody you'd like to act as a guide.[1]

NEIL: It's an old man, shabbily dressed in a brown coat with long white hair. He has a kind expression, and his eyes are like pools of wisdom. He doesn't have a name. I know he can be trusted. I'll call him 'Friend'. I have a tremendous feeling of awe in the forest. Friend gives me a medallion made of stone. On it is carved a plain circle. Nothing much seems to be happening.

---

1   It is curious, but never in all the years of using imagery, has a client chosen me as the guide. I don't think this is anything to do with lack of trust, but rather more with that I would possibly intrude into the imagery. I think also that to have me as their external guide and internal guide could create too much tension and ambiguity.

WILLIAM: Somewhere you will encounter an obstacle, and your guide will help you.

NEIL: I see a big rock, like a stone table, with some writing hidden by moss. I scrape it away, but all I can make out is the letter 'R'; there is other writing, but I can't read it.

WILLIAM: Ask Friend if he can help you.

NEIL: He says just to relax and it will become clear.

Session 5

WILLIAM: Here you are again, Neil, at the strange stone, with the letter 'R' on it. Have you had any thoughts about it?

NEIL: Looking at it now, it reminds me of a tombstone. It stands on three steps.

WILLIAM: Can you find an entrance anywhere?

NEIL: That's really frustrating, there isn't one.

WILLIAM: Is Friend able to help you?

NEIL: He's changed too. It's somebody different, dressed in bright clothes, he says his name is Neil. He takes the medallion from me and places it on the 'R', and a door opens. Guide Neil is leading me down a few steps. I feel afraid, but I know I have to go on. That's what I'm here for.

WILLIAM: What would help you to feel less afraid?

NEIL: Guide Neil now has a torch, and I feel more comfortable. He's leading me down a long, steep passage that's going deeper into the earth, it must be about a hundred feet long. We come to a fork in the tunnel. I don't know which to choose.

WILLIAM: Ask Neil.

NEIL: He won't tell me, he says it's my choice. I'll choose the left hand one. It leads into a chamber which is dark, but the torch gives some light. I see three openings. The one on the right seems to be lighter than the others, so I'll choose the right-hand one. This leads me into an immensely spacious cavern. There are lots of lights around and an empty throne. I don't think I should be here.

WILLIAM: What does Neil advise.

NEIL: He doesn't know either. I'm looking at my own mind, and that's too scary.

Session Six

WILLIAM: I thought I'd better ask you about last week, and if you feel like continuing with the journey.

NEIL: It was pretty scary, and I've thought a lot about it since. It seemed to be about opening doors, didn't it.

WILLIAM: I wondered, too, if the throne was something to do with taking possession of what was rightly yours?

NEIL: You mean, be king of my own mind?

WILLIAM: That's a good way of putting it, yes. Now to continue. I'll take you back to the fork in the passage, and this time I suggest you take the right side. Just check with Neil if that's OK.

NEIL: He says, it is OK, and says, that to explore one and not the other might lead to disappointment. The right side is dark and quite narrow. The walls are made of stone.

WILLIAM: Do those stones have any message for you?

NEIL: No, only that this passage is durable, and won't easily crumble. This is a really long passage, and now I come to a room, like a mediaeval banqueting hall, with a long table, but no chairs or benches. By the huge fireplace are two chairs. One straight and uncomfortable to sit in; the other has cushions, that is comfortable.

WILLIAM: Any ideas?

NEIL: Oh, yes, they're something to do with my father and mother. As different as those two chairs. Father's as hard as nails, and I don't feel comfortable with him, never did. Mum's different, soft and cuddly.

WILLIAM: Anything else about the room?

NEIL: There's a door in the corner. I'm knocking at it, but there's no answer.

WILLIAM: How do you feel about exploring what's there?

NEIL: That feels OK. I don't need to asks permission this time. There's a spiral staircase leading up. I see other doors that I know haven't been opened in centuries. Now I've come into a modern lighthouse, and I can see night and day simultaneously.

WILLIAM: Can you imagine you are travelling with the light beam?

NEIL: This is wonderful, exhilarating! It's not the light that's lighting the darkness, I am. I can be a light. Now I'm travelling through outer space, and find a star. But I'm disappointed, really disappointed. I

	thought it would be warm but it's cold. I meet lots of spherical people up there.
WILLIAM:	You really did sound disappointed. Lots of spherical people? Any ideas?
NEIL:	It shows we're all the same.

Session Seven

WILLIAM:	How do you feel about going back into the big hall where the chairs were?
NEIL:	I'd like that. There's some unfinished business, I think. I'm back there, and find myself sitting in 'father's' chair. I feel guilty, and very uncomfortable.
WILLIAM:	Stay with it and let whatever is to happen, happen.
NEIL:	The chair is growing bigger, very big, and I'm small. I've got butterflies in my stomach.
WILLIAM:	Let the butterflies come out and fly around. Describe them, and what happens.
NEIL:	They're ordinary butterflies, some white, some coloured.
WILLIAM:	Go into them, become them.
NEIL:	They've flown out, and I'm now in a wood with a woman, though I don't know who she is; she's about nineteen, and very attractive. We're standing beside a lake, and see a reflection of the moon.
WILLIAM:	Let her take you somewhere.
NEIL:	She leads me to a bedroom and we make love. I don't understand this, suddenly she's changed into a cross, lying on the bed, then quickly back again to a woman. Most odd. She tells me it's time to go.
WILLIAM:	What do you want to do with her?
NEIL:	Protect her.
WILLIAM:	I suggest you absorb her into yourself.
NEIL:	We're back by the lake, and we move towards each other, and then she's gone, and I know she's within me, and I feel comfortable with that.

Comment

Neil was an introverted and intuitive man who hated being pushed by deadlines, rules and regulations. He hated planning, and this was something that caused him concern about the course.

His 'trial run' in imagery demonstrated an unusual ability to use constructive imagination. His whole presentation was so swift and vivid, smell, hearing, colour. Not everyone can become microscopically small as he did. At that stage it was not necessary to go into psychological explanations about descending into the unconscious, and finding union with Mother Earth. His intuition told him enough, and I was certain that the experience would develop within him, and he would become aware as and when it was necessary for him to do so.

When a people have been on a 'trip' of such intensity, and depth, and particularly where they have become small or large, it is vital to make sure they are returned to 'normal'. I have taken this stance from my work with hypnosis, where the subject may retain some traces of, for example, anaesthesia, or heaviness of limb, unless everything is 'put right' before coming out of the trance. The deeper the exploration under imagery, the further the journey, and the longer the time spent, the longer it seems to take many clients to return to the present. For many it is like awakening from a deep sleep.

I would like to examine the significance of Neil's journey from the meadow to the house, by way of the stream. It is not unusual to encounter another symbol, which must be explored before moving on. There was something about the quality of the word 'paddling' that urged me ask the age, for paddling is more a word a person would use when recalling childhood memory.

The circle on the medallion probably represented the sun, and this ties in with the letter 'R' which stands for fire and for regeneration. Friend said it would become clear; it may not have become clear to Neil, for at the time I didn't know the meaning. It was not until some years later, however, when I was researching this book, that the significance of those two symbols became clear to me. What we both felt, intuitively, was that there was a link, and certainly there is a clear symbolic link between fire and regeneration. Once again, here is what seems to be clear evidence that Neil was dipping into archetypal images.

The stone turns into a tombstone, representing death, depth and the unconscious. The change of guide is not unusual, for it would appear that a new guide brings a different message and serves a different function. The new guide, with the same name, is possibly telling Neil that he has it within himself to find out; he can rely on his own strengths. The opening of the door, with the medallion, suggests one of those mystery keys, where both parts are required. Now the connection between Friend and the new guide becomes clear; each brings a part·of the mystery that opens the door and opens the unconscious.

Neil's choice of the left hand tunnel represents the choice to explore the less dominant function, and possibly the feminine principle. The choice of the right-hand opening seems to suggest that he wants to explore the dominant, the ego. He was stunned by the vision of the expanse of his mind, and abruptly ended the journey, and it took him some time to gain his equilibrium. A phrase that came to both of us, as we talked, was 'mind blowing'.

The throne represents the ultimate in authority, and an empty throne suggests that Neil hadn't yet taken possession of his inheritance, his kingdom, his right.

In my notes for that session I wrote, 'I was very conscious of having to hold him in check, though obviously I didn't succeed. I wonder if he'll come back'.

I was impressed that Neil hadn't taken fright, and that indicated a high degree of motivation and persistence. My rationale for taking him back to the fork in the passage was the abrupt ending of the previous session, suggesting unfinished business. The new tunnel, with its passages leading off *to the left* suggests that there was still much to explore about his inferior function, or his feminine principle.

The absence of people in Neil's journey is worthy of comment. One can see where they have been, or should be, but they are absent. This could reflect Neil's introversion; it could also suggest that the places and rooms are waiting to be occupied, just as the empty throne.

Three openings, or three doors represent past (left), present (centre) and future (right). They may also represent unconscious, preconscious and conscious.

The ascent of the spiral staircase suggests an ascent into the upper realms of the intellect, or into the realm above the conscious, the spiritual. This seems to be confirmed by the lighthouse, with its symbolism of light dispelling darkness, and providing safe passage. Neil identifies with the light, then 'takes off' into the heavens. However, that ends in disappointment, which 'brings him back to earth'.

I want to say a word here about synchronicity. I wrote the Dictionary, the companion volume to this one, first and then Part One. One evening, there was a television programme on lighthouses; this reminded me that this was one subject I had forgotten to include, so I entered it. One of the surprising things about imagery is that I can recall much of the client's imagery for years afterwards. This was so when I was writing the Fourth Journey, and included the bit about Neil and his cavern, although I did this without reference to the notes from which the *Dictionary of Images and Symbols in Counselling* (Stewart 1996) has grown; Neil had been my client almost five years before. The reason I think the images remain is because they have become a part of my own collective unconscious. Be that as it may, those images remain far, far longer than the recall of words. When I reached his sixth session, I was astonished to read the bit about the lighthouse. Although it had gone from my conscious memory, was my unconscious prompting me? Did it alert me to watch the TV programme so that the image of the lighthouse was included in this book? I leave you to judge, but I know what I think.

In session seven, Neil found himself in his father's chair – in his father's place. The 'growing bigger' could be symbolic of his father's personality, presence, authority, control; everything about being masculine. In Freudian terms, the 'growing' relates to the erect penis; and possibly Neil felt inferior to his father's masculinity. although this was never discussed.

The image of the butterflies is an example of externalising an image. It could have been done from within, but again I acted on intuition. Butterflies are made to fly, and I wondered where they would take him. The previous discussion about sexuality seemed to tie up with this new image of the girl and of making love. So he moves from his father's chair to being his own man, making love in his own way, without feeling the constraints of his father's presence.

The lake with the reflection of the moon. Both represent the feminine principle. The image reminds me of Narcissus who fell in love with his reflection; in Neil's case, he could well have been having a glimpse of his feminine part. The image of the cross replacing the girl possibly speaks of moral injunction and prohibition. It could also symbolise the guilt of illicit sex. Certainly, it seems to have a religious symbolism. Perhaps he was saying that he deserved to be crucified for his act.

Neil came for one more session, and reported one last bit of imagery: that he felt he had moved from wandering in a fog, to walking in the sunlight. He was meeting deadlines more better, and felt he understood himself much more.

Sophia
Lost in a Fog

I am Sophie, aged 30, and my home country is Mauritius. I did my nurse training in England, and am one of two sisters looking after elderly psychiatrically ill people. I enjoy my work very much, but recently I have been very unhappy, because the manager wants to move me to another ward where other people are in charge. It was because of my sadness that I asked to speak to the counsellor. I agreed to come weekly for six sessions.

We spoke a lot about my work and my feelings at being downgraded. My work is always of a very high standard, so it was very difficult for me to see why I should be moved. I know I get cross when work is not done to my standards, and sometimes I have to do what others should do. I cannot leave it undone. For me, expressing anger is difficult, but William encouraged me to do this. As I did express the anger, William wrote on the board, 'Sophia is not OK'. This brought the tears, and when William asked me how I felt, I realised I was very angry. He then asked me where I felt the anger. It was in my throat, almost choking me. He instructed me to open my mouth and let the anger out. When I did that I started to cry, really cry, and the anger slowly left me.

We talked about this anger, and for the first time I realised that work was only one cause of the anger. What I was even more angry about was the way other people used me. My brothers and sisters use me. Some of them still live in Mauritius and expect me to support them. They think that everyone is wealthy here, and that because I live and work in England that I must be wealthy too. I do own my own house, but only because I've worked really hard since coming to England. They expect me to send them money whenever they want it. My sister in Canada even wanted me to remortgage my house to give her £4000. I told her 'No', then felt very bad. I still want to be the good little girl, and do what they want. William asked me to think of some goals, but this was too difficult. I would like to go and live with a friend in America, but I don't know if I could risk that. Also I felt trapped in my work, I'm afraid of the manager's power and I want to escape. I thought I'd taken a big step forward when I was able to write on the board, 'Sophia is OK. I am OK'.

One session will always be with me. My ward move was coming closer and I was feeling very anxious. William explained imagery to me.

WILLIAM: You were talking just now of feeling trapped. Can you imagine what sort of trap that is?

SOPHIA: I see myself surrounded by fog, isolated and unable to move.

WILLIAM: That sounds really scary, like there are no boundaries or landmarks any more.

SOPHIA: Yes, that's right. It's late afternoon in winter. The awful feeling is so real. I've never been in one of the London fogs I'd read about, but it's just like that. I can't get any sense of direction, behind or in front.

WILLIAM: I know it's frightening, and you feel as if you're frozen to the spot, but don't fight the feeling. Stay with it, experience it.

SOPHIA: I want to run away, and I know I could, but I'll stay and fight this thing.

WILLIAM: Good on you. You're coping well. Now I'm going to suggest that the sun will appear. Describe what's happening.

SOPHIA: Slowly, oh, ever so slowly, the sun is breaking through the fog, and I feel the breeze, and I am bathed in bright sun. The scene has changed to spring time, with flowers and blossom everywhere. I feel happier. There are people, houses, and birds singing, but the way ahead still looks uncertain.

WILLIAM: Is there anyone you want to take with you?

SOPHIA: I don't want anybody. I find it difficult to reach out, William.

WILLIAM: Try, Sophia, just reach out your hand and see what happens.

SOPHIA: My mother has appeared, and I can see myself as a little child.

I cried, very much, for I realised how much I was still a child at heart and how much I wanted my mother. William held my hand as I cried, not something I find easy. I always have to be in control. There was something about the atmosphere that made me start to talk about trusting people and being used by people. An example of this is that a girlfriend wanted me to marry her brother just to keep him in England. I couldn't do that, but it made them angry with me. I wasn't sure who I could trust. By trusting William, I felt that I was starting to trust other people.

I really cannot say what it was, but I just knew that my future home would be in America, and I started making plans for later in the year. As a gift to my parents I would have them over to England for a holiday before I left for America. I think what happened is that my energy had been trapped by my anger, so that when I came for counselling, I was tired and felt unable to cope. The fog was very real, and I realised that I had the power to change things, even though perhaps I would have to experience being vulnerable again. I feel now, that I was very near to a breakdown, and if I hadn't sought help, I don't know what would have happened to me.

Comment

My impressions of Sophia in the first session were that in her personal life she was very unassertive, and found it difficult to say 'No', particularly to her relatives. At work, however, I felt she was a very powerful woman, very judgmental and intolerant. At work she likes to run a well-ordered ship, and her opposite number is a lot more casual. From what she said, I detected a strong degree of obsessiveness, and I thought she could be quite difficult.

Again from what she said, added to my observations, I thought she was quite introverted, which means that others would find her difficult to get to know; she was a very private person. Counsellors must always be aware that introverted people tend to be very private, especially about their feelings, so the motto has to be 'softly, softly'. Sophia also came over as not being a very happy person, at least in the early stages of counselling, although I didn't think this was her true state.

I was in no position to *know* the rights or wrongs of the work situation; what I thought was important was to try to understand it from her point of view. Her feelings were of loss of esteem, of being downgraded (even though her rank would have been the same), and of loss of identity. All this was coupled with a massive upsurge of vulnerability. Sophia had achieved a great deal since coming to England, and probably her way of keeping all this together was to be rigid and demanding of herself as well as of other people. It is possible, although once again I have no means of knowing, that her rigidity, her judgmental attitudes, and high standards could turn her into a tyrant; when one is ruled by a punitive conscience, this is often the visible behaviour.

It is also interesting that although she really was angry about the job, much of her anger, and sorrow, was tied up with the way her relatives used her, and her feelings of not being able to do anything about it. She still had to be the 'good little girl', and 'good' means doing what other people wanted of her. Sophia said she took a significant step forward when she could write on the board, 'I'm OK'. Some people with low esteem find it difficult to say 'I'm OK'. While none of us is perfect, or totally satisfied, or have a completely full self-esteem bucket, most of us, for most of the time, feel OK. So, even without any direct work on esteem-building, Sophia felt more OK.

Sophia's imagery was important. Her image of the fog, that grey, featureless, isolated state, spoke very much of depression. People who are depressed very often speak of feeling grey. It was also important to allow her to experience feeling lost, bewildered and afraid, without rushing to her rescue.

Although Sophia had never been in a London 'pea-souper', what she described reminded me of a time during the blackout in 1943, when I was walking across London, and was totally lost, and frightened. That experience gave me an insight into her feelings. And although we were in a cosy little room, for her the experience was as real as mine had been, all those years before. By allowing her to 'feel' the experience, it was then all the more dramatic when she was able to visualise the sun as it dispelled the fog. With the sun came the spring, with its flowers and birds; all the things that had been obscured by the fog in her emotions.

The appearance of her mother within her image surprised Sophia; she was particularly surprised by her realisation of how much she needed her mother. It was as if by stretching out to her mother she was admitting her vulnerability and her willingness to shed some of her independence. In imagery, it is often helpful for the client to be accompanied by someone else. Sophia's reluctance to stretch out was possibly an indication of her independence, and maybe her lack of trust in others. To reach out and accept help from another person demands a great deal of trust, not only in the other person, but in oneself. Sometimes it is not a person: it may be an animal, or in some instances, a favourite pet or toy; whatever gives comfort, and in whom the person finds comfort and strength.

Sophia did go to the States and was able to start making a new life for herself.

Norman
The Jigsaw

I am Norman, aged twenty-nine, and this is my account of what happened to me in ten months of counselling. I am in the Army and at the time was stationed in Winchester. Life hadn't been going too well for me. One night I stupidly became involved in a pub brawl with my ex-girlfriend – I'd drunk too much – and hit her. The police were called and the upshot was that I was hauled before the commanding officer (CO) on a charge, and told that this was my last chance, and that one of the conditions of my staying on was that I go for counselling. It wasn't the first time my drinking had caused problems for me. So, I found myself making a call to William. The CO was a friend of William's, and the Army must have paid a packet for me to see him.

There were many things I felt angry about. One of them was having to come for counselling. I resented that – I wasn't going to any shrink. William took me by surprise immediately by asking me how I felt coming to him under some sort of compulsory order. I let off steam, and felt better. I was also 'cheesed off' off at having had to go to an Army psychologist. His report said that I was immature and psychopathic in my relations with women.

Within the first session, trust was starting to build up between William and me. That was a surprise, for I don't find it easy to trust people. I was able to talk about my affair with Chris and how it had ended. It had taken me a long time to get to know her, and now that it was over I was feeling bitter and had retreated into my shell. At the end of the first session I knew I wanted to come again, if I wasn't in prison.

By the time we met again, the Court case was looming, and I asked William to help me write to my solicitor. That was useful for me, for it helped to sort out the major issues in my mind. My parents divorced when I was three. I lived with my father, and never saw my mother again until I was twenty-one. My father remarried, and mother remarried, too. I never got on with my step-mother. My mother never told David, her new husband and her daughter, May, that she had a son – me. When I knew, I felt like a spare part; a skeleton in my mother's cupboard. My father and step-mother had two more sons, Neil and Andrew.

I'd never considered myself an angry man until I started counselling. That sounds funny, now, because I'd been involved in many fights before coming into the Army. Glasgow was like that; you had to be tough to survive, and I was very tough.

WILLIAM: Just now we were talking about anger. Can you imagine what that anger looks like?

NORMAN: That sounds weird. I've never done anything like that before! But I'll go along with it.

Norman sat with his eyes closed.

I said it was weird. Something's hit me straight away. I imagine a raging forest fire. The flames gradually form the word 'hate'. I don't like that word.

WILLIAM: Do you know the bottlebrush bush in Australia? No, right. The bottlebrush bush has attractive red flowers that look like bottlebrushes. The seeds need to be exposed to the heat of the fire in order to germinate.

NORMAN: I like that bit.

WILLIAM: Now can you look at 'hate'; what does it feel like?

NORMAN: I feel very uncomfortable in my stomach. What I imagine is a furnace, stoked up and ready to blow.

WILLIAM: That's a very powerful image. How do you feel it relates to you?

NORMAN: I feel that my hatred gives me energy.

WILLIAM: Hate could also lead to murder.

NORMAN: True, but I don't like the idea of that either.

As counselling went on, I knew my anger was reducing. I suppose my job as a soldier made use of my anger, but I also knew it got in the way. I'd left school with good grades, and had taken two A levels in the Army. I'd been all set for promotion several times, but lost it because I couldn't control my temper. It always happened when I'd had too much to drink. I knew I was winning the battle when I was able to go out with some friends, have a drink, feel angry over some incident, but not blow up. I reported this back to William; he was as pleased as I was. Towards the end of counselling, William asked me to look again at my furnace, something we hadn't done for several months. I was surprised to see it completely disused, with cobwebs everywhere, and the fire, although still alight, was just smouldering. At that stage I felt in control.

My main reason for coming to William, or so I thought, was Chris. I've said that it wasn't easy for me to trust people, and I couldn't understand why she'd gone off me. I'm not sure what I expected from William; that he would look into my brain and drag out the things I'd kept hidden away. It wasn't like that, of course. Sometimes it seemed so slow to get anywhere, although I wasn't sure where I wanted to get to. In an early session, I'd been talking about my mother, when William said something like, 'Is there any connection between how you feel towards your mother and how you feel towards Chris?' Now, I'm no psychologist, but the minute he said that, I knew he'd hit the mark.

I'm not really sure how I felt about my mother. I knew what I thought, but, as William said, that's not the same thing. He was right; my feelings about her were pretty foul. I'd never given myself a chance to 'work through' them, as William put it. Whenever I thought about her, the furnace would start to blow. So, I'd learned not to think about her or my feelings. That's probably why, at one stage, William commented that whenever I spoke about mother, I never showed any emotion. I was afraid to. I just knew I needed to know my feelings.

For years I felt in the middle; between my father and my stepmother, on one side, and my mother and David on the other. I was twenty-one before I met my mother again, and sometimes I wish we'd kept apart. Both sides snipe at the other, and I get caught in the crossfire. In a strange way, I've taken on a lot of my parents' problems, and get caught up in their rows and acrimony. William put it neatly when he said, 'Like a pack-horse'. That is how it was; I felt weighed down by them. 'David's OK, he's a nice guy', I once said to William. He challenged me about that, and linked it with something I'd said in a previous session. 'David took your mother away from you and your father.' I then felt angry at William for putting my thoughts into words. I thought I had to be nice about David, for if I felt angry I might do or say something bad.

By admitting my true feelings about David, I was able to relate that to Chris going off with her new chap. I'd been angry only with her. So, I gradually came to accept that my anger towards Chris *was* probably something I felt towards women in general, and specifically towards my mother. Linked with that was the fact that I felt I couldn't trust them, any of them. Mother had let me down, and so had Chris, and there were others. That's how I thought at that time.

It wasn't easy talking about my feelings, and this was something William challenged me with early on. He said that I pushed everything up into my head. That has been the major gain for me; to be able to say how I feel. A lot of the time I didn't know how I felt. I agreed with William that a lot of my time was taken up with, as he called it, negative thinking. He taught me how to control this by substituting positive thoughts. That really did help. Many of my negative thoughts were to do with my mother, something I'd been only dimly aware of before. It's a funny thing, but although I didn't get on well with either of my parents, I hadn't told them of my latest escapade; I didn't want to lose their respect, or incur their censure. When I said that, it really surprised me. For the first time ever, I think, I was prepared to admit that I did need them, both of them.

I'd been with William for three months before I plucked up courage to talk about my darkest secret. It had been heading in that direction for weeks. I suppose I'd been holding back until after the Court case. I got a year's suspended sentence.

WILLIAM: We were talking about your life just now. How about trying to
           imagine what it looks like?

NORMAN: I see a jigsaw scattered on the floor; some of the bits I've picked up
           and pieced together. But there are other pieces I knew were there,
           but wasn't yet ready to look at.

WILLIAM: That's OK. You'll know when the time is right.

NORMAN: Thanks, that's reassuring. I had a funny dream. I was in a brick
           maze, right in the centre, with no obvious way out. I punched a
           hole in the wall so that I could see the exit.

           We just started discussing this when Norman stopped me short.

           I've just had a flash. I saw myself hanging by my teeth on the end
           of a rope. Voices were telling me to let go, but the drop seemed
           so vast.

WILLIAM: It sounds as if part of you is wishing to let go, but can't.
           Something is preventing you.

NORMAN: I know the usefulness of that rope is over; I've come to the end. I
           can't hang on by the skin of my teeth for ever.

The following session

NORMAN: When I went away last time I knew I couldn't put it off an
           longer. Oh, God, I feel bloody uncomfortable. I've come to the
           point where I have to risk letting go; risk jumping across the gulf.

WILLIAM: Norman, whatever is there is obviously very painful. And the
           image I have is of little boy lost, curled up on the pavement, head
           on knees, almost too sad even to cry.

NORMAN: That's very accurate, you know. But I'm scared as well. Did I tell
           you about this girl I've met? Nothing serious. I'm not ready for
           any real commitment.

WILLIAM: Norman, it sounds as if you would rather talk about the possible
           happiness with this new girl, than talk about what's really on
           your mind.

           *Norman and I spent a long time in silence in that session. There was
           nothing awkward about the silence, although Norman fiddled a lot with
           the seam of his trousers. Even that was significant.*

WILLIAM: It looks as if by concentrating on the seam you'll find out how
           things are joined together, kept them together. If there was no
           seam, something would be revealed.

I kept looking at my problem and how to talk about it. That silence was valuable
for me; it gave me an opportunity to think through. At the start of the next session
I told William I'd made my decision; I was going to pick up the piece of the jigsaw.
I drew a brief family tree on the board, and drew a dotted line between myself and
May, my half-sister.

When May and I met, she was 19 and I was 21, we fell head-over-heels in love
and had an intense sexual relationship for about three years. We'd grown up without
knowing about each other, and although we both knew the relationship was wrong,

we felt helpless to do anything about it. May had to have two abortions. We eventually told our parents, and they blamed me for everything.

Yes, I was partly responsible, but so were they. May and I felt victims of a horrible plot, conceived by some malevolent being. They said to me 'You've only done this to get back at us.' After the second abortion, we both knew it wouldn't work out, so we split up, and I withdrew into myself again, and joined the Army, to get away from Glasgow and all the memories.

As I told William all this, I was taken aback to see tears in his eyes, and he said, 'I feel so sad for you both'. No one had ever said anything like that to me, not that many people knew about our incestuous relationship. There was no judgment, no censure, no blame, just an overwhelming feeling of being cared for.

What I hadn't realised is that I'd never given myself a chance to grieve. I'd lost something precious in my relationship with May, yes, but there were also the two abortions. Two children we could have had. Oh, I know it couldn't have worked, but the feelings as I talked it through with William were overpowering. Slowly, but surely, I was getting in touch with all the feelings that for so long I'd pushed up into my head; feelings that all fuelled the fire in the furnace. When I met Chris, I thought it was love, but now I realise that there was far too much anger in the way of loving anyone. When that session ended, I wondered why it had taken me so long to talk about it. William said, that's the way it had to be; that there is a natural flow in these things.

In the first session I told William about my brother Neil who had been killed in a motorcycle accident fifteen months before. My father was ill at the time, so all the funeral arrangements fell on me. It's awful to say, but I wished it had been Andrew; he and I didn't get on very well. We do now, but at the time, no. I was angry and deeply hurt by Neil's needless death, and very angry at the lorry driver. As I talked it through, although it was almost five months before I felt safe enough to talk, William and I came to the conclusion that here was another strand to my anger. I liked Neil, and he was killed. I didn't like Andrew very much, and he lived.

But there's a rub there; it was only just before Neil was killed that I'd made any effort to get on with him. William wondered if my grieving over Neil was not being completed because of my anger over Chris. So, I suppose what we had been doing was untangling all these feelings, and dealing with them separately. I didn't do much crying with William; I did that privately.

Several times William asked me if I wished to continue counselling. We'd agreed on eight sessions, but as time went on I knew I was getting so much out of it, that it would have been silly to stop before we had picked up all the bits of the jigsaw. As it happened, I never did, completely. By the end, the picture had grown from the centre outwards, although I realised that the edges of the jigsaw were missing, and that the picture would go on being completed all through my life, and that it was very much up to me what sort of picture was painted.

William and I got on really well. At first I was wary, and I didn't have to tell him so. I found him very open in his feelings towards me. Two or three times he said something like, 'I feel there's something happening within you, that makes me want to hold you'.[1] When this happened it was spot on, for I was feeling pretty low, and at one time I knew I was feeling like a little boy again, needing comfort. Although part of me wanted to, I couldn't reach out to him. My goals in counselling were to come to terms with my feelings of anger and loss, and to be able to react appropriately to feelings. I wouldn't say I've reached those goals, but I've started, and have gone quite a long way along the road.

One reason the relationship meant so much to me is that William knows far more about me than any other person alive, and I feel comfortable with that. There was one occasion when I rejected what he was offering me. It was at the time when I was struggling with having to disclose my relationship with May. He leaned forward towards me, and with much compassion said, 'I feel, at the moment, of a need to give you a great deal of love'. It was that word 'love' I rejected. Something to do with never having had much love from a man before. I turned it into 'support'. I could cope with that. At the same time, and now reflecting on it, I know he was talking about a love deeper than at that stage I could understand.

I feel that William allowed me to travel towards my goals at my own pace, in an atmosphere of total acceptance. Our final session wasn't easy. We'd planned it over four months, by only coming monthly and for two months before that I'd been coming every other week. I realised that these ten months were probably the most significant in my life, for I'd learned so much about myself. It would be trite to say that I was a different person, but in many ways I'd changed. My CO was pleased with me and my progress. The Regiment was soon to be off to Ireland, and I'd been told that if I kept my nose clean, they would consider me for promotion. Saying goodbye to William wasn't easy, and yet in a strange way I was glad to. That part of my life is finished, yet somewhere within me there is a part that is warmed whenever I think about that relationship.

Comment

My work with Norman is something I shall remember for a long time to come, for a number of reasons. In my experience as a counsellor, this was the first time I'd been used as part of a disciplinary procedure. As a psychiatric social worker in the Army I had become used to working within the constraints of the Army Act, and the discipline involved therein. I felt decidedly uncomfortable at first, and it took me a few days before agreeing to the CO request. There are many people in the social work field who have no option. Probation officers, for example, are part of the legal system, and have to exercise a controlling function. Those caring for children and mentally ill people often have to protect clients by the use of court orders, and at the same time, establish and maintain a caring relationship, in much the same way as I did with Norman. Having explored this with Norman, we settled down to a long and fruitful relationship.

Norman has already said how he had difficulty with feelings. People who have suffered great trauma, particularly from an early age, often experience this. Intellec-

---

1   See footnote 1, p.222 for comment on touch within the therapeutic relationship.

tualisation is frequently used as a defence. It's safer that way. However, we must not despise thinking. A person's thoughts often lead us into feelings. So, we start where the client is, not where we would like her or him to be. I have found imagery to be a useful link between thinking and feeling.

Images, initially, bypass thinking, and Norman, much to his surprise, was adept at imagery, some of which he has mentioned. One often gets a clue to how easily a client will use imagery. Norman's use, quite early on, when he was talking about his mother, of 'I was a skeleton in her cupboard', immediately creates an image, so I thought he would probably use this medium very well. In session four, I asked him to imagine what his life looked like. He imagined a troubled sea, with the sun rising over it, and a lighthouse on the shore. His interpretation of this was a picture of hope.

Another image we shared was of limbo. Norman was a nominal Roman Catholic, so the concept of limbo would be reasonably familiar. There was something about the way Norman was relating his state of mind that conjured up Limbo in mine. Norman experienced this; separation from his family, but also separation from part of himself. When I first met Norman (and I commented on this in my notes), I was struck by his eyes. They were incredibly sad eyes, yet within them there was a deep fear. If he was experiencing limbo, then his eyes would reflect something of what I picked up. Although this image wasn't pursued, it might have been fruitful to liken Norman's journey with Dante's *Divine Comedy*, and the passage through Limbo, Hell, Purgatory, then to Paradise.

In session four, Norman spoke of limbo as a white room with many locked doors; none of the keys he found fitted. This image speaks of frustration and lack of control; that he did not possess the answer. A room frequently represents the unconscious, or something not easily accessible to the conscious mind. A function of a key is to either lock (to make secure, to hide) or to unlock (to reveal, or make visible). The finding of a key that fits a treasure box often features in mythology and fairy tales.

It is possible that the reference to limbo awakened something in Norman's mind. The Church of Rome teaches that the Virgin Mary is the 'Gate of Heaven'. If Norman felt himself to be in limbo, an appeal to the Virgin Mary might be the key to open the gates and release him. Many people think of limbo as being a place of darkness. White suggests timelessness and, at the same time, is more positive than black, more hopeful. One can also look upon limbo as a state of suspended judgment. Perhaps Norman felt alienated on account of his 'sins', deserving of punishment, yet not totally guilty.

At one stage Norman was feeling emotionally low. In imagery he saw himself as a tramp, wandering in the rain. He was free and yet not without his problems. The feeling that we discussed was that of loneliness and isolation; of not fitting in, of rejection by society.

One of the significant sequences of working with Norman was the tremendous feelings his struggle generated within me. This, I think, was important for both of us. I want to link this to the period of about six sessions when he knew there were parts of the jigsaw he would have to pick up. His struggle became mine. As he was unwilling to disclose, I was unwilling to force disclosure in any way. It was at that time when I told him of my need to give him love, the word he rejected and for which he substituted 'support'. Two sessions before he spoke of his incestuous affair, I ended my notes with, 'I must guard against pushing him into disclosing something, merely because of my curiosity'.

There is always an ever-present danger of doing just that. One becomes intuitively aware of something significant hovering just on the brink, and one feels that if only the client will let go, everything will drop into place. Yet, it is at such a time that one is often wiser to hold back and to stay with the struggling client, with all that that means.

Norman recalls the silence during that particular session, silence that gave him space and time to work things through. During such silences, it is of vital importance for the counsellor to be in total attendance, though this is not easy. It is much easier to allow one's thoughts to be a thousand miles away. When we break contact by allowing our thoughts to wander, there is an intuitive break in the slender thread that holds client and counsellor in rapport. Such a break will interfere with the client's inner concentration, although the cause of the break may not become evident to the client.

Norman's pain about his relationship with May was tangible, and it caught me somewhere in the solar plexus. Much of what had transpired over the previous thirteen session dropped into place, for him as well as for me. This was no tragicomedy of the opera stage; this was tragedy in the raw, a sadness that tore Norman apart as he spoke of their happiness and loss. A relationship that had all the seeds of destruction inherent within it: a relationship that could never be.

Norman was not the sort of man to respond to my physical contact; we'd discussed that early on. I felt, at that stage, that I was the one needing to be held. I wasn't at all sure how to reach out to this man in such despair. My tears did that. The sharing of those tears emphasised vulnerability, his and mine. In the next session he disclosed how he felt empty in the pit of his stomach. This was probably to do with the amount of feeling he had discharged in the previous session. After gaining his permission, I put my hand on his head and as I suggested he fill the empty chamber with warmth and light, he became aware of flashing, bright lights, then the sun filled his whole body. The feelings he identified with were hope and light.

In one imagery session, Norman found himself guardian to a lost little boy, who just wanted to go home. Later on, around a lake, he met lots of people. I asked him if they had anything to say to him. He asked if they were dead. Their reply was, 'If being dead is not living, then we are dead'. His interpretation of these two separate, but linked, images, was that he needed to find and care for the child within him. The second part he interpreted as his past was dead, and he had to leave it behind. I wondered if there was part of him that had been dead, emotional, spiritual, intuitive, that needed to be brought alive. He looked very thoughtful as that session ended.

The penultimate session was close to the second anniversary of Neil's' death; that seemed a hurdle for him to get over. Although we talked about Neil, it seemed that by the time we did, much of his anger and hurt had been explored. It is interesting that he decided to talk first about May, and only then could he talk about

Neil. I had known from session one of his bereavement, and guessed at the depth of his feelings, but my instinct to leave it to Norman to work towards proved to be right. A premature exploration could have turned the course of counselling in a completely different direction.

Norman related an experience that was both cathartic and therapeutic. We had a break for one month about half-way through, while he went on holiday. One night, while listening to a record, he saw himself riding across America on a motorbike. Somehow, as often happens in these reveries, his journey became mixed up with Neil's fatal crash. In the security of his room he wept, and with the weeping came healing. The previous session, one month before, had prepared him for this. Not everything takes place within the counselling session! This is an important fact to bear in mind.

In the second session, Norman had talked about his second self, his 'alter ego', whom we decided to call N2. N2 had been around for a very long time, in fact he couldn't remember a time when he wasn't there, although his presence had become more pronounced over the past ten years. Norman described N2 as angry, immature, childish, ugly and horrible. 'He feeds off me like a parasite, and is just waiting to take over. He's not someone you'd like to meet on a dark night.' At one stage Norman used the word 'scapegoat' referring to N2. Norman hadn't exiled N2, hadn't driven him away. There was something in the way Norman was relating this that prompted me to ask if he thought N2 felt lost. He wasn't sure about that. Neither was he sure about the distance between him and N2. I related N2 to Jung's concept of the 'shadow', and the need to work toward integration to achieve wholeness.

The discussion about N2 took place in session two; thereafter he was not discussed until session fifteen, three months after the start of counselling. By this time Norman didn't feel so separated from N2, although he was still reluctant to integrate him totally. I suggested that N2 didn't only represent his bad feelings, but also some of his tender feelings. Norman had the characteristic of thinking deeply about my comments; on this occasion, it took quite a long time for him to respond. I think he genuinely did agree; he was not just giving assent. He recognised the truth of my remark. Then Norman made a profound statement; N2 only separated himself when Norman was under threat of some kind. This was a tremendous insight, and when it came, his face lit up with that delightful expression when revelation dawns. When that happened, I, too, was caught up in the feeling.

Norman and I did very little direct work on N2 there was no further mention of him and throughout the remaining nine sessions. It seemed as if the revelation achieved in session fifteen worked its own integration.

As Norman said, we had agreed to reduce the frequency of the sessions, as a preparation for the final one before he went to Ireland. Reducing the frequency may sound logical, but it presents its own difficulties. For both of us it was often not easy to pick up the threads again. In a certain sense it was as if every session was a first. But that's how Norman wanted it to be. The final session of a long-standing relationship is seldom easy, for either person. Norman had experienced so many traumatic endings to relationships; perhaps this ending, planned as it was, would, in some way, help him to work through some of the others.

Sandra
The Horse Called Freedom

I'm Sandra, I work as a secretary in local government. I came for counselling because of not being able to get over my divorce. I had psychotherapy after that.

I have one son, Jan, who now lives with me. My GP referred me to William, to see if he could help me with my stress. It was interfering with work, and I was having too much time off.

I told William that I had been sexually abused by my great-uncle when I was a child, although I knew I'd blocked most of the memories out. My ex-husband, an alcoholic, was a violent man, who sexually violated me. When it came to the separation and then divorce, he threatened to reveal my 'murky past', as he put it, if I contested his claim for custody of Jan.

I gave him custody, but after six months, he said I could have Jan as he couldn't cope with looking after him on his own. I'm now living with Ben, a black African, and we all get on really well. I feel really secure at home, although I've had to put up with a lot of prejudice over his colour.

It was brought to a head when I visited my grandmother for her ninetieth birthday and my great-uncle was there. It's the first time I've seen him since I've been grown up. All the old terror came back, but more than that, all the disgust about myself. I just knew I had to do something.

WILLIAM: Sandra, as you were telling me your story, you were obviously finding it very difficult. Your hands were on the move the whole time, and you look really very tense just now.

SANDRA: That's how it is most of the time. Sorry.

WILLIAM: No need to apologise on my account. Stress gets us like that, and we can't keep still. What I suggest is that I work through some relaxation with you.

SANDRA: The psychotherapist did that, but go ahead.

When Sandra was in a relaxed state, we continued.

WILLIAM: Sandra, when you were telling me about your traumatic life, starting with your childhood, and then your abusive husband, you related it all without much feeling, a bit clinically.

SANDRA: That's me. I don't let myself feel much, my way of coping. My psychotherapy helped me deal with my anger, now I want to get in touch with my other feelings.

I introduced Sandra to the meadow, the usual image of a bright, warm, sunny afternoon. It is not unusual for someone whose mood is low not to be able to feel the warmth, or see the sunshine, so one has to be prepared to work with what the client imagines.

WILLIAM: Can you tell me what you are imagining right now?

SANDRA: It's a cool, autumn day. I think it must have been a hot summer, for the grass is brown and dry. I can't see anything of what you suggested, for this little patch of grass is stuck right in the middle of traffic, like an island, with roads and cars and buses hurtling past.

WILLIAM: That sounds as if it's noisy, and smelly, and not very safe.

SANDRA: Oh, it's safe enough; they can't get me here.

WILLIAM: So, having people whizzing past, looking out from bus windows, all give some sense of security.

SANDRA: That's it. Safe, surrounded by concrete.

WILLIAM: Not exactly a place to lie down and rest.

SANDRA: Oh, I don't want to rest. Why should I rest?

WILLIAM: How did you get in there?

SANDRA: That's funny, how did I? Can't see any path or anything. No tunnel. How am I going to get out?

I detected a note of anxiety in her voice, and her hands tightened.

WILLIAM: I want you to imagine some steps and a bridge. Go up the steps and over the bridge, and tell me where it goes.

There was a distinct 'Phew' from Sandra as she said.

SANDRA: Oh, yes, there they are. I'm climbing the steps and on to the wooden bridge. It's a very long bridge, and as I get half-way over I look back at the grass and can see that it's much greener than I thought it was. That's nice. The bridge leads me right over the traffic and down the other side to my house.

WILLIAM: Now you're back home, my guess is that you feel really secure.

SANDRA: Yes, and there's Jan and Ben waiting for me.

Session Two

WILLIAM: Sandra, when you think of your self-image, what do you imagine?

SANDRA: I know it's not going to be very pleasant. I'm not sure I want to look at me.

WILLIAM: You're afraid that what you see will be repulsive, so you'd rather not look.

SANDRA: Yes, but that's silly when I hear you say it. Now that's funny, really funny, it's not me at all. It's a red apple. Oh dear! It's got a nasty blemish on it, and I just know that it goes right inside. Is that me, bad all the way through?

WILLIAM: That's not how you want to be, so let's see how we can work to change that image. Take the apple with you into the meadow, and tell me how it is this week.

SANDRA: It's changed slightly, the grass looks greener, and the whole patch seems much larger. It's not so noisy, either. Oh, yes, I walked across the bridge to get here this time.

WILLIAM: It sounds as if you feel secure in that image. What about the apple?

SANDRA: I'm holding it, but I don't want to. It feels bad. I want to throw it away, but I can't, it's stuck to me.

WILLIAM: However much you might want to get rid of it, you can't. Perhaps that's telling you something.

SANDRA: I can't reject myself, that's what it is.

WILLIAM: Tell it you're not going to reject it, not going to throw it away, or destroy it, then put it gently down on the grass and watch it grow.

SANDRA: It's grown to about half my size. Now what?

WILLIAM: Go into the apple and tell me what happens.

SANDRA: I feel quite comfortable here, no smell, but it's dark.

WILLIAM: Somewhere there is just enough light to let you see the way. Now travel through the pulp to the core of the apple. Now that you've reached the core, become the core, so that the core is you and you are the core. Feel the seeds within you, feel the power of those seeds, the power to produce many more apples. Now imagine a bright light shining on the core, and slowly the core is transformed, then the pulp, then the skin, transformed into a beautiful, wholesome apple. You are now outside, looking at it. What do you want to do with that apple?

SANDRA: Hug it.

WILLIAM: I suggest you do that, and tell it how you love it.

SANDRA: I'm doing that, and it's starting to shrink to its normal size.

WILLIAM: Now what do you want to do with it?

SANDRA: Eat it.

WILLIAM: As you eat it, watch as it is absorbed into your body, and transported to every part of your body. There it brings wholeness and transforms what is not whole. How do you feel, now that is over?

SANDRA: Strong and much bigger.

WILLIAM: Is there anyone else with you in the meadow.

SANDRA: Strange! The meadow's changed, it's not where it was. It's now a place I used to go to as a little girl. Yes, there's a white horse with me. I'm patting him and telling him how much I love him.

WILLIAM: And what does he say?

SANDRA: He tells me how much he loves me, and that feels really good.

WILLIAM: Ask him what his name is.

SANDRA: He says he is 'Freedom'.

WILLIAM: Get him to take you for a ride.

SANDRA: It's very difficult to get up. My uncle, father and husband's faces keep appearing. They're trying to prevent me getting up. They don't want to me have my freedom. But I'm determined, and I manage it. Oh, this is lovely. (*From the way she said it, Sandra was a child again.*) He's taking me across a bridge and upstream, through a ploughed field and into a cornfield, then to the foot of a mountain.

WILLIAM: Ask him what he wants to do.

SANDRA: He says he doesn't want to take me up the mountain. I've got to do that for myself.

WILLIAM: It's now time to say goodbye to your friend, but not goodbye to freedom. And in your own time, return to this room.

Session Three

I felt much better about myself after the second session, now I seem to have other things to cope with. Over a long time I've become really fed up with my work. It's not that I don't like it, I do, but it means I'm away from home a lot, and there's much I could be doing there. However, Ben is obsessed with money and having a nice home, so he wants me to keep on working. I wouldn't mind taking a lower paid job a bit nearer home that would give me more free time.

WILLIAM: Can you imagine two traps, one that represents your work and the other for your relationship with Ben?

SANDRA: Yes, quite easily. The work trap is a large animal trap in a wood, and I'm caught by my right leg. It's very painful. Ben is trying to help, but he's caught in a mud trap. I want to pull him out, but I can't. So we're both stuck.

WILLIAM: Is there anyone else who could help both of you?

SANDRA: A male friend of Ben's comes up and after a struggle gets Ben out. Ben then tries to prise open the teeth of the trap. But it does hurt so.

WILLIAM: Here is what I suggest. Look around and see if there is anything that will heal the wound. (*Hesitation*) Look for a pool of water, bathe in it and get healing. Take Ben with you. Now look at the trap and see if has changed.

SANDRA: It has. It's lying open, broken, useless.

WILLIAM: What about the trap of the relationship with Ben?

SANDRA: That's a domed cage, made of steel. That's probably of my own making, a protection against being hurt. I know I relate to Ben and other people through the bars.

WILLIAM: As you did with the other trap, see what emerges to bring healing with this trap.

SANDRA: My white horse, Freedom, flashed across the image, and with it the faces of my husband, father and uncle. I know they don't want me to have my freedom. They want me to remain trapped. I feel trapped by those early experiences. I want to tell them, to confront my father and my uncle, but I can't. Father is blind and we're not close enough to tell him how I feel.

Comment

Sandra's image of the 'meadow' was rather bleak and quite the opposite of the normal meadow scene. My private interpretation was that this patch of grass represented her past and her present. Autumn after a hot summer might suggest happier days, and this is backed up by the grass. The closely confined grass suggests a shrunken inner world, kept secure by the circle of roads. Her 'They can't get me here', was a possible reference to her abusers, for if there was no way in, and if she was being observed by people on the roads, then she felt safe. It is also possible that the traffic and the people represented the chaos of his her inner world.

However, not knowing how she got there was suggestive of some sort of blockage, possibly lack of insight. Also, I felt I needed to provide a way of escape, rather than increase her anxiety level. I felt she had enough for one day. There could have been a number of ways out of that enclosure; a tunnel, a path, or she could have been rescued by a helicopter. All of these were possibilities. I suggested the bridge, because a bridge connects two different points; it carries the person over something, from something towards something else. The bridge is suggestive of the past and the future.

It was interesting that the grass had changed to being slightly more green, which seemed to suggest new growth. Landing at her own front door speaks for itself, and if one takes the symbolism of the bridge one step further, the bridge connected the enclosure with her own front door. And all the movement there was that day was from the one to the other. My hunch was that as they both symbolised security to her, that it might take some time before she felt secure enough to leave her own front door to venture into the wider space of her inner world.

The red apple with a blemish represents spoiled potential, as if the flesh has been bruised. The representation would have been different had she bitten into the apple and then discovered, for example, that a worm had eaten part of it away. So it is important to distinguish that although Sandra saw the blemish going right through, that it came from outside in, and happened *after the fruit was formed*. When an image is presented in this way, I always think it better to continue developing the theme, rather than to enter into 'discussion'. Sandra was screaming out for reassurance, and I felt that it was more appropriate to use imagery to help transform the image into something more acceptable.

The return to the meadow is an important part of the journey. In a way it is a partial regression, a going back, and often going back is necessary to move forwards. A second point is that the meadow is familiar ground, and while some clients may cope perfectly well with exploring new ground, Sandra's first encounter with her meadow would suggest that she would feel safer with what she already knew. It is also significant that she recreated the bridge. The green she had already imagined at the end of the first session had remained, and that was a healthy sign.

The image of entering the apple may seem odd, but I saw the apple as representing the unconscious, and so it was no more odd than entering a cave. In some ways the image of the apple makes more sense than entering a cave, for if we accept that fruit speaks of fertility, and is associated with the womb, then entering an apple could very well symbolise entering the womb.

It is always wise, although it doesn't always happen this way, to 'bring the client out' from wherever she has gone into. This is symbolic of bringing out from the unconscious back into the conscious. This part of the journey illustrates integration and absorption of the good. It is significant that when Sandra re-enters the meadow it, too, has been transformed.

Naming an object is often a way into the symbolism, in this case 'Freedom'. The three significant men in her life all conspired to prevent her gaining her freedom. Her father, with whom she has little contact now, had persistently put her down and always told her she was illegitimate. The link with her great-uncle and husband was obvious.

One of the essential characteristics of imagery, indeed in all counselling, is to get the client to be specific. By my pressing Sandra to be specific about the traps she provided clues as what could be done to rescue her from them. Taking the first trap, it could represent the mouth – jaws and teeth. For it is what people have said that created that trap. Animal traps such as she visualised are vicious; the tongue is also vicious. She is caught by her right leg; the right side could represent her logical brain.

Ben was caught in mud. Mud is a totally different sort of trap, very difficult to get out of. In a way, the mud trap is more passive in nature, and yet more frightening. Ben needed the help of a male friend, someone outside of the situation. So, she could only get out of the work trap with Ben's help, with his agreement and co-operation. Her steel-domed trap symbolises fear. There is a difference between this trap and the bird cage; this one keeps people out; the bird cage keeps the bird in. Sandra and I discussed much of this, and though only some of it seemed to fit Sandra's particular circumstances.

Jack
Repairing the Reservoir

I am Jack, a self-employed builder, aged 28. I fell in love with Jess and very quickly she became pregnant. I was thrilled and thought she wanted what I did, to marry, settle down, have a family. Without speaking to me, Jess had an abortion, and only told me when it was all over. In the first session with William I wept for a lot of the time. No woman had ever drawn such love out of me in the way that Jess did. Now I just feel bitter and so hurt. I know a little about counselling, from when I was a Samaritan.

I think the relationship breakdown is irreversible. She's decided to go to Australia in three months for a whole year. Somehow I have to try to pick up the pieces of my life, but I'm so afraid that this will get in the way of other relationships.

Session Two

JACK: What can I do with this pain? At times it almost chokes me.

WILLIAM: Spend a few minutes on your breathing, and relaxing, then I'll take you into some imagery, and see if we can get at the pain.

I had introduced Jack to relaxation in the first session, and he had taken one of my relaxation tapes.

Now that you are nicely relaxed, imagine the breath entering your nostrils and watch it leaving them. Get this rhythm going. Now watch the breath as it enters and starts to go down the tubes into the lungs. Imagine as it gets there that it is bringing peace as it bathes the tissues. Watch it now as it travels from the lungs to the heart. Imagine you are looking at the heart from the inside. What do you see.

JACK: All I can see is blackness, I can't see the lungs or any of that. What I can see is a black shape on the wall, it must be my heart, but it's held there, like a plaque.

WILLIAM: Touch it: what does it feel like?

JACK: It's smooth, moist and warm.

WILLIAM: And how you feel as you do that?

JACK: Strange, but it seems it wants to say something.

WILLIAM: Talk to it. Love it, show it you care.

JACK: I'm doing that, and I stroke it, so it's changing. The black is slowly changing to grey. It's like it's struggling to change into a colour.

WILLIAM: Imagine a bright light shining on to it and you, and with that light will come healing.

JACK: It's working, it really is! The light's coming from outer space, you know, something like a laser beam, directed at the centre of the heart, and the light is spreading from the centre. Oh it's lovely. I'm going to cry again, but I don't care.

I felt really good at the end of that session, and very relaxed, and somehow clean. We talked about how vulnerable I felt and kept everybody, as it were, outside castle walls. William smiled and said, 'You've let me in, and thank you'. I don't ever remember crying so much with anyone before, but it felt really good.

Session Three

JACK: You know, William, in spite of all that's happened, I still need to have hope, but I'm not sure what's happened to that.

WILLIAM: Let's try some imagery. Imagine there is a reservoir, and you give it the name of Hope. What do you see?

JACK: I'm remembering a reservoir in Africa, when I was doing VSO,[1] it was outside a small town. Now I see the water level dropping, and I know if the leaks aren't stopped, the people will die. I must repair it.

WILLIAM: How will you do that?

JACK: I'll get in. There's a big hole, bigger than I thought. I don't know how to repair it. I feel so helpless.

WILLIAM: Who can you get to advise you?

JACK: Dave appears, he's an old friend. He advises me to make the hole a little bigger, and to round it off, get rid of the rough edges. He's helping me repair it with a sort of plastic cement that fills the hole. I'm now getting out and looking at the water. Oh, dear (*crying*), we've blocked that hole but there's still a small trickle of water from somewhere else.

I reached out and held his hand, which he gripped very tightly.

WILLIAM: What do you want to do now?

JACK: I'll leave it for today, and maybe come back and have another go.

---

1   Voluntary service overseas.

That session really gutted me. I felt so optimistic that I'd be able to repair the hole and stop the water escaping. I felt quite exhausted after all that. I know it was all imagination, but it really did feel like I was in the water, and I know I was having to keep my cool and not panic. We discussed what it all meant, and came to the idea that the hole was some really big wound I've been carrying around, although maybe it's not just to do with Jess, that wouldn't be fair. I knew there's been a lot of healing taking place over these three sessions, and we agreed that I'd stop there, but I could always come back if I felt I needed to.

Comment

The imagery of the breath and the heart is one I frequently use, particularly where the person is feeling constriction or pain. Most people enter into this very well, and I think this is so because breath is vital to life. I also find that immersing the client within the body in this way helps to deepen relaxation, thus allowing the imagery to work more effectively. In Jack's case, all he could imagine was a 'black heart', hanging on the wall. In discussion, I said, 'It sounded like it was somebody's trophy, you know, like a stag's head'. Although he smiled, it was without humour, as he acknowledged the truth, of the situation; that Jess had 'bagged' his heart, now he was having to reclaim it.

One session of imagery should not be divorced from the imagery in other session, for just as individual dreams often have a common thread, so in imagery. In Jack's case, the image of the heart, essential to life, then became linked with the imagery in the third session. The fact that I had introduced the idea of the reservoir is an example of how I think my unconscious was working, and making links, for I was not aware that I consciously thought of the two images being connected.

Water is also essential to life, and Jack's experience of Africa emphasised this importance. Developing the link between the heart and the reservoir, it would seem appropriate to suggest that the 'hole' was in his heart, that he was still 'bleeding' from the 'wound'. Instinctively he knew that if that hole was not repaired then he (the people of the village) would not survive. And in order to survive he had to have hope.

The sadness Jack felt when he realised that although that hole was repaired, there was still leakage somewhere, seemed as if was coming from the very depths of his soul. He realised that at some stage he would have to work on that. Here seems an appropriate place to talk about tears. Tears are not uncommon in counselling, and are often associated with healing, certainly with release of tension. What I have noticed is that in imagery, tears seem to come from much deeper.

Many people struggle against crying, but when they do allow themselves to cry, their tears often turn to weeping. My thoughts on this are that the imagery is working at such a deeply unconscious level, and tapping into archetypal images that they cannot help their tears. And when these deep images are tapped into, they invariably bring healing *deep down*.

Jack discovered that although he had 'plugged' one hole, there was other work to do. It is highly unlikely that any of us could ever plug every hole, heal every hurt, but that does not invalidate the work of healing.

Drawing the Threads Together

In the second part we journeyed a little way with 18 people and shared some of their joys, pain, frustrations and tears. We experienced how some of them felt trapped by their circumstances, and we saw how through imagery they felt empowered to move forward, and how many of them left counselling with their self-esteem bucket more full than before they started.

We saw how Bill dealt with a crossroads experience, and how Alan became more accepting of his sexuality, and how he began to take control of his life. For Arran, his journey into the depths of his lake was scary as he confronted his shadow in the form of the monster.

Andy experienced the healing touch of his inner priest. Tracy's journey was longer than the others, but like all the others there was a steady move towards integration. It is a paradox that before integration could take place, Tracy had to experience separation from Auntie Joan and from her mother through rebirth.

Imagery can take many forms and directions, as we saw with Hazel and the brass candlestick which represented her hopelessness. The work with Hazel demonstrates how it was necessary for me to be prepared to experiment with different techniques.

Janice described herself as a 'woman who loves too much', and this had led her into many disastrous relationships with men. As she moved towards reconciliation with her parents, and accepted that she was not to blame for their divorce, some repair work was done on her self-esteem bucket.

Lily's journey speaks of a descent into the unconscious, the opening up of the psyche and the ultimate union of the human with the wider universe.

Meg experienced healing on the beach, as the waves washed away the pain and the dirt she felt she had been carrying, particularly related to her rape and abortion.

Moira discovered her 'pearl of great price' in the most unlikely of places, deep in a well.

Neil, in his journey, found two different guides as he travelled the vast distance from his roots into outer space.

Sophia found herself lost and trapped in a grey, lifeless, sunless and frightening fog, which had some semblance of depression. Fog which was dispelled by wind and sun.

Norman's journey illustrates how 'passing through the fire' of grief and loss brings refinement.

Sandra experienced a dramatic contrast between the meadow scene – an island in the middle of thundering traffic – and the freedom of riding her horse. Being freed from her past opened the way for her to work on freeing herself from the traps she felt herself and her husband to be in.

Jack covered a great deal of ground in a few sessions, and did a lot of repair work on his broken heart and on the leaky reservoir, which, if not repaired, would have led to drought and disaster.

In none of these illustrative cases do I talk about 'cure' or 'success'; all the clients left with much work still to be done. The journey towards wholeness and integration is never complete. Jack probably sums it all up best: 'I've plugged one big hole, but there are others, and another day'.

In the *Dictionary of Images and Symbols in Counselling* (Stewart 1996) you will be able to identify many of the different symbols that have been used in this book. You may also find that you want to extend the imagery by introducing inner pictures of your own. I hope you do, for this extending of ideas will be a fruitful for you.

Examples of Archetypes

1. One:
   The origin, the essence of nature.

2. Two or twofold structure:
   masculine/feminine.
   Animus and Anima.
   Positive/negative.
   Light/dark.
   Yin/Yang.
   Inner/outer.

3. Three or threefold structure:
   the Trinity: Father, Son and Holy
   Spirit.

4. Four or fourfold structure:
   North, south, east, west.
   Summer, autumn, winter, spring.
   Childhood, youth, adulthood, old
   age.
   Fire, water, air, earth.
   Ego, shadow, Animus/Anima, self.
   Thinking, feeling, sensation,
   intuition.

5. Other symbolic models:
   The *I Ching*.
   The chakras.
   The kabbalah.
   The planets of the Zodiac.
   Gods and goddesses.
   Demons and angels.

6. The hero, for example:
   King Arthur.
   Jason of the Argonauts.
   John Wayne – the example of
   rugged, honest American
   manhood.

7. Search for food and shelter.

8. Daily rhythm of work and sleep.

9. The search for a mate.

10. Ideas:
    Plato believed that reality consists of
    archetypes, or forms, beyond human
    sensation, which are the models for
    all things that exist in human
    experience.

11. Art:
    van Gogh's work represents the
    archetype of expressionism, the idea
    of emotional spontaneity in painting.

12. Great Mother, from whom the world
    sprang; who fertilises every living
    thing.

13. Father, representing all that is strong;
    that which endures.

Make your Imagination Work for You

- On wakin z, and often during the day, repeat – aloud if possible – 'My mind is under my control'.

- Learn to use deep relaxation positively. When relaxed, repeat, 'My mind is under my control'.

- Before you start doing anything that requires concentration, repeat inwardly, 'Now, concentration'.

- On a sheet of paper draw a number of columns and divide them into one year periods of your life. Start with the current year, and gradually work backwards, recalling specific incidents, people, places and events associated with a particular period. Be precise. Recall colours, smells, tastes, sights, sounds and touch.

- Recall the first time you were allowed to choose and buy your own clothes.

- Recall your first kiss. Who, where, when?

- Recall the first time you deliberately disobeyed an order of your parent or teacher.

- Think of a 'trigger' word, for example 'home', and let your mind conjure up every association linked with that word. Pay particular attention to the images linked with the five senses. Choose another trigger word, such as 'cat', 'dog', 'cow', and experience the different images that are associated with it. Then get a sheet of paper and write the trigger word in the centre of the page and write the words that came into your mind when you were using association. Are you now able to add any more words? While doing any of these exercises, note when you allow your mind to wander. Gently bring your mind back to the last association. When the association is finished, think around those times you allowed your mind to wander and try to discover the reason why. By recalling in this disciplined way you are controlling your mind.

- Let your imagination work *for* you, not *against* you.

- Spend time every day concentrating on any of the mandalas included in Appendix 7.

- Sit in a park, by the sea, or in some other place of nature, close your eyes and for five minutes listen to all the sounds around you. At the end of the time, write down what you heard. Repeat the exercise whenever possible and try to increase the number of sounds you can recall.

- Sit in a shopping precinct and count the number of people who pass you in the course of five minutes.

- Count the number of people you observe wearing a particular item of clothing, or wearing spectacles, or carrying a particular article.

- Sit with your eyes closed (never mind if people think you're odd!) and try to identify different smells.

- Lay 12 small objects on a table and cover them with a cloth or leave the room for at least ten minutes. When the time is up, look at the objects table for two minutes, then move away and recall the items on the table. When you can recall all twelve, draw their positions on a sheet of paper. When you have mastered this, ask a friend to lay out twelve different items, and repeat the exercise.

- Scatter a box of matches on the floor. Place the empty box on the table and pick the matches up one by one and put them in the box. Try not to hurry the exercise. This exercise induces calmness

- Create an imaginary scene in which you were forced to say that you had lied, when you had in fact told the truth.

- Imagine a huge hole in the sky, and then fill it up with imaginary objects.

- Imagine yourself creating a masterpiece of great art.

- Imagine finding a map of Treasure Island, then set out to find the treasure.

- Imagine walking along the street and coming face to fact with your double.

- Imagine coming face to face with someone you thought was dead.

End of Session Exercise

Each time you engage in exercises involving imagery, I suggest you finish off with the following routine.

1. Rapidly sketch over the session in your mind.

2. Make a few notes of what took place and any insights you have received.

3. Go round and touch various objects to 'ground' you.

4. Stand upright, stretch your hands above your head, and as you slowly lower them to your sides, repeat, several times, 'I am... Today's date is...and I am here (name of the room and place).

Make your mind a willing partner, not a fettered slave!

APPENDIX 4
Biofeedback

Our body responds dramatically to our thoughts. Thoughts are powerful, and to a certain extent they determine our body functions. If our thoughts can make our body tense, the power of the mind can also help us to relax.

Find a quiet place and relax, using a relaxation tape or earplugs to cut out noise if you find these things helpful. Sometimes you may be aware of trying to relax and yet your body and mind seem to be racing. Use your power of imagination to help yourself to slow down.

Visualise yourself running: experience the raised heart rate and increased breathing, then consciously slow the pace of the run, over several stages until you are walking briskly.

The next stage is to slow the brisk walk down to a stroll and then from a stroll to an amble until finally stand still. Find a quiet place to sit or lie. By this time your body will be relaxed; it has responded to the feedback you have given it.

When you are relaxed, let your imagination take you to a place that is beautiful, quiet and peaceful. Lie down and let the sun warm you. Listen to the sounds of nature – the birds, bees, the wind in the trees and the grass around you. Listen to the sound of a brook somewhere in the scene. Get up, wander to the stream, take off your shoes and paddle. Feel the coolness of the water, see the slightly brown, rusty deposit that comes from high up in the peat hill you see in the distance. Put on your shoes and decide to explore the distant hill. Let your imagination take you where it will. Give this place a name. It is your place, your retreat, that no one else can enter or violate. It is your haven to retreat to when you are feeling under pressure.

Usually your body will tell you when it is time to end this exercise, either as you become wide awake or sigh deeply. Learn to listen to your body and you will have mastered one important step towards balancing of body, mind and emotions. Remember that balance in nature is a transitory state, not a perfect one that lasts for ever. That would be static. Whenever we achieve balance, however transitory, that is perfection. Savour those moments. When we experience many such moments, we will have travelled a little further along the road of managing pressure and preventing stress and breakdown.

APPENDIX 5
Exercise in Focused Attention

Focused attention is a useful exercise to use in pain relief or the relief of tension. Many of us shy away from pain, and try to dismiss it. What I suggest here is that we should do the exact opposite: imagine you are the pain. Pain is something we all experience and is the body's means of communicating some message to us. Persistent pain, however, should not be ignored, and medical advice should be sought. But very often, even after having consulted a doctor, all that we are offered is pain-killing medication. What I am suggesting is an aid, not a cure.

When you are nicely relaxed, imagine you are sitting on the grass in your meadow. You put your hand down by your side, and feel the sharp pain of thorn as it pricks the tip of your right index finger. You jerk away in pain. You hold your finger, then stick it in your mouth to find relief. You really can feel the throbbing, and the finger looks red.

Now concentrate your whole attention on the spot, see the blood as it oozes out. Feel the throb as your whole body takes up the throb of the pulse in the finger. Your attention is now truly focused. Now start to feel the pain lessening, gradually, little by little. The throbbing becomes less intense, the angry red changes gradually to a more normal colour. You can no longer feel the pulse in the finger. You are back to normal.

This visual exercises can be used for any part of the body, and is simple enough to pass on quickly to someone who is in pain.

Affirmations

Using Affirmations

Read through the affirmations listed here, and note any that you think you would have difficulty believing *about yourself.* Go over the affirmations to which you cannot give wholehearted assent.

When you have done this for all of the affirmations you query, choose one, and ask yourself why, and write down your reasons. Use your imagination to go back in time and try to find out why you cannot affirm yourself. Whose voice do you hear? What words are they saying to you? What figures do you see? What gestures are being used? Being able to affirm ourselves invariably has its roots in how other people approve of us, and vice versa.

Changing a non-affirmation into a positive affirmation will not be achieved easily; however, if you believe you can change it, you will end up believing in yourself.

Affirmations

- I am me, and in all the world, there is no one else exactly like me.
- I am unique.
- I own everything about me – my body, and everything about it.
- I own my mind, including all my thoughts and ideas.
- I own my eyes, including the images of all they look at and see.
- I own my feelings, whatever they may be – both positive and negative. I might like some and not others, but they are still mine.
- I own my mouth, and all the words that come of it, polite, sweet or rough, correct or incorrect.
- I own my voice, loud or soft.
- I own all my actions, whether they be to others or to myself
- I own my fantasies, my dreams, my hopes, my fears.
- I own all my triumphs and successes, all my failures and mistakes.
- Because I own all of me, I can get to know myself intimately, and use all of me to work in my best interests.
- There are things about myself that puzzle me, and others I yet do not know. But so long as I am friendly and loving to myself, I can courageously and hopefully look for the solutions to the puzzles and for ways to find out more about myself.
- However I look and sound, whatever I say and do, and whatever I think and feel at any given moment, that is the unique and authentic me.

- When I think about how I looked and sounded, what I said and did, and how I thought and felt, I can discard anything I choose. I can keep that which proved appropriate. I can invent something new for that which I discarded.

- I can see, hear, feel, think, say, and do. I have the tools to survive, to be close to others, to be productive, and to make sense and order out of the world of people and things outside of me.

  - I own me, and therefore I can change me.

  - I am me and I am okay.

  - I forgive myself for every mistake and offence against myself.

  - I forgive all hurt other people have caused me.

  - I accept the responsibility for my own life, and affirm that no one has power over my decisions without my full agreement.

A quote from Gibran's *The Prophet* brings this appendix to a close.

> You are not enclosed within your bodies,
> nor confined to houses or fields.
> That which is you dwells above the mountain
> and roves with the wind.
> It is not a thing that crawls into the dun for warmth
> or digs holes into darkness for safety,
> But a thing free, a spirit that envelops the earth
> and moves in the ether. (p.108)

Mandala Number 1

This mandala is more than a simple pattern; it is the first step toward control of your right, creative hemisphere. You may well find that your verbal left brain will become frustrated because it cannot deal with the spatial relationship and it will stop paying attention. Then your right-brain can begin to take over. The mandala will help you find the silence that lies deep within you.

Sit comfortably and hold the drawing before you. Focus on the centre of the figure, and observe the pattern. Feel the sensations caused by the pattern. Plan to stare at the centre of the mandala as long as you feel comfortable doing so. The visual patterns will seem to shift as you concentrate on the centre.

The mandala will help you to:

1. Centre your attention.
2. Quiet the chattering of your inner dialogue.
3. Distract the left hemisphere, which cannot deal with spatial relationships.
4. Allow the right hemisphere to dominate for an extended period of time.

Mandala Number 2

Sri Yantra, the most revered of all mantras, is composed of interlocking triangles based on a single, downward-pointing triangle, symbol of female creativity. From it, or her, all male and female life forms develop, shown by upward- and downward-pointing triangles, spreading like concentric ripples in water.

Mandala Number 3

The *Rose Window* of a Christian cathedral normally faces west, the direction of paradise, in ancient pagan tradition. West is also the mysterious sunset land that medieval mystics converted into the fairy land ruled by its divine queen.

Christian congregations turn their backs on the female rose in the west window and face the male symbol of the cross in the east window.

References

Aeschylus (1979) *Oresteia* Translated by Hugh Lloyd-Jones. 3 vols. Electronic Text.

Aeschylus (c. 450 BC) *The Furies.*

Assagioli, R. (1965) *Psychosynthesis.* Wellingborough: Turnstone Press.

Assagioli, R. (1969) *Symbols of Transpersonal Experiences.* London: The Institute of Psychosynthesis.

Assagioli, R. (1976) *Transpersonal Inspiration and Psychological Mountain Climbing.* London: The Institute of Psychosynthesis.

Bacon, F. (1672) 'The New Atlantis.' Cited in *Great Literature* (CD-ROM). Parsippany, NJ: Bureau Development Inc.

Blake, W. (1993) Cited in *Oxford Dictionary of Quotation and Modern Quotations. Electronic Edition* (1993). Oxford: Oxford University Press.

Bolen, J.S. (1984) *Goddesses in Every Woman.* New York: Harper and Row.

Bolen, J.S. (1989) *Goddesses in Every Man.* New York: Harper and Row.

Brown, M. (1983) *The Unfolding Self.* Los Angeles: Psychosynthesis Press.

Browne, T. (1643) 'Religo Medici.' Cited in *Great Literature* (CD-ROM). Parsippany, NJ: Bureau Development Inc.

Buber, M. (1937, 1987 print) *I and Thou.* Edinburgh: T and T Clark Limited.

Bunyan, J. (1678) *Pilgrim's Progress.* Glasgow: Richard Griffin and Co.

Campbell, J. (1959–1970) *The Masks of God.* New York: Viking.

Cary, H.F. (1923) *The Vision of Dante* (Trans.). Oxford: Oxford University Press.

Chetwynd, T. (1986) *A Dictionary of Symbols.* London: Palandin.

Crampton, M. (1974) *An Historical Survey of Mental Imagery Techniques in Psychotherapy.* Montreal: Quebec Centre of Psychosynthesis.

Dante (c.1307) *The Divine Comedy.*

Desoille, R. (1966) *The Directed Daydream.* London: The Institute of Psychosynthesis.

Fabricius, J. (1989) *Alchemy.* London: Aquarius Press.

Ferrucci, P. (1982) *What We May Be.* Wellingborough: Turnstone Press.

Fierz, H. (1991) *Jungian Psychiatry.* Einsiedeln, Switzerland: Daimon Verlag.

Fancis, J. and Beaumont, F. (c1610) *Philaster or Love Lies -A-Bleeding.*

Freud, S. (1900) 'The interpretation of dreams.' *Standard Edition* (Vols. 4 and 5). London: Hogarth Press.

Gallegos S.E. and Rennick, T. (1984) *Inner Journeys.* Wellingborough: Turnstone Press.

Gibran, K. (1980) *The Prophet.* London: Heineman.

Grimm, The Brothers (1812–15) 'The Valiant Little Tailor', 'The Sleeping Beauty', 'Hansel and Grethel', 'The Frog-King'. In Grimm's *Household Tales (1812–15).* Cited in *Great Literature* (CD-ROM). Parsippany, NJ: Bureau Development Inc.

Hammer, M. (1967) 'The directed daydream technique.' *Psychotherapy: Theory, Research and Practice 4,* 173–81.

Irving, W. (1832) The Alhambra: *The Enchanted Soldier.* Cited in *Great Literature* (CD-ROM). Parsippany, NJ: Bureau Development Inc.

Jung, C. (1953) *Psychology and Alchemy.* London: Routledge.

Jung, C.G. (1962) *Commentary on the Secret of the Golden Flower.* London: Routledge and Kegan Paul.

Jung, C.G. (1969) *Man and his Symbols.* Garden City: Doubleday.

Jung, C.G. (1958) *The Collected Works – Psychological Types* (Vol. 6) London: Routledge and Kegan Paul.

Kelly, G.F. (1972) 'Guided fantasy as a counselling technique with youth.' *Journal of Consulting and Clinical Psychology 19,* 355–61.

Klein, M. (1930) 'The importance of symbol formation in the development of the ego.' In *Contributions to Psychoanalysis.* London: Hogarth Press.

Kosbab, F.P. (1974) 'Imagery techniques in psychiatry.' *Archives of General Psychiatry 31,* 283–90.

Lass, A.H., Kiremidjian, D. and Goldstein, R.M. (1989) *Dictionary of Allusions.* London: Sphere Books Limited.

Leuner. H. (1984) *Guided Affective Imagery: Mental Imagery in Short-term Psychotherapy.* New York: Thieme-Stratton.

Lyles, J. (1982) 'Efficacy of relaxation training and guided imagery in reducing the awareness of cancer chemotherapy.' *Journal of Consulting and Clinical Psychology 50,* 509–24.

Milner, M. (1955) 'The role of illusion in symbol formation.' In M. Klein *et al. New Directions in Psychoanalysis.* London: Karnac, Maresfield Reprints.

Morris, A. (1970) *Chronically Sick and Disabled Persons Bill. Hansard.*

Ornstein, R.E. (1975) *The Psychology of Consciousness.* Harmondsworth: Pelican.

Orwell, G. (1945) 'Animal Farm.' Cited in *Oxford Dictionary of Quotation and Modern Quotations. Electronic Edition* (1993). Oxford: Oxford University Press.

Oxford Dictionary of Quotations and Modern Quotations, Electronic Edition (1993). Oxford: Oxford University Press.

Renan, E. (c. 1856) 'The Poetry of the Celtic Races.' Cited in *Great Literature* (CD-ROM). Parsippany, NJ: Bureau Development Inc.

Satir, V. (1972) *People Making.* Palo A, to CA: Science and Behaviours Books.

Shorr, J.B. (1974) *Psychotherapy Through Imagery.* New York: Intercontinental Medical Book Corporation.

Singer, J.L. (1974) *Imagery and Daydream Methods in Psychotherapy and Behaviour Modification.* New York: Academic Press.

St. Augustine (1838) *The Confessions of St Augustine.* Translated by E. B. Pusey. Cited in *Great Literature* (CD-ROM). Parsippany, NJ: Bureau Development Inc.

Stewart, W. (1985) *Counselling in Rehabilitation.* London: Croom Helm.

Stewart, W. (1992) *A–Z of Counselling Theory and Practice.* London: Chapman and Hall.

Stewart, W. (1996) *Dictionary of Images and Symbols in Counselling.* London: Jessica Kingsley Publishers.

Walker, B.G. (1988) *The Woman's Dictionary of Symbols and Sacred Objects.* London: Harper and Row.

Woolman, J. (1772) 'The Journal of John Woolman.' Cited in *Great Literature* (CD-ROM). Parsippany, NJ: Bureau Development Inc.

Zdenek, M. (1983) *The Right-Brain Experience.* London: Corgi.

Zolar's Encyclopaedia of Omens, Signs and Superstitions (1989) London: Simon and Schuster.

Index

Printed in the United Kingdom
by Lightning Source UK Ltd.
134913UK00001B/441/A

Printed in Great Britain
by Amazon